Murders on the Nile

MURDERS ON THE NILE

THE WORLD TRADE CENTER
AND GLOBAL TERROR

J. BOWYER BELL

ENCOUNTER BOOKS
SAN FRANCISCO

First edition published in 2003 by Encounter Books, an activity of
Encounter for Culture and Education, Inc., a nonprofit tax exempt
corporation.

Encounter Books website address: www.encounterbooks.com

Manufactured in the United States and printed on acid-free paper.

The paper used in this publication meets the minimum requirements of
ANSI/NISOZ39.48-1992 (R 1997)(*Permanence of Paper*).

Library of Congress Cataloging-in-Publication Data

Bell, J. Bowyer, 1931-
    Murders on the Nile, the World Trade Center and global terror / J.
    Bowyer Bell
    p. cm.
    Includes bibliographical references and index.
    ISBN 1-893554-63-5 (hardcover : alk. paper)
1. Terrorism—History—20th century. 2. Islamic fundamentalism—
    Egypt—History—20th Century. 3. Terrorism—Prevention—
    Government policy—United States. I. Title.

HV6431 .B425 2003
303.6'25'0962—dc21
2002040885

10 9 8 7 6 5 4 3 2

For
Ambassador Tahseen Basheer, 1925–2002,
who has always been there in
Cairo, London, Cambridge, Washington and New York
and
Amos Perlmutter, 1931–2001,
who improbably I once met wandering down
Shari el Tahrir in Cairo, on the first day Israelis could visit Egypt.

CONTENTS

PREFACE

Just before nine on the morning of September 11, 2001, I was sitting by the radio outlining a new chapter of this book, which I had let slide over the summer in Ireland, preferring to chat with idle IRA gunmen rather than continue writing about new zealots. What I intended in this book-in-progress, at that point two years in the works, was to trace the course of righteous murder as it moved from Egypt to Manhattan, indicating why Americans had so much difficulty in understanding the dynamics of political violence and devising an appropriate response. History had not ended with the Cold War; instead, driven by the American example and influence, it was moving toward a new global order. It was the direction history was taking, in fact, that motivated those who shattered the American calm that September morning. The Islamic terrorists lacked the assets to reverse the course of history, but not to engage in spectacular violence. They wanted to find a future in the past and at the same time punish the power of the present, as embodied by America. These were the new *jihadi* of Islam, engaged not simply in a terror crusade but rather in a great battle, as they saw it, between good and evil, between the way of Allah and that of the infidel. They were true believers, and unlike previous terrorist sects—the anti-imperialists in Algeria or Aden or Cyprus, the IRA or Italy's Red Brigades, the *fedayeen* of Palestine—they were also very interested in discussing their beliefs.

I had written up to the point in the narrative at which the *jihadi* were spreading out from Egypt to New York, where they would bomb the World Trade Center in 1993. Then the radio music was interrupted by an announcer with confused reports that something was going on at the World Trade Center at that moment. Like tens of millions of other people everywhere, I switched on the television. On the screen I saw the long plume of smoke floating across the bright blue skyline and heard that an airplane had hit one of the towers. I remembered that when I was a boy, an army bomber had crashed by error into the Empire State Building. However improbable, perhaps this was a reprisal of that event. But reports from the ground indicated that the plane had been large and painted in airline colors. Airliners do not fly down the Hudson, much less plow into a skyscraper on a sunny day. And so this had been no accident. I knew immediately that the Middle Eastern zealots I had been writing about had come to New York. And given the nature of the impact shown on the television screen, it appeared they had killed thousands of people.

From my research I knew that the evacuation procedures from the Twin Towers had been improved since a bomb went off in the parking garage in February 1993, the denouement of my book at that time. But experts still had doubts about the dangers of a bomb or a fire. A glance at the television showed that the impact zone was huge and the fires, fed by jet fuel, were beyond reach and so beyond control. I knew that in their preparations, the Port Authority security at the Trade Center and the federal government had not envisioned such an attack. Nearly everyone who worried about weapons of mass destruction assumed that the assault would come in the form of plutonium, plague or nerve gas—not an airliner turned into a missile. New York would have to cope with the situation without any effective standard operational procedures, without guidance, and without a clear sense of the possible.

Like everyone else I remained in front of the television, hour after hour, horror after horror. From my windows near Riverside Drive, five miles from the World Trade Center, nothing was visible. Soon the acrid smell of the fires wafted up from the tip of the island, but that was all. The streets of the Upper West Side of Manhattan were quiet. Later on, people emerged to stock up on bottled water and groceries, but quickly returned home to follow the crisis on television. There was no traffic on the West Side—no traffic in or out of Manhattan, no downtown subways—and nobody was walking dogs or paying visits.

One catastrophe followed the next, each played and replayed on the screen. The second Boeing crashed into the south tower. First one and then the other tower imploded in a great cloud of smoke and dust. Far away in Washington, the Pentagon was hit.

The day stretched on into night and another day. The war on terrorism was announced. And in New York, people simply watched—bottles of water in the closet, emergency food waiting to be eaten, the future in doubt. After a few days, events slowed down and life drifted back toward normalcy, but I realized that my book would have to be revised.

I had spent two years investigating the nature and impact of the *jihadi* who had bombed the World Trade Center in 1993 and how we had responded. And here was the next time that no one had really believed possible: a catastrophe not caused by a home-made nuclear bomb or a deadly virus, but something more like a scenario from a video game. What would be the American response? What would be done in the short term to prevent a crisis and, more important, what would be done in the long term to manage the terror threat so that America remained an open society? The title of my book stayed the same; and so, for the most part, did the focus on past events, although the narrative had to be adjusted to account for what had happened on that fateful morning when America changed forever in ways we have barely begun to grasp.

The persistence of political violence without closure—a peace process here and a new terror war elsewhere, some gunmen ambushed and others emerging from the underground—has given me a continuous supply of material for my studies into the influence of the gun in politics. In fact, I have spent most of my adult life investigating political violence: small wars, armed struggles, coups and guerrilla campaigns, largely by talking with those involved. I have wandered through the garden spots of violence in Africa, the Middle East and Europe chatting up gunmen and guerrillas, as well as their opponents. I began this before many of the current generation of Islamic terrorists were born, spending a lifetime amid those who smell of cordite and believe they possess the absolute truth. Some are decent, some not, and many are hostile to questioning. And, as well, I have invested time in those who defend order: police, soldiers and politicians, some congenial, others not.

In Egypt, the unchanging focus of this book because it is where the new *jihad* arose, I began my visits before the 1967 war with Israel. Over the years I have talked with Egyptian nationalists in the lobby of the old Semiramis, gone to a reception with Nasser, and met with *fedayeen* who fought in the Suez Canal Zone in 1953–1954. I have talked with Egyptian diplomats and generals inside and outside the country, and with figures like Osama el-Baz before he was national security advisor to Presidents Sadat and Mubarak, and with Defense Minister Abdel Halim Abu Ghazala. I have interviewed those who felt that radical change was needed in the Egypt of Nasser and then in the Egypt of Sadat and finally in the Egypt of Mubarak—in some cases the same people. I have met Arab socialist theorists and Egyptian communists, Moslem Brothers, retired gunmen of Young Egypt, police officials, all sorts of bureaucrats, editors and journalists, the cousins of the famous and the families of the powerful, professors and men on the wanted list. In Israel I have interviewed most of the survivors of the Stern Gang terrorists including the three-man high command that directed the assassination of Lord Moyne—one of whom, Itzhak Shamir, became prime minister of Israel. I have lectured in Jerusalem, Tel Aviv and Haifa, in Egypt at the research center at *Al-Ahram*, the great Egyptian newspaper, and at the Foreign Ministry. In the course of my Egyptian travels, I have benefited particularly from the aid and comfort of two shrewd observers: Mahmud el-Okdah, first met at the Arab League office in New York, who died far too early; and Taheen Bashir, first met at the Egyptian embassy in London, who as Ambassador Bashir became the sage of the Nile, a required stop on any investigator's trip to Cairo, and who died just as I finished this book.

It is, of course, not easy to find either wisdom or access among those dedicated to the gun. It is also very difficult to blend into a crowd on a Cairo evening in an area where tourists seldom go and almost no one is a WASP over six feet tall, pale and blonde and as visible as a zebra. Little boys in ragged pajamas have thrown pebbles, not from malice but because my presence is so unnatural.

Even when all obstacles dissolve and someone drives you down dark streets to meet a source, matters do not go as planned, even in broad daylight. I once sat in powerful heat at a table in an empty nightclub by the Nile and, for reasons too complicated to explain, received a complete briefing on the illegal communist party. The briefing was largely wasted because a jazz band was practicing just behind me and I could hear nothing.

In some cases, the obstacle was neither the acoustics nor the authorities nor the degree of underground cooperation, but my own failure to ask the right questions. One is likely to discover that what is not said is often more significant than what is: the party line, the list of grievances, the dream that all want to explain. Nobody wants to talk about money problems, arms routes, blunders, the erosion of morale. So the view from the underground is often self-serving. There are always those who believe that the truth sets them free—to lie. Yet I found a remarkable number of diverse individuals willing to talk about their cause.

The basis for this work is not simply those involved in Egyptian politics and ultimately global terror, but also all the others in the Middle East and beyond who are dedicated to the gun as a political instrument. Old terrorists can sometimes be found in the presidential palace; but most, especially if they are still engaged in their vocation, must be sought out in strange places not unlike the seedy nightclub by the Nile where the jazz band played. A great deal of time must be passed in the lobbies of small provincial hotels waiting for someone to drive you to see someone else who is not inclined to be very forthcoming. Now and then things go wrong. On the other hand, the aggrieved have sent people with guns to insist that I come with them for a second visit. And in the Middle East, along with all the usual obstacles, many do not want to talk to Americans who might read their intentions or gain insight into their movement.

It is better not to attempt to see those who prefer not to see you. And there are adventures best avoided. In Yemen I was briefly kidnapped, more as amusement than as an ideological gesture. And in Jordan, because one set of *fedayeen* did not like me talking to another instead of to them, they took me away to their headquarters at gunpoint. By the time I began work on this book, most of the American *jihadi* conspirators were no longer available. It was too late to see Sheikh Rahman, whose address was in my computer. I had postponed that venture in part because I was not yet working on the *jihadi* and in part because the wilds of Brooklyn and the streets of Jersey City seemed less familiar to me than Cairo or Aden. In any case, I missed the sheikh, if not his colleagues, rivals and enemies—Arab zealots and Western police officers and government representatives.

I have also spent a considerable amount of time engaged in one way or another with the Western national security community that is concerned with political violence, terrorism and insurgences—remote and unpopular themes until recently. Beyond the West, the authorities are different in that some have recourse to repression and often exist in societies without law or civil justice, although theoretically cherishing the same values as are found in Washington or Rome. My research and writing at Harvard, MIT and Columbia always dealt with the unpleasant aspects of national security. I have written thousands of pages on terror, publishing twenty books and more articles than I can bear to think about, besides writing special reports, project outlines, options, all the usual byproducts of an academic and analytical career. I have run simulations, consulted, lectured and so on. Some of this has been reporting from the terror front, but increasingly I have been concerned not only to portray the reality of the armed struggle, the dynamics of the underground, but also to analyze the appropriate response for an open, democratic society. What should we do when confronted by murderers with an unshakable belief in the righteousness of their cause?

In 1978 I wrote about these issues in a book called *A Time of Terror*, referring to when the Palestinians went international and gunmen appeared in Milan and Berlin. Over the years, between small wars, coups and the Irish Troubles, I have persisted in offering advice to those who generally intend to persist in their usual way of dealing with unconventional threats. I have lectured to the most diverse audiences at conferences, at research institutions in Great Britain and Israel, at the International School of Disarmament and Conflict in Italy. I once gave a lecture to a closed session of Provisional Sinn Fein in Ireland, and another time, to expatriates in Rhodesia. Not many in my audiences seemed to find my perspective convincing.

For this book I have spoken not only with eminent Egyptians and their neighbors and to people of importance in Washington and New York, but also to people without titles and political power, including firemen, detectives, doctors and security officers. The specifics of the text, however, rest on more conventional sources: the printed word and interviews with the responsible parties. I have also had the advantage of seeing special papers done by members of my spring class on Terrorism and Irregular War in the School of Public and International Affairs at Columbia University. Having announced my book-in-progress, I indicated that papers on what had been learned about the World Trade Center bombing of 1993 would be welcome as long as they were based on interviews with people involved. I received four excellent papers by Joshuah Berman, Joseph Blady, Andrew Galliker and Ronit Golan.

In addition, I am a consultant for the law firms representing the victims of the 1993 bombing and the massacre on top of the Empire State Building in 1997. I have benefited from the international academic and analytical communities concerned with internal war and terror, through seminars, lectures, gossip in the halls of think tanks, programs and conferences both open and closed. Over the years, and for this book in particular, I have benefited from the views of a few special individuals. I especially appreciate the wit and wisdom, the sources and insights provided by Dr. Neil Livingstone of Global Options in Washington, the center of his own intelligence web.

One of the joys of growing old is that you can dispatch your children to arenas without proper plumbing or cold beer, so this book benefits from a daughter, Elizabeth Hill Carter Bell Meaney, who reported to me on anthrax from her position at the Centers for Disease Control in Atlanta. Unlike her earlier reports from India, where she was stamping out polio, and from Nepal, where the royals were slaughtered down the street, the news from Atlanta was often hectic.

On technical matters, because this work is intended for a popular audience, I have tried to pare down the conventional scaffolding of footnotes without leaving the reader in the dark.

The "Sources" section indicates the provenance of this work as well as the nature of the pertinent literature—the good books and the bad. Second, I should note that one of the unchanging, if minor, hobgoblins of writing on the Middle East is the transliteration of Arabic names. The most recent, and often the best, systems transform familiar proper names into new and sometimes unappealing configurations. So I have instead used what is familiar; Nasser is still Nasser.

I would like to thank again the kind hearts at Earhart Foundation who for a very long time have had the courage to fund my convictions. And on more personal matters, special thanks should be offered to my former student, friend and now agent Tony Outhwaite, who as always offered encouragement, a close reading of the text, and the latest news from the despots of Africa and from the pitching staff of the Baltimore Orioles. Meeting a hard and unforgiving deadline meant sitting before a computer, day after day. Because my editor at Encounter Books, Peter Collier, proved assiduous and painstaking, these computer days continued for some time, hopefully to the advantage of the final text.

During the whole project, as always I could rely on the encouragement of my Kerry wife, Nora, who had her own anxieties resulting from the daily journey to the wilds of the Bronx to teach many who did not choose to learn. And as always she coped; for the Irish, especially the Kerry Irish, remain indomitable and, like Nora, delightful.

J. B. B.
New York and Dublin

PART ONE

PROLOGUE

Egypt has always been a romantic and mysterious country. Postcards show the great Pyramids, the Sphinx, the date palms, Ferdinand de Lessup's famous canal, the ruins along the Nile. History textbooks offer an intriguing cast of thousands: Ramses, King Tut, Moses in the bulrushes, Cleopatra and Marc Antony, Nasser, Napoleon, the fat King Farouk. General Rommel and St. Louis of France spent time in prison in Egypt. Winston Churchill and Lawrence of Arabia had their photographs taken in front of the Sphinx.

Egypt is *Umm al-dunya*, "Mother of the World." For centuries, it has remained the heart of the Arab nation and a great center of the Islamic world, mentioned eighteen times in the Koran. Sooner or later everyone comes to Egypt: fakirs and prophets, Armenian traders, the King of Greece, Lord Nelson and Menachem Begin, Christian saints and heretics, Japanese tour groups. There are camels in the streets and Mirage jets in the sky. Exiled Yemeni poets and Syrian radicals at odds with Damascus sit in hotel lobbies. The students at the American University in Cairo study postmodern theory, while those at al-Azhar University find all that is relevant when they read the Koran. Each sees a special Egypt—miserable crowds of the poor, the Pyramids and ruins, a strategic asset, a risen people, decayed mosques, the home of the Arab League, the feluccas sailing on the river, the Sphinx as promised by the guidebook.

Other ancient civilizations are rubble, covered with jungle in Cambodia or sand in Libya, scattered stones in the dust; but through four millennia the Pyramids have cast long shadows.

1

None who built them would have been surprised: they built for the ages, for the pharaoh and for the gods.

Since the ninth century, Cairo has been the great Arab and Islamic city, built, rebuilt, ruined and extended, cut by the Nile. It is a complex of palaces and gardens, penury and slums, mosques and fortresses. Beyond this are the endless, brutal apartments; and always on the periphery, beyond the cemeteries and the suburbs, is the desert. In the spring, the winds of the *khamsín* bring the desert into Cairo, leaving hot, dry dust everywhere, wearing away the edges of ancient stones, the cheap paint on the mud and concrete, and wearing on the nerves as well.

North of Cairo, the Delta dangles from the long thin thread of the Nile that twists south slowly through the desert of Upper Egypt to disappear into Sudan, the Ethiopian highlands and central Africa. For millennia the river imposed seasons on the people, offered riches to the few and demanded incessant stooped labor from the many. Troubled times meant fewer canals and fewer acres planted. There was no wealth without the water. That water now accumulates behind the Aswan High Dam before spilling out across Upper Egypt. Now industry and manufacturing, services and remittances make the country viable, but the river still marks seasons and pace. For thousands of years, the Nile has passed the ancient, battered temples of Idfu, Kom Ombo and Luxor. In places the barren sand of the desert comes down to the riverbanks.

And finally there is Cairo. There beside the Pyramids at Giza and Sakkara begins Lower Egypt, the lush Nile Delta, a maze of mud and canals and tiny villages. For thousands of years, regular, predictable floods have spread silt over the fields—low, flat, rich land planted in date palms, cotton, fruit, vegetables and grain. The Delta mud generated all the wealth of Egypt, made the pharaohs and pashas possible, supported the *fellahín*, the peasant workers, funded the temples and mosques, kept the merchants and bankers of the cities comfortable. Even with new industries, furniture factories, power plants, paved roads, clinics and railways, the Delta still matters.

For over five thousand years, the *fellahín* of Egypt worked the rich Delta, their lives shaped by the seasons of the Nile, the whims of overlords and the imperatives of the gods. Century after century, life in the Delta villages persisted, each generation different but the same. So the *fellahín* remained within their mud villages, assured that tomorrow will be like yesterday and that little really changes. The temples of the pharaohs ran to ruin, but the Nile rose and fell as always. The Christians came, and then in 640 the Arabs and Islam. Then the great city was built. Egypt remained open to the faithful and the heretics, Moslems, Jews and Monophysites, each denying the other's doctrine but adopting some of its superstitions.

Everyone came to Egypt—Ottomans and Seljuks, Armenians, Sudanese and Arabs—but many did not stay. Even in modern times the French, the British, Italians, more Greeks, more Jews, adventurers from the Balkans, Cypriots and Lebanese came to Cairo. They spoke no Arabic, kept to themselves, bought land but rarely came to the countryside. The rich lived in the cities, in Alexandria on the Mediterranean, and especially in Cairo.

The Nile Delta has always been a maze of twisting waterways, unpaved roads, canals, tiny lanes; it has always been home to the village, real home for most Egyptians, no matter the disruptions of war or forced service, the opportunities elsewhere, the appeal of the cities or the charms of emigration. Each of the little villages is special—not simply a few mud houses, a tiny mosque, a shop on the rough road through the fields, but home, unlike any of the other five thousand or so villages, each of them a gift of the Nile. There the people live in mud-brick houses, gray, unpainted, rough, squalid. Until very recently, a water buffalo might have lived with the family. The children work instead of attending school. The land is owned by others; the date palms are owned by others; the wealth goes elsewhere. The village is still in many ways the same as it has been. Until recently, few of the men telling the same stories their fathers and grandfathers told in the cool of the evening were literate or healthy. Today the Egyptians of the village eat food that is little different from what fed their ancestors: beans, salty white cheese, perhaps *houmos* from chick peas, *frisikh* (dried fish), vegetables and few savories. Thick black tea is the great and necessary luxury.

In the past there were goats and donkeys, cheerful children and everyone a cousin. There were also plagues and river parasites, rotten teeth, no doctors, no sewers, filthy water and many risks for children. There might be a holiday, annual trips to the tomb of the local saint, perhaps time smoking a *narguilas*, a water pipe. Not until after the 1954 coup did Egyptians—General Mohammed Neguib, Colonel Gamal Abdel Nasser, Colonel Anwar Sadat and the other officers—finally rule the nation. Then there was real, if slow, change in the village: clean water, visiting nurses, schools and electricity.

Today the village nights twinkle with fairy lights on Aswan power; battered pickup trucks come and go; and even the very poorest are familiar with events in Cairo and beyond. But the village is still the village; the *fellahín* persist in traditional ways shaped to Islam while they adapt the new world of films, space vehicles, radical ideas and Arab nationalism. Each village is still cherished as home by those who, with talent and luck or out of desperation, move on to the cities or beyond.

In one of these grimy little villages in the Delta, al-Gamalia by name, Omar Abdel Rahman was born on May 3, 1938. His prospects seemed limited. As it had been for generations, Egypt was controlled by foreigners: the British in offices and palaces along the Nile, and their ally, the young King Farouk, the last of a dynasty established by the Albanian Mohammed Ali after Napoleon had withdrawn. The dynasty had begun with violence when Mohammed Ali murdered the last of his Mameluke predecessors in 1811. His successors had modernized the country, but at the price of British intervention. In time, Egypt evolved into a British protectorate with a king in the palace in Cairo.

The villages in 1938 were hardly just the same as in the days of Mohammed Ali, but change had come very slowly over the century. Once Islam had largely converted the Delta a thousand years before—even if the Christian Copts remained a large minority and the Jews were tolerated—the strictures and attitudes of Islam shaped the *fellahín* of al-Gamalia as they did all Egyptians. The result was a society that was narrow, devout, obedient to the religious law, the *shari'a*, often acquiescent, on occasion violent—and yet remarkably tolerant, docile and genial. There seemed little that could change fate, and so Egyptian heretics, fanatics and zealots were rare. The devout villagers might be inspired to momentary violence, but by nature they remained long-suffering and limited in their aspirations and expectations.

For the baby Omar Abdel Rahman, even conventional expectations disappeared. He lost his sight by the time he was eleven months old. Perhaps this was the result of diabetes, although Egyptian rural society was afflicted with a spectrum of diseases. Bilharaziasis was endemic and preventive medicine unknown, and so blind babies were no novelty. Unlike many others, Rahman survived his first years. As he grew older, he was encouraged to seek a future in Islam. Unable to see the outside world, the child could concentrate on the world of the spirit, memorize the True Word, and grow in piety. He was often told that the blind are able to see in other ways.

As soon as he was old enough, the child was taken to the local mosque and taught the Koran. Islam has no hierarchy, for man needs no intermediaries, and anyone may preach within the mosque on Friday. Some become popular saints and others become sheikhs, respected and esteemed. Soon, for Abdel Rahman there was a vocation truly discovered. He was clever, bright, curious and pious. He could see a promising future, even if he could not see the river and the fields that dominated the future of others.

By eleven he had memorized the Koran and had gone on to an Islamic boarding school. Then he went on in triumph to al-Azhar University in Cairo. Al-Azhar was ancient and famous, the greatest Islamic educational institution, attracting students and scholars from far away. For many of the devout, it was ground zero of the Islamic world. But although traditional in custom and curriculum, it was an enormous distance within Islam from the cadences of the Koran as heard in the village of al-Gamalia.

After his graduation in 1965, Abdel Rahman preached in a small mosque along the main road of Fedemin on the outskirts of Fayoum, sixty miles south of Cairo. It was a very traditional place, and also very dirty in the harsh white light of day. The men wore tattered *galabayas* and broken sandals, the women were in black, the children were cheerful and ragged. There were flies and open sewerage. As in all the villages, life was coarse and hard. The new money from Cairo, the investments of the nationalist government, had made a difference; the new rulers in Cairo extolled progress, development and new habits over the radio and eventually on television; but change did not come quickly.

Fedemin in 1965 was no place special. There were only a few shops, with naked light bulbs and pigeons on the roofs. By the time Abdel Rahman arrived, however, the outside world had begun to intrude. Cairo was no longer another realm, but the capital city where the corrupt Farouk, last of a foreign dynasty, had been expelled and the British driven from the country by the new warriors, chief among them Gamal Abdel Nasser—Egyptian hero, prophet of nationalism, voice of the Arabs and key to their future. His government, the first truly Egyptian once since the pharaohs, reached out to all the villages. The land was ineffectually redistributed, and the *fellahín* became tenants of the state. Medical officers and nurses stopped by. Disease was curbed. Wells were dug. More teachers arrived. The great singer Oom Khaldum could be heard on the radio, with her long, complex songs not only of love but also of pride: Glory to Nasser and Arab Socialism and We Built the High Dam. There were Nasser's own speeches in dialect so everyone could understand. So in the village there was a feel of triumph and change: tomorrow had arrived.

And there by the mango trees, far beyond al-Azhar and the notice of Egypt, Omar Abdel Rahman preached against Colonel Abdel Gamal Nasser, the most popular Arab of his day, the most popular Egyptian in a millennium. According to the zealous young cleric, Nasser was the wicked pharaoh, not a hero but a secularist leading his people to perdition. The Koran might be read on the state radio, but Nasser's dream was secular, corrupting, in violation of the fundamentals of Islam. For Omar Abdel Rahman, Islam was not merely his religion—a tradition, rituals and public piety—but an imperative. For himself, for Egypt, for the Arabs, for the world, Allah was the answer, not the secular dreams of Nasser and the officers, not the triumphs of technology and not the advent of global culture. Democracy, development, nationalism were mere words—glittering mirages covering an impious lack of faith. Islam didn't need the West, nor did the people need a false prophet.

Abdel Rahman found in Islam all that was needed to create a seamless society formed by the law of the prophet, the *shari'a,* and focused on the eternal, fundamental revelations of the Koran. All that was necessary was already written down, available and applicable. All else was false and forbidden. In this belief, Abdel Rahman had ancestors and allies, but little impact on the villagers who looked for tomorrow in the dreams of Nasser and the Arab nation.

So in 1965 the Egyptians had Nasser. The tiny village of Fedemin had an obscure, blind cleric whose Friday sermons resonated only with a few other clerics. The Egypt of the masses, the new Egypt, had become a presence in the modern world. Egypt mattered. The great dam at Aswan was in construction. Nasser was a power in the nonaligned world; the Russians were allies and the West was frustrated because Egypt was no longer a client. The British and French had been confounded at Suez in 1956. The old Egypt was gone: the debauched court, the corrupt king, a foreign elite, landowners, bankers, Greeks, Armenians and Jews and Turks who spoke no Arabic and did not attend the mosque, the government ministers who wrote Arabic poorly and spoke French at home. In its place, the dream of the nationalists, a new and virile Egypt, had emerged.

So in Fedemin few heeded the call to the fundamentals of the faith. Yet the young sheikh in the small mosque dreamed of speaking to a different Egypt, long ignored and denied by the powerful and the rich. The nationalists, the politicians and the officers wanted Egypt to be modernized, Westernized, prosperous and respected. Sheikh Rahman wanted Egypt to be Islamic. He was dedicated, uncompromising and isolated, one of the few Islamic voices still crying in the nationalist wilderness. And he was noticed by authorities who recognized him as a harbinger of an alternative reality with enormous potential. His sermons were summarized; a file was opened.

ONE

RIGHTEOUS MURDER: EGYPT OF THE NILE

For two millennia Egypt had been a prize rather than a nation—a conquest, a strategic necessity for foreigners. They came and ruled and exploited the people. This Egypt was a matter of administration and taxes, foreign titles and oppression. The West knew Egypt primarily from engravings of the temples Kom Omba or Karnak; the Sphinx, partly covered in sand; and the Pyramids, one of the wonders of the world. A few tales and ancient historical texts circulated, but through the centuries Egypt remained a mystery, an exotic oriental backwater.

For those in Arabia and the Middle East, the Nile was of more consequence. The Arabs first arrived in 639 with the army of Amr Ibn el-As, a force out of the desert, alien and ambitious. An Islamic conquest in 642 transformed the residue of ancient Egypt ruled by Levantine foreigners. The military city of Fustat—now old Cairo—had been built and control established over the local authorities, the docile peasants—the *fellahín*—and the Coptic Christians. The Islamic dynasties that followed, at times operating independently and at times nominally in control of other Islamic rulers, were always imposed.

Cairo became a great city, the country prosperous and sophisticated, though often riven by internal war, and always a prize. Saladin ruled in splendor for a while. Then in 1250 came the Mamelukes: proud, avaricious and cruel Turkish mercenaries, revitalized by new slave levies. They flourished, ruling even after the Ottoman Turks under Sultan Selim I had annexed Egypt. Sovereignty might be elsewhere, with the caliph, but Egypt was Mameluke.

8

Over the centuries Mameluke feudal lords became more greedy and brutal but also less efficient. Without much Turkish interference, they indulged in their quarrels and their increasingly haphazard exploitation of the weak. The poor simply endured as always, in wretched exhaustion and pious docility. By the end of the eighteenth century, Mameluke Egypt was neglected and isolated, inhabited by the urban destitute, the Islamic imams and sheikhs of al-Azhar, and the *fellahín*. Egypt was a squalid oriental despotism erected on ancient ruins, an arena for the deadly quarrels of an elite of Mameluke beys and pashas fighting over scarce spoils.

Change came to Egypt in 1798 with the unexpected arrival of Napoleon. At the Battle of the Pyramids, in June 1798, the Mamelukes discovered the modern world. The battle, an afternoon's slaughter, was a bloody farce. The last medieval cavalry charge transformed all of the Mameluke splendor—the glittering armor and whirling swords, the cries of arrogance and defiance—into heaps of bloody bodies piled helter-skelter amid maimed horses and abandoned weapons.

Occupying Cairo, the French found only shoddy ruins and slums. The streets were filthy, the buildings dilapidated, the crowds in rags. Outside the city, the great ancient temples were covered in sand. The countryside was unproductive. And for those among the masses who noticed them at all, the French were merely bizarre, strangely dressed infidels come to rule. Nothing else would change.

The French scientists and other experts were eager to investigate the past, change the present, assure progress toward a modern future. They found that the Nile Delta had increasingly become fallow as the canals filled with silt. The people lived in squalid tenements or with their animals in mud huts in mean villages. Alexandria, ancient glory long gone, proved to be no more than a shabby town of fifteen thousand. Cairo was filthy, raucous and vile, its unlighted and unpaved streets filled with sewage, slop dribbling down walls, garbage dumped from windows, dead rats in the gutters. No one seemed interested in razing the fetid slums, widening the dark streets or repairing the canals.

Napoleon wanted to reach out to Islam; he had come as a

liberator, after all. Cairo was tidied up, the filth removed, new streets opened, order encouraged, reformed regulations imposed. Licenses and permits were required. There were new taxes. Change was embodied by pink-faced men in military uniform and scientists at work measuring temples and water levels and naming plants. But the French did not stay. In 1799, Napoleon returned to France and other wars and adventures. On June 14, 1800, his successor, General Jean-Baptiste Kléber, was murdered in Cairo.

Napoleon's adventure had revealed to only a few Egyptians what the modern world looked like: how wars were won, how nature was harnessed, how cities were governed. Revealed as well were the power of reason, the glory of science and the cost of Egyptian feudalism—mean, sterile and squalid. Most Egyptians took no notice of this interlude of European enlightenment. The Koran supplied all necessary answers, while penury eroded all curiosity.

Still, Egypt was never the same after Napoleon; modernity had been set loose in the land. Following the French came the British, intervening for narrow strategic purposes without romantic notions about the Pyramids and without reaching out to Islam. They simply wanted no one else to use Egypt—not even the sovereign Turks. They didn't want to rule or administer, but they couldn't find capable Egyptians to rule for them. They muddled through for a time, wrangling with the sultan, coping with the surviving Mameluke beys, arguing with each other and with their own experts.

In March 1803, the British left Egypt to the surviving Mamelukes. Egypt was again in the hands of the rapacious and incompetent. The sultan could not impose authority, nor could the Mamelukes run the country. An ambitious and ruthless Albanian adventurer, Mohammed Ali, saw opportunity. Egypt could matter; it could garner respect and power. So Mohammed Ali betrayed his allies, murdered his rivals, played off one Mameluke bey against another, roused the mob in Cairo and put his trust in cruelty and guile in order to seize absolute power. It was the Egyptian way.

Mohammed Ali had himself elected pasha of Cairo almost at the same time as Napoleon became emperor of France. He was the only viable alternative to anarchy and exploitation. Only a few opposed him, while many admired his cunning and brutality. In 1811 he lured the last forty Mameluke survivors to the Citadel overlooking Cairo and had them all slaughtered. Then he ruled Egypt without rival, becoming the khedive and modernizing the country.

Taking Western advice, Mohammed Ali introduced cotton as a major crop, transforming the Delta and therefore Egypt. A vast network of new canals was constructed. Soon there was an export crop: cotton drove out all else but assured huge sums from foreign sales. The state now had money to spend. Wealth flowed into the growing Egyptian middle class and into the accounts of a growing number of immigrants and investors. For the *fellahín* the patterns of work in the field and the daily round changed; even if the work required longer hours, there was more to eat and more children survived. The newly rich and comfortable needed their houses swept, messages delivered, laundry done. By the time of Mohammed Ali's death in 1848, cotton had made Egypt, if not all Egyptians, far wealthier; had tied the country to European markets; and had funded a centralized government that maintained an effective military force.

Mohammed Ali's heir, Ibrahim Pasha, was determined to press forward the transformation of Egypt as quickly as possible. He invested in a new army and proved a skilled military leader; all of Egypt's neighbors feared him. He also took foreign advice, expanded the canals, and encouraged the production of still more cotton. Between 1853 and 1870, the income of the *fellahín* increased threefold. The cities grew. The population rose from three million in 1830 to seven million in 1890. A continuing stream of émigrés, investors, tradesmen and adventurers arrived. Land was bought, railways built, banks opened, stores staffed and gardens laid out. Opportunity drew the skilled and ambitious, among them Cypriots, Syrians, Maltese, Lebanese, Orthodox, Jews and Aryans.

Visitors still were stunned by the poverty, the flies and open sewers, the primitive villages, the crippled beggars and medieval customs; but they had never seen the utter misery of Mameluke times and didn't realize how awful things had once been. The next khedive, Ismail, ruling from 1863 to 1879, oversaw another great thrust toward modernity. Egypt suddenly had gaslights and the telegraph. The railway was extended. The great squares and boulevards of Alexandria were completed. When the cotton money ran short, the British and others lent funds to the khedive. In Cairo the opera house was finished and Verdi was commissioned to write *Aïda* to commemorate the opening of the Suez Canal. Khedive Ismail felt that all had been changed: Now, we are no longer part of Africa but part of Europe.

Impatient to join the modern world, Ismail ran up debts that Egypt could not immediately pay. He opened the door to bankruptcy and so to foreign intervention, especially by the British and the French, who wanted to protect their shares and control in the Suez Canal. In 1882, to keep others out and to see debts paid, the British reluctantly returned and initiated a veiled occupation, shutting out all others including the French. There would be a British resident, imported bureaucrats and specialists and an administration largely directed by those seconded to Egyptian service.

Some found the arrangement insulting. Nationalism had come to Egypt along with gaslights and international debts. It seemed to the new patriot class that the country had been occupied by stealth and without consent. In 1882 the new Egyptian army under Colonel Arabi Pasha revolted and was promptly defeated by the British at Tel el-Kewbir. The British representative, Major Evelyn Baring, became consul-general, one of the great imperial overlords, absolutely confident in his policies, honored and admired and eventually titled: Lord Cromer. Isolated in the Residency, dedicated and hard-working, Lord Cromer introduced fair and efficient administration, along with a host of new initiatives to transform the lives of the natives.

As resident, Cromer pursued growth, prudence and the payment of old debts. The palace still offered pomp and ceremony, but the resident made the real decisions, imposing policy by influence, logic and the reality of British power. For the few middle-class Egyptians, politics was limited to palace intrigue and resentment, with no prospects of power, no parties, no institutions of governance and no opportunities for dissent. From 1885 to 1910, modernization included an improved army, a fairer tax structure, reformed courts, a modernized police force, new construction and increased cotton exports (in 1885 the value was £9 million and in 1910 it was £29 million). Sudan was brought under an Anglo-Egyptian condominium and French influence once again was frustrated.

Immigration stepped up, meaning more Greeks and Italians, more new ventures and enterprises where no Arabic was spoken, more banks, large department stores and paved roads. Those eager for advantage and profit—speculators from Malta, agents from Salonika or Naples, Balkan merchants with funds to invest—all wanted to be in Egypt. They didn't want to be Egyptian, but rather to benefit from the privileges and exceptions offered to foreigners. So they came and prospered. Modern luxury hotels were built with Swiss managers and German waiters. The Egyptians were found in the scullery, carrying messages, sweeping out.

The foreigners shaped their own Egyptian world in Cairo and Alexandria, imported their cravats and novels and manners, kept their own language and religion, gambled away fortunes at San Stefano Casino. The immigrants with more menial jobs and no capital to invest also lived apart from ordinary Egyptians, spoke no Arabic, and saved to go home again to a comfortable old age.

The Egyptians, few having an education or money to invest, only gradually moved away from the old economy, the street stalls, the date palms and the miserable slums. While appealing, the modern world was for most still alien and would continue to be so. Few Egyptians studied abroad, accumulated capital or bought land, practiced law or medicine, or published a newspaper.

The khedive, the Egyptian Legislative Assembly and what there was of Egyptian opinion also accepted the benefits of British administration. Modern politics had come to Egypt but the palace had no power, the lawyers could not enact laws, the politicians had no parties, and the men with new university degrees had limited prospects. The sheikhs and imams offered no opposition to the British. The new army was co-opted. The palace was content with stipends and titles. These new Egyptians accepted the British position papers and development programs, smoked cigarettes and read the newspapers, sent out for coffee, collected their salaries. Yet they resented English condescension as much as the students and the radicals in the tiny middle class.

At the beginning of the twentieth century, the aspiration for a powerful, independent Egypt faced severe obstacles: a population only superficially Western, an economic system that relied on one crop, limited technical and political talent, and a society ignorant of Western norms of efficiency and responsibility. Much had been accomplished. Cotton had proved enormously profitable. The army looked like an army. The centers of Cairo and Alexandria were not unlike Palermo or Nice. Canals and railways and gaslights were visible. But the *fellahín* had too few primary schools and so remained illiterate, superstitious, volatile—the stuff of mobs. And there were too many secondary school graduates who were underemployed, underpaid and resentful. Prosperity was unevenly distributed; the reduction of the Egyptian debt had meant little for those on the edge of penury.

The British associated with their own. They saw all Egyptians as simply natives: the clerks, the peasants, the palace officials and the lawyers. They knew only their faithful watchman, the habits of the khedive, and their bureaucratic contact—a small man in a badly cut suit, often with a fez and an odd accent, who had to be monitored for sloth. They had seldom met an Egyptian socially. Those in charge chose to ignore the international community of bankers and merchants—Levantine, louche, mere immigrants. They regarded most of the locals as incompetent, superstitious, often corrupt; the palace as exotic and irrelevant; and the international caste as necessary but unsavory. And this was quite often accurate.

With each new year of the new century, it was reasonable to expect that tomorrow would be like today. There was stability and routine; schools were built, documents were initialed, orders were given as suggestions. There were no threats, no Islamic zealots, no danger from the palace conspiracies, no way to organize the poor. Egypt was wretched, but also seemed romantic and eternal.

Everything fell apart unexpectedly at a small mud village called Dinshawai. In the summer of 1906 a party of British officers, none of whom spoke Arabic, were on a pigeon shoot while their troops marched from Alexandria to Cairo. They had camped in Menoufiyya on the way to Shibin al-Kom and five or six had gone after the local pigeons. The angry village *fellahín* protested; pigeons were a large part of their meager diet. There was a crowd, and then a scuffle, with shouts and screams. A gun went off. The wife of a local leader was wounded. The crowd pummeled the British, injuring two of them. There were no local police about. The officers began to run; one who had been hit on the head suddenly collapsed and died on the road, felled by sun stroke and shock as much as from the clubbing. A young man from the village who rushed to help him was seized by the British soldiers and beaten to death.

Fifty-two Egyptians were arrested, the convenient suspects along with the guilty. The incident at Dinshawai became the imperial topic of the day as rumors circulated in Cairo and the newspapers cleared their pages for fresh revelations: the mob had murdered a British officer. The London press was hysterical. The British in Egypt were outraged. The authorities acted swiftly and vigorously.

Something had to be done immediately; someone had to be taught a lesson. Egyptians were Orientals, assumed to be limited in moral capacity and needing a firm hand as well as guidance; thus an example had to be made. Lord Cromer established a special court with British and Egyptian members. The chairman was a notable politician, the minister of justice, Boutros Pasha Ghali, who was also an Egyptian and a Copt. Elegant and well educated, he was a friend of Britain. The purpose of the court was not to seek justice or weigh guilt, but to teach the illiterate and ignorant villagers and all Egyptians that violence did not pay.

On June 26, 1906, four of the arrested *fellahín* received death sentences and three of these were to receive in addition fifty lashes each. A number of others involved were given long terms at hard labor. Lord Cromer confirmed the sentences from his isolation in the Residency and they were promptly carried out. The lesson learned by the *fellahín* and the new nationalists was that the British were hypocritical tyrants, modern in dress but otherwise no different from beys, Mamelukes or local despots when irritated or insulted. They ruled not by right or by law, but through state violence. The British had offered other values, but Dinshawai revealed them to be camouflage for arrogant self-interest. Those like Boutros Pasha Ghali who had cooperated with the Residency were discredited. The stock of the nationalists rose.

The illiterate *fellahín*, al-Azhar, the palace and the nationalists were as one on the need for action. Some wanted respect, some a concession, others advantage and the more militant among them freedom. When Lord Cromer retired the next year, he was content with his record and with the status quo: "I shall deprecate any brisk change or any violent new departure." Yet while the British officers were shooting pigeons at Dinshawai, new local classes were maturing all but unnoticed: Egyptians educated at the Sorbonne, lawyers who had learned about the rights of man and the age of reason from English political philosophers like John Locke and John Stuart Mill, accountants and clerks and engineers. Many had become nationalists. Some were patient and saw the advantages of the British Residency. Others were not, but acknowledged the reality. As is always the case, a few zealots wanted to act at once. All these Egyptians, even the poor and illiterate, had been outraged by Dinshawai. Resentment, however, did not translate into power, only into painful grievance. For the devout Moslems and the Egyptian nationalists, one option was to delay violence but secretly prepare for the future—deception as duty. The other was to risk immediate action. All tradition favored delay.

The faithful who found the answer in Allah were poorly organized. The imam and the sheikhs wanted to continue to enforce orthodoxy, study Koranic law, and persist in the face of British insults. A holy war, a *jihad,* against British power and presence was beyond imagining. In the cities, the nationalists, the politicians and the students had no power. The Legislative Assembly was a chamber for debate and agitation, not governance. Nobody wanted to see a mob in the streets.

Yet some saw in the miasma of grievance after Dinshawai an opportunity to act. Politics in Egypt was increasingly played out on two levels: the conventional and visible world of parties, receptions and speeches, and the hidden world of cabals and intrigue, secret schemes that generated a sense of threat, if no real evidence. Stones were thrown, fires set, threats made. Now, suddenly, the streets felt unsafe. The British, like the hidden zealots, sensed a time of change, and unlike the conspirators, they acted immediately. They offered concessions and gestures. Boutros Pasha Ghali was made the first Egyptian prime minister. True, he was a Christian and had been chairman of the special court for Dinshawai, but he was still an Egyptian. There had already been other concessions: a new university, for example, which would absorb the energies of the secondary school students. British bureaucrats were instructed to interfere less in routine administration.

The number of incidents declined. The conspirators and zealots were apparently neutralized; and for a while the anger and resentment seemed to evaporate. The militants, however, had not gone away. They read concessions as signs of British vulnerability, not strength. Then Boutros Pasha Ghali announced that in return for a higher Egyptian share of the profits, he favored extending the concession of the Suez Canal Zone another forty years after the existing terminal date of 1968. This meant generations of occupation, the indefinite postponement of freedom. On February 9, 1910, the Legislative Assembly voted against any such arrangement. This was the way of the new politics: constitutional, moderate, electoral. But the next day, Boutros was murdered. The killer was immediately seized and promptly confessed. He was Ibrahim Nasser al-Wardani, a young Moslem zealot who belonged to a tiny secret organization called Tadama—more a shifting group of the pious than an underground cell. As for the murder, al-Wardani explained that he had acted for Allah and for Egypt, and was guilty of no crime save patriotism and piety.

The deed unnerved the moderates and frightened most nationalists and all the Copts. The very spontaneity of the murder was unsettling. The punishment that followed was inevitable: a new criminal conspiracy act, a press censorship act, a school discipline act. The futility of violence was the lesson taught in the aftermath of the murder, and many Egyptians, fearful of a time of terror and assassination, quite agreed. National dreams might easily become nightmares. Vengeance by Islamic fanatics might have no bounds. None with power or wealth, influence or property wanted new risks. The militants, Islamic or nationalist, found no friends and could do no more than wait, organize, conspire and hope.

There was in fact a new Egypt with modern cities, an acceptable social and economic infrastructure, with income from the canal and from cotton. There was the elegant Khedival Sporting Club and the familiar Shepheards Hotel, the polo fields and nightclubs. There were Greek poets, elegant cotton brokers, new banks—even an Egyptian bank, al-Misra. Yet the curve of the public cornice along the Nile was broken by the walls of the British embassy's garden, tangible evidence of imperial priorities and power.

Then in August 1914 came a European war. As the months passed, the prospect of a short and salutary battle faded. The West was mired in a long, miserable, lethal conflict that destroyed whole classes and, by 1918, great empires. The war brought a pause to Egyptian events. National aspirations and agitation were postponed. Politics was shut down. Egypt was technically a Turkish province and Turkey was about to become a British enemy. So London decided to break the connection and declared a protectorate. Britain deposed the Khedive Abbas Hilmy II and placed his uncle Prince Hussein Kamal in the palace as sultan. Upon Hussein Kamal's death in 1917, his brother Ahmed Hussein succeeded him.

By the time the armistice was signed on November 11, 1918, the world was upside down. Five emperors, eight kings and eighteen dynasties had been swept away. The German empire was gone, along with the Russian tsars and the Austrian Hapsburgs. New states appeared and disappeared: Armenia, Tannu Tuva, Bavaria, the Free City of Trieste. There were small wars and insurrections. Communism had been set loose. Turkey collapsed into the chaos and turmoil of internal war. In Cairo the militants, the lawyers, even the effendis wanted Egypt for the Egyptians. But the British did not want to abandon the strategic advantage of the canal and of Egypt as the great base on the way to India. Egypt was crucial to Britain's new treaty empire in the Middle East.

Egypt's premier nationalist politician was now Saad Zagloul Pasha. Born in the Nile Delta to a landowning village leader, he had gone to al-Azhar University and been exposed to Western ideas, learned French, become a lawyer, and married advantageously in 1906 to the daughter of the pro-British prime minister, Mustafa Fahmi Pasha. A dedicated reformer, he had been appointed minister of education at the urging of Lord Cromer the same year, and for four years he introduced new programs. He became minister of justice, serving until 1913, when he resigned and was elected to the Legislative Assembly as the most prominent nationalist. Essentially a moderate, experienced in two ministries, competent and honest, Zagloul had shaped himself as the most prominent and available Egyptian political leader.

After four years in the assembly and with the war over, Zagloul was still dedicated to negotiation and accommodation, but he believed that Egypt had a right to independence. He was supported by the new middle class, the lawyers and politicians, and their allies in the countryside. They said they didn't want gradual concessions—independence on the installment plan. Those who followed Zagloul organized in 1918 as the Wafd Party, seeking an end to British tutelage. Few anticipated instant independence but most expected concessions. The British exiled Zagloul to Malta for a month so he could reconsider his demands.

Just as the incident in Dinshawai had provoked anger and resentment, the end of the war and the use of the forbidden word "independence" encouraged the most ambitious. Beginning in November 1919, the various nationalists resorted to random terror. On November 22, a British officer caught alone on the street was killed, and the next day four British soldiers were shot and wounded. The numbers might be small but the impact was considerable. In 1920 there were two bomb attacks on Egyptian cabinet ministers. Negotiations led nowhere. When the violence erupted again, Zagloul was again exiled in December 1921, sent first to Aden and then on to the Seychelles. Nothing was solved. At this point the British recognized that there would have to be a new arrangement. Zagloul was allowed to return.

Over the next two years, new and old politicians, the British, the traditionalists and the palace maneuvered through a series of governments, proposals and confrontations. In the palace, the Sultan Ahmed Fuad sought to enhance his own power and protect the dynasty that stretched back to Mohammed Ali. From time to time there were violent incidents, undertaken more to concentrate minds than to open a prolonged armed struggle.

On March 15, 1922, Egypt's independence was declared.

Britain, now represented by a high commissioner, would control the Suez Canal Zone until the concession ran out in 1968, would dominate Egyptian politics and supply the personnel and skills to administer the country—all this under the green flag of the newly declared King Ahmed Fuad. Even after the 1924 election, when the Legislative Assembly had a huge Wafd Party majority, the Egyptians did not have an effective government or real control of their destiny. The British army was stationed in the country, British officials were seconded to all the ministries, British money and influence were used to manipulate the politicians and limit the ambitions of the king. Egypt had a king and a flag, and issued postage stamps, but was hardly independent.

Those who had opted for violence accepted that the prospects for revolution were poor. The prospect of punishing the alien occupiers, however, was appealing. Honor at least could be salvaged and shame avoided by action. The fanatics looked for a symbolic target, another victim like Boutros Pasha Ghali. Soon they decided on Sir Lee Stack, the *sirdar*, commander of the Egyptian army; as a foreigner, he was an affront. Stack was also governor-general of Sudan, where the Egyptians had been denied control by the British.

On November 19, 1924, Sir Lee was to be driven as usual from the Ministry of War in Cairo to his home on Gezira Island. Along the way his driver noticed some kind of scuffle on the street, and slowed the car. There was a small crowd, mostly young men dressed like students. The limousine crept along, and suddenly the "students" rushed the vehicle. Stack looked out of the window. People leaning out to watch from the buildings nearby heard shots. The car had stopped. Seven "students" turned from the limousine and began to run, leaving Stack crumpled up in the back of his state car, and then the killers disappeared into the crowd.

This was not just another murder on the Nile—not just an Egyptian, even an important Egyptian official, killed or a British soldier ambushed. Stack was a powerful imperial figure, friend of the ambassador, Lord Allenby, friend of royals, and star of the British establishment. With his murder, the assassins had swiftly and truly made their point about the Agreement of 1922 and sham independence. The imperial infidel was not immune to Egyptian vengeance. Zagloul rushed to apologize for Egypt, but apologies alone would not do.

British vengeance was swift and nearly absolute. There was no negotiation, only an ultimatum: the Egyptian government must apologize, must bring the criminals to justice with the utmost energy, must suppress all popular agitation. The Egyptians must pay a fine of £500,000 and end opposition to the rights of foreigners in the country. Worse, the Egyptian army had to withdraw from Sudan, leaving only the British in charge:

> *His Majesty's Government consider that this murder, which holds up Egypt as at present governed to the contempt of civilized people, is the natural outcome of a campaign of hostility to British rights and British subjects in Egypt and the Sudan, founded upon a heedless ingratitude for benefits conferred by Great Britain....*

Compliance meant accepting that national politics was a futile exercise. For a decade there had been revolving Egyptian prime ministers, repeated palace conspiracies, the corruption of the Wafd, a new constitution, and discussions with the British about a future treaty and general tranquility. But nothing had really happened in terms of the real transfer of power. During the independence years no Egyptian wanted to risk the cost of British intervention. The great agitator Zagloul had died in 1927 and with him militant nationalism.

But in fact, significant events had been transpiring quite out of sight of the major actors. In the provincial town of Ismailiyya in 1927, a primary school teacher named Hasan al-Banna—devout, shrewd and enthusiastic—organized a small group called al-Ikhwan al-Muslimon, the "Moslem Brothers." He wanted to engage faithful Egyptians into a social force as brothers, *al-ikhwan*. He insisted that Islam required action and commitment, not simply habit and attendance at the mosque. Allah, not elections, would be the answer to the power of secularism; the faith would replace political parties. There had been other Islamic societies—Zagloul himself had belonged to one; but the new brotherhood was special, offering a role to those who had left their villages or were confused by novelty. Al-Ikhwan offered a mission.

There were rituals and purpose and a sense of righteousness. The secret brotherhood proved so attractive that the next year al-Banna was able to move his headquarters to Cairo. Al-Ikhwan—part political party, part guild and welfare organization—was a net of cells, and also a way of thinking that gave meaning to narrow lives shaken loose from the old sureties. There was a place for the educated, the urban worker, the clever villager. Branches began to open all over Egypt, each reporting to the center. The poor gave a few coins and the comfortable more; charity was a duty.

Intense and charismatic, Sheikh Hasan al-Banna, now known as the Supreme Guide, traveled constantly but secretly, often hidden in a red cloak, to spread the faith and urge a return to the fundamentals as a road to the future. Allah was the solution to the challenges of contemporary society, the only force that could counter the appeal of the secular West and correct the flaws of Arab society.

The Moslem Brothers continued to expand. A small room could become a mosque, and clubs and schools opened with little investment. Teachers of the Koran were easy to find and rooms were readily offered. Welfare programs and disaster relief were organized. Appealing to traditional Koranic law, the *shari'a*, al-Ikhwan called for a return to the customs of the past and avoidance of alcohol, the cinema and immodest dress. In the grubby slums, in the neglected towns of Upper Egypt, in classrooms and law offices, Islam suddenly mattered again. The poor were attracted because the Brothers gave life meaning; the educated and ambitious were attracted because the organization offered them a forum and a means to act.

For many, the long and fitful independence struggle was more readily seen as a way to reestablish the cherished values of the faith. Egypt didn't need Western values and didn't have to compete with the West. Everything of value could be found in the Koran, everything proper in the customs and commands of Islam. The brotherhood and the Supreme Guide offered pride and perhaps power, and did so largely without any notice by the authorities, the police, the palace or the British. The Brothers had no interest in conventional politics—the old nationalist Wafd Party, the communists, the xenophobic cadres of Young Egypt, the conservatives and radicals, all the factions shaped by reaction to the West. The brotherhood offered tradition, faith, exultation, strictures with daily pertinence.

The spread of al-Ikhwan hardly touched the visible political life of Egypt as the established parties and the British continued to focus on adjusting national interests to British requirements. To assure more effective governance, the British had decided to negotiate an accommodation. These negotiations ultimately culminated in the Anglo-Egyptian Treaty in August 1936. To Egyptians, the new treaty was a grand concession, a farce, an insult or a stroke of diplomacy, depending on viewpoint. The British assumed that with Europe entering troubled times, Egypt was at last secure and nationalist agitation blunted.

Five months after the treaty was signed, on his eighteenth birthday, Farouk succeeded his father as the new king. Egyptian political and public opinion had hopes for the young King Farouk. He was attractive, slim and eager, and had maneuvered himself into power early. The British thought he would be useful to them; the nationalists hoped he would press for greater independence. Farouk was soon addicted to power, and especially the ability it gave him to make marginal changes, to thwart the ambitious, and best of all to reward his friends. For him, politics was a game, not a means to some higher end. Increasingly capricious, he manipulated and corrupted politicians and savored the tangible pleasures of power.

Despite his increasingly obvious flaws, however, the king had support. For some time, Farouk could rely on al-Azhar—the scholars of the *ulema*, the doctors of Islamic law, along with the conservative army officer class—and rely too on his friends and his own talent at conspiracy in order to survive. In any case, the alternative to the existing Egyptian balance of power was either conspiracy or protest, and protest had proved futile.

In 1935, the year before King Farouk's ascension, the Wafd leader Nahas Pasha had delivered a fiery speech against British domination. The crowd was delighted. In response, the students rushed into the street and provoked the police. One of those in the mob was an unknown young man named Gamal Abdel Nasser, unremarkable in academic achievement but strong in nationalist commitment. Like others of his generation, he was eager to act. During the riot, the police batoned the students and Nasser ended up in a hospital with a skull fracture.

The new Anglo-Egyptian Treaty had been negotiated in hopes that such displays as this one could be forestalled, that conventional politics would absorb national interests and that in time the king would become more responsible. But the new generation of nationalists had no intention of accepting such a system. So now there was a cadre of young men like Nasser with scars and vague plans for the next time.

Nasser and his nationalist friends could riot only so often. The revolution sought by the militant Moslems did not even have a spokesman. Al-Ikhwan worked out of sight, far from power, transforming the attitudes of ordinary people, while Egyptian politics evolved into a struggle between Farouk in his Italianate palaces and the politicians in the baroque Princess Chivekiars palazzo housing the Assembly of Ministers. In any case, as the prospect of another world war grew, British concerns in the area were no longer focused on Egyptian politics but on potential adversaries: the Italians in Libya, German agents in Syria or Iraq, Zionist dissent and Arab nationalists in the Palestine Mandate.

The British had frozen into caricatures of late Victorian imperialism, dominated by precedence and protocol, appropriate form and dress, and the cutting edge of social categories: rank, accent, ancestry. For the representatives of empire, the babble in various tongues of the cosmopolitan caste of émigrés in Farouk's Egypt, the fancy balls, the French novels, elegant boutiques, perfumed cigarettes, sophisticated chatter about profit and card games—all held no charms. The rich, often Levantine émigrés wore tailored clothes, consummated cunning business deals, attended tea dances and had assignations. They drank iced coffee in the heat of the day, had aperitifs at Baudrot and ate cream cakes at Groppi's.

Like their Victorian predecessors, few of the British administrators at the Residency or the engineers overseeing the canals knew any more about the bankers and effendi than they did about the *fellahín*. Even in 1939, the British in residence saw less of the country than a tourist saw. So the British initialed their documents, met at dances and polo matches, shot pigeons and maintained standards. The secretary of the Royal Yacht Club in Alexandria in 1943 turned away the king of Greece, Noel Coward and Lord Keyes because they were wearing white naval shorts. Even war allowed for no exceptions to convention. All of those with power and position—the Armenian merchant bankers, the British cavalry colonel, chattering women in summer dresses at café tables, the secretary of the Royal Yacht Club—so comported themselves as to provoke most Egyptians, who as "wogs" felt isolated in their own country, patronized and scorned by foreigners. They were not welcome at the Khedival Sporting Club or the Union Bar, or for that matter at Shepheards Hotel.

In September 1939, when war again came to Europe, Egyptian anxiety and demands were pushed into the background by Britain's focus on the war effort. With the early triumphs of the Axis, Britain by June 1940 was alone and beleaguered, with a vast treaty empire to defend. Egypt had been far away from the great events of Europe, but there was war in North Africa and the Middle East as well. Yet even after the collapse of France, the Italian threat from Libya proved chimerical. The Germans did not win the air battle for Britain, and in September 1940 the invasion, "Operation Sea Lion," was canceled. In the Middle East the British held firm, occupying Iraq and deposing the pro-Axis regime there. Germany's ally Vichy France was driven out of Syria and Lebanon.

Then, the German Afrika Korps under General Erwin Rommel arrived in Libya. Unlike the Italians, the Germans were a serious threat. The war in the Middle East had now truly come to the borders of Egypt. British and Commonwealth troops flooded into new British bases, into the Suez Canal Zone, into the streets of Cairo and on out to the desert. Rommel's success seemed inevitable. The British lost Tobruk and could not hold the frontier, but in Cairo many Egyptians didn't care who won the war as long as Egypt benefited. Some bet on the Axis, the Germans, and Rommel's panzers. On May 16, 1941, the British arrested the former Egyptian chief of staff, Ali al-Masr, just before his plane—Farouk's own private aircraft—was to take off secretly for Beirut. Al-Masr had been involved in contact with the Germans and the British suspected he intended to aid them. A few Egyptian officers, including a young nationalist officer named Anwar Sadat, had also become involved. There were secret meetings, attractive women, spies hidden on a Nile houseboat, until the British arrested them all and Sadat was imprisoned.

The students took to the streets shouting "Rommel! Rommel! Rommel!" Names were taken, arrests made, protests monitored. Such choreographed riots were, however, no real threat. British counterintelligence smashed the plots and al-Masr ended up in prison.

Farouk had persisted in exploiting what he imagined to be an opportunity. His support of ministers sympathetic to Germany was neither subtle nor long tolerated by the British. At the beginning of February 1942, Prime Minister Hussein Sire Pasha resigned after the British forced him to break off relations with Vichy France. The king bitterly resented this British interference. In retaliation, he then tried to arrange the appointment as prime minister of Ali Maher Pasha, one of the most pro-Axis politicians and so quite impossible as far as the British were concerned.

Farouk was delighted with British discomfort. On February 3, 1942, the British ambassador, Sir Miles Lampson, visited the palace and informed the king that the only satisfactory appointment as prime minister was Nahas Pasha. If this was not accomplished by six o'clock in the evening of the next day, the king must expect the consequences. Farouk decided that the best alternative was to do nothing, to delay, quibble and wait for the inevitable consequences to disperse.

At nine in the evening of February 4, British infantry and a squad of Stuart Mark 3 tanks moved into the square in front of the Abdin Palace. Inside in his office, Farouk could soon hear tank motors turning over. Outside, the British ambassador's yellow Rolls Royce Phantom III pulled to a stop. An armored car smashed down the gates. The palace guard were promptly disarmed. Ambassador Lampson and the new British commander in Egypt, along with eight officers with drawn pistols, made their way through long, dimly lit corridors toward Farouk's study. Farouk was furious. He waved a revolver, threatening to resist. His aides fluttered and appeased. A wrong move and the dynasty was finished.

The king sat behind his desk glowering as the British entered. He immediately announced to Sir Miles, "We have already instructed Nahas Pasha to form the government of his choice." There was nothing else to do. The crisis was over, and so too were Farouk's remaining feelings of responsibility for the Egyptian dynasty. He began devoting more time to exploring the charms of nightlife and ladies, and dabbling desultorily in conspiracy on the side.

The British intrusion became a national symbol—not because the now fat king had been insulted but because Egyptian illusions were gone, pride was lost once again, the nation was shamed. Some wanted instant retaliation. Several young officers, including Anwar Sadat, now out of prison, Abdel Latif Boghdadi and Saleh Salem, offered to undertake a suicide mission against the British.

Increasingly the models that appealed from the secular West were radical ideologies: communism, fascism, permanent revolution or revolutionary anarchism. In the past, provocative violence had been largely symbolic, assuring vengeance and honor but at great practical cost. Those who resorted to such violence, like Sadat and his colleagues, were few. Mostly, Egypt waited out the war. The politicians hoped for national vindication, the radical imams and sheikhs for a return to Islam and the everyday people for very little.

Meanwhile, to the blind child of four, Omar Abdel Rahman, all this was another world. In his parents' small house, gray-brown and bleak, he had only the Koran, his family and the familiarity of the village. This was all that most of Egypt's poor possessed. But after the gates of the Abdin Palace were smashed in February 1942 and Farouk was humiliated, this was not enough. It was not enough for Nasser's Free Officers underground group nor for the other conspirators, not enough for the resentful and the ambitious nor for the mob or the students, not even for the *fellahín*. The poor might not understand revolutionary rhetoric or political strategies, but even they recognized that Egypt was in the hands of infidels.

TWO

ZION ON THE NILE:
THE MURDER OF LORD MOYNE

F ar from Cairo, across the Sinai Desert, the British presence
in the Palestine Mandate had become strategically
significant. Palestine had become a nexus of routes, military
bases and influences, a protector of the route to India, a front line
in the campaigns against Lebanon, Syria and Iraq, a presence in a
volatile and vital Arab region. The British had divided the Mandate. The east across the Jordan River became the independent
Arab state of Transjordan, while the Arabs and Jews in the west
remained London's mandated responsibility. The Jews had been
promised a national homeland by Britain with the Balfour Declaration on November 2, 1916. Arabs opposed any such homeland
and each year would demonstrate on November 2, Balfour Day.

In the Palestine Mandate after 1918, the British had to balance Arab and Jewish interests with their own, a process
complicated by the pressures of Jewish immigrants fleeing European anti-Semitism. The Arabs wanted no more Jews. The
Mandate had become a country twice promised. There were incidents, Arab attacks on Jews and the creation of an underground
Jewish self-defense army, the Haganah. Then in 1936, a widespread
Arab revolt against the British began: riots, ambushes and snipers,
arson and road closures. The British responded with an effective,
if protracted, anti-insurgency campaign.

By 1939 the British had finally put down armed resistance
and then offered the Arabs concessions in the White Paper of 1939.
Nonetheless, until the battle of El Alamein in 1941, the Arabs of
Palestine had been fascinated with the prospect of a British defeat
by the Germans. In Iraq, Syria and Lebanon, the Arab nationalists

had in many cases made common cause with Britain's enemies. In Palestine the Arabs were more discreet, although the leader of the Arab Revolt, the grand mufti of Jerusalem, was known to be pro-Axis. The mufti was a handsome, clever nationalist, a cunning agitator, an effective conspirator who had been accepted by the British in hopes of co-opting him. The mufti disappointed them. He had continued agitating for British withdrawal and had encouraged Arab rural habits of violence to frustrate the British forces from 1936 to 1939. London hoped that the White Paper of 1939 would limit his capacity for causing trouble. The British, in any case, would try to ignore Arab provocation in order to assure a stable base area for the war. Since the Zionist settlers could offer London little but complications, the Arabs were favored despite the mufti's and the Arab nationalists' past record.

So at the very time that the Jews most needed a refuge in Palestine, their prospects were poorest. The war had gobbled up Zionist assets in Europe, filled concentration camps with Jews and left the Jewish settlers in Palestine isolated and impotent. The Arab Middle East was strategically vital to the British war effort and Arab support was a real factor in resisting the Axis. The Zionists became more and more cut off from European events, involved in illegal immigration but unable for the most part to take action against the British—Hitler's enemy. Some of the more militant Zionists had launched attacks against the British before 1939; but with the beginning of the European war, many Zionists joined British units to fight Nazi Germany.

A tiny minority of Zionist zealots, however, persisted in their campaign against the immediate enemy, the imperial power. Their anger was stoked because the British denied refuge in Palestine to endangered European Jews. The small, radical LEHI (the Hebrew acronym for Fighters for the Freedom of Israel), led by Avraham Stern Yair and so known by the British as the Stern Gang, had continued their armed struggle. As urban gunmen and guerrillas, LEHI engaged in bank raids, urban ambushes and gunfights, amusing the Arabs who could now watch the Jews alienate the British. Even the sympathetic revisionist Zionists in the Irgun Zvai Leumi underground saw the LEHI violence as counterproductive, at least until the arrival of their new leader Menachem Begin in 1943. The great majority in the Jewish Agency, like its leader David Ben Gurion, adamantly opposed the adventures of the zealous Stern Gang.

Stern himself was a charismatic leader, handsome and talented, a poet and theorist who spoke many languages and, most of all, had the capacity to inspire dedication and sacrifice. He had a seriousness of purpose and a presence that touched all those in the underground. Yet the constituency of the LEHI was tiny. The few LEHI gunmen were perpetually on the run. Stern himself had no place to stay. His followers were shot or arrested one by one. By January 1943 hardly anyone was left. Stern slipped silently through Tel Aviv, carrying a folding cot with him to sleep in the few rooms still open to a fugitive. In February he was killed trying to escape from the last LEHI safe house at 8 Mizrachi B Street in the Florentine quarter of south Tel Aviv. By then, most of his followers were intimidated, dead or in prison. The Jews in Palestine had been either more daring or more foolish than the nationalists of Egypt.

Few in Egypt other than British security police even knew about Stern. Britain was focused on the real war. Prime Minister Churchill had considered Egypt so important that he appointed a minister of state, Lord Moyne, to oversee Egyptian events. From a well-connected Anglo-Irish family, Moyne was for a time the center of events. He had an agenda filled with far more pressing matters than the minor trouble caused by a few Zionist gunmen. So none but the most concerned in the British Palestine police noticed when several of the LEHI hard men, the prime gunmen and organizers, escaped from prison. Everyone in Palestine, in Egypt, in the Middle East was concentrating on the global struggle and, as the tide turned in favor of the Allies, wondering what would come with peace.

The LEHI militants didn't want to wait for the Nazis to kill the last Jews, or for the British to make their plans without recognizing the legitimate demands of the Zionists. In 1943 several key LEHI leaders escaped from British detention camps and contacted sympathizers. They revived the organization and, reinforced by other escapees, turned it into a classic revolutionary organization.

During these years of despair, the Stern Gang members lived

on nerve rather than hope. They had no prospects or assets, possessing only a few weapons, a clandestine radio, the faith and a compelling conviction to act. They began again to function as urban guerrillas, a few gunmen in the streets of Tel Aviv and Jerusalem. In 1944 the Irgun Zvai Leumi underground led by Menachem Begin also began an armed struggle, but at first its actions were limited. The violence alienated nearly all Palestinian Jews and the orthodox Zionists, hardly damaged the British, and did the Arabs no harm.

As news of the Holocaust continued to reach the Mandate, the pressure to act intensified. The Allies seemed uninterested in the fate of European Jewry. The British, still pro-Arab, persisted in treating the Mandate as a strategic matter. In Cairo, Lord Moyne hardly considered Zionist rights or aspirations. He had far more pressing priorities. The LEHI leaders knew that to have an effect on events, they would have to resort to personal terror, a conventional Eastern European strategy. They would have to strike at the heart of the occupying power.

They didn't have the assets to wage guerrilla war or a congenial context for revolt, as the Arabs had between 1936 and 1939. In fact, they had no more than a few absolutely dedicated, if untrained and unprepared, faithful to wage any sort of campaign. So LEHI chose strategic terror, using assassination as a means to punish the British and publicize their grievances. The three-man LEHI High Command focused on the high commissioner, Sir Harold McMichael. He was an obvious target, an arrogant man with a gift for the hard word, sympathetic to Arab over Jewish interests, and suspected of being personally anti-Semitic. But none of the LEHI and Irgun assassination attempts worked. McMichael completed his term and flew out of the Mandate back to London, leaving behind a moderate, Lord Gort, with no record to engender distaste. The symbol of repression having been replaced by an administrator whose death would not be worth the risk, the LEHI High Command decided to target the most vulnerable British symbol available: Lord Moyne, British minister of state and resident in Cairo. The three-man command chose two young militants, Eliahu Hakim and Eliahu Bet-Zouri—the two Eliahu, as they became known—to go to Cairo and kill Moyne.

In the autumn of 1944, the sprawling, filthy city of Cairo was filled with American air crews, Sikhs, soldiers from Manchester, Greeks of uncertain origin, warlords of the black market, Nubian waiters. The city absorbed one more exotic, Eliahu Hakim, a prospective assassin dispatched by LEHI. For Hakim, that Cairo autumn was a strange, unreal time, stretching him between his Palestinian past with his friends in the dingy rooms of the underground, and the looming deed that would change history. On arrival in the city, he began the traditional rituals of the assassin—wandering about on the victim's trail, seeking patterns and rumors. Where did Lord Moyne eat? When did he leave the office? Where did his limousine park? Who was always at home? Who guarded him? Who visited him?

Hakim's mind was filled with abstractions of history and destiny. A thin young man with a dark mustache, wearing a blue shirt, he spent hours walking beside a dark-haired girl called Yaffa. He loitered near the Nile Cornice, not far from the British embassy. He was aware that he and she were not ordinary people; they were instruments of fate.

From a previous visit to Cairo, Hakim was familiar with the LEHI organization in the city, the strange aliases, the safe rooms, the tiny circle of the trusted, the double and triple life of the underground. It was easy to hide in the autumn of 1944; the British didn't even know he was in the city. He went dancing, ate in restaurants, walked with Yaffa along the river. Each night he returned to his small room at 4 Shari'a Gheit el-Noubi in the Mouski district, far from the elegant embassies and tidy gardens along the Nile. By the end of October, he knew Moyne's patterns and chose his moment. His colleague Bet-Zouri, the other Eliahu, arrived. Hakim's drifting was over.

On November 2, 1944, Hakim walked past Lord Moyne's residence once more. His plan was simple: Each working day, Moyne was driven home to his garden for lunch in his Packard limousine, without fanfare or protection. Once the limousine stopped in the garden, Moyne would be vulnerable to the two Eliahu—stationary, undefended, unprepared. They could be in and out in minutes. The pistols were loaded. The bicycles were hired. The safe house was ready. The deed that seemed so unreal when the two young men accepted the mission in Palestine had come down to a matter of timing and distance.

At 1:00 P.M. on November 6, 1944, accompanied by his personal secretary, Dorothy S. Osmond, and his aide, Captain A. G. Hughes-Onslow, Lord Moyne left the building as usual to be driven across Cairo for lunch. It was a ten-minute trip, a welcome break from the office routine. Moyne's black Packard Saloon, driven by Lance Corporal A. Fuller, soon edged through the impossible traffic and crossed the Nile bridge into Gezira. At 4 Shari'a Galabayas, Fuller turned the car into the walled yard, drove on past the underground garage, and pulled up before the three steps leading to the front door. Hughes-Onslow popped out of the right front seat and ran up to the front door, reaching into his pocket for the key. Fuller opened his door and got out. He snapped shut the front door of the Packard and started around the back so he could open the door for Moyne.

Hughes-Onslow was about to take the door key out of his pocket when he heard someone say, in English, "Don't move. Stay where you are. Don't move." Fuller had reached the rear of the Packard. He stopped. Bet-Zouri raised his revolver and fired directly into Fuller's chest. The slugs tore through his body, severing the right internal iliac artery, and then smashed against the far garden wall. Fuller collapsed in the driveway, sprawled on his back, and quickly bled to death.

Inside the car, Dorothy Osmond leaned forward at the sound of the shots. She heard Fuller groan but could not understand what was happening. She saw a young man of medium height, about thirty, wearing gray trousers and a lighter jacket and tie. He was standing back from the car, holding a revolver. Another man, taller and darker, moved up to the Packard's rear window next to Moyne. Hakim had finally reached the target. He looked once at Dorothy Osmond and said, "Don't move."

Moyne began to open the door. Hakim thrust his revolver toward him and started firing into him, slowly and deliberately. The first slug hit Moyne in the neck on the right side, just above the clavicle, jerking his head around. The second ripped into his abdomen near the twelfth rib, becoming embedded to the right of the second lumbar vertebra. Before Hakim fired again, Moyne raised his right hand to ward off the shots. The third slug ripped across his four fingers and tore in and out of his chest, leaving a superficial wound. Hakim stepped back. Moyne managed to cry, "Oh, they've shot us!" as blood spurted out of his neck. Hakim drew further back and moved away from the car. Moyne slumped forward, unconscious.

By the time Dorothy Osmond could grasp what had happened, Hakim and Bet-Zouri had run out of the yard and off the grounds. They jumped onto their rented bikes and began pedaling madly down Shari'a Galabayas toward the Samalek Bridge. Once across and into the traffic, they could simply disappear in the crowds. Chasing after them, Hughes-Onslow rushed out the gate and stopped at the sentry box to give the alarm. Hearing the hue and cry behind them, Hakim and Bet-Zouri peddled off into a side road, Shari'a Bahres Amer, and then turned again by the residence of King George of Greece. They were very nearly away, but suddenly, just at the bridge, El-Amin Mahomed Abdullah, a member of the Ministerial Protection Squad, appeared on his motorcycle. He ignored a volley of warning shots fired into the air—Hakim and Bet-Zouri were determined not to injure any Egyptians in their operation. Others rushed up. The two still would not fire on Egyptians, and so they were captured.

In the meantime, Dorothy Osmond had run into the house and telephoned for help. She also asked the duty clerk to send for the police. After raising the alarm, Hughes-Onslow hurried to the nearby Gezira police post and phoned the Fifteenth Scottish Hospital to arrange for a doctor and an ambulance. By the time he returned to the yard, Major H. W. Forester, alerted by Osmond's telephone call, had already arrived from the ministerial resident's office. It was just 1:15. Air Vice-Marshall Nutting and Major Woodford appeared. Forester walked over to Fuller, who was lying on his back in a pool of blood, obviously dead. The three British officers stood there appalled. Suddenly Major Woodford noticed that Moyne's hand had moved.

When they rushed over to him, he regained consciousness but seemed confused. He asked Forester if he could be moved to his room, as he was feeling rather uncomfortable. Soothing him, Forester suggested that they wait until the doctor arrived. Moyne asked several times in a low voice when the doctor would arrive. In a very few minutes, the doctor and ambulance appeared. Moyne was driven straight to the hospital and admitted at 1:40, just forty minutes after he had left his office. He had lost a great deal of blood through gross hemorrhaging and was still bleeding. His pulse was imperceptible. He was in shock. At 1:45 he was given the first of three transfusions. The doctors could not reverse the decline and, at 8:40 that evening, Lord Moyne died. The deed was finally done.

British security forces and Egyptian political circles were thrown into chaos. No one had expected assassins in Cairo, foreign or Egyptian. No one knew who the two men were, who had sent them or what they represented. All that was known was the names they gave, Saltzmann and Cohen; but the authorities were uncertain: was it Zalzman? During the afternoon and evening of November 6, the authorities continued to interrogate the two men.

The Egyptian government reacted to the news of the assassination with deep horror and immediate panic. Everyone still remembered the British reaction to the assassination of Sir Lee Stack Pasha. That one mad moment in 1926 had cost the Egyptian monarchy an empire to the south, in Sudan, which might never be regained, and had set back the nation's march toward independence. Neither King Farouk nor Prime Minister Ahmed Maher Pasha wanted another such disaster in 1944. Amid the confusion of the moment, the Egyptians finally learned the only good news of the day: the assassins were not Egyptian.

The British soon decided that one of the young men, first identified as Moshe Cohen Itzak, might actually be Private Eliahu Hakim, who had deserted from the British army on February 9. The other remained an unknown. Although both suspects admitted the deed, Saltzmann to shooting Lance Corporal Fuller and Hakim to shooting Moyne, they were forthcoming with very little else. Their silence gave the other LEHI people in Cairo time to go underground. On Tuesday, November 7, after nearly twenty-four hours of questioning, the two finally announced that they were members of LEHI and that what they had done was done on the instructions of this organization.

In the meantime, British police had uncovered ample and

grisly evidence of LEHI's involvement. Ballistics tests on the bullets from the two pistols were checked with files in Palestine. The results indicated that the weapons had been repeatedly used in LEHI's armed struggle against the police in the Mandate. Bet-Zouri's 1916 Parabellum had been used to murder Constable Zev Flesch in Ramat Gan in March 1944. The report on Hakim's Nagant 7.62 revolver was more startling: it had been used in the murder of Ibrahim Hassan el-Karam in Rehavia, Jerusalem, on November 14, 1937; the murder of another Arab, whose name and dates had disappeared from police files; the murder of a Constable Caley on March 23, 1943; the murder of Inspector Green and Constable Ewer in Haifa on February 14, 1944; and the murder of another constable in Tel Aviv on May 10, 1944. As recently as September 26, the gun had been used in Jerusalem to murder a top LEHI target, Constable J. T. Wilkin, who had arrested Avraham Stern Yair on February 12, 1942, at 8 Mizrachi B Street in Tel Aviv and then had left the flat before he was killed "attempting to escape." The macabre Nagant revolver was in fact a major artifact of LEHI's terror campaign. The weapons had never been discarded because the organization had no replacements. LEHI had taken on an empire with a handful of mismatched weapons, the absolute dedication of a few, and a strategy of personal terror. There were zealots in Cairo who noted the example.

The two men did not act like terrorists nor did they fit into comfortable categories. They had killed Fuller and Moyne but would not kill Egyptians to save their own lives. They realized the cost of not shooting El-Amin Mahomed Abdullah off his motorbike, and they explained why: it would have been killing a potential ally, another victim of British imperialism, and would have alienated Arab opinion. Moyne was guilty. El-Amin was not.

On January 10, 1945, the assassins were in an Egyptian dock, charged with murder. They were placed behind an iron grille overlooking the courtroom. Those in the crowded courtroom saw two rather conventional young men, the taller, Hakim, in a jacket, and Bet-Zouri in an open-necked shirt. Both stood calmly manacled between a group of Egyptian guards with red fezzes. Both were—and had been since their capture—self-possessed, almost serene. They had, of course, no defense, only an explanation:

Our deed stemmed from our motives, and our motives stemmed from our ideals, and if we proved our ideals were right and just, then our deed was right and just.

We don't fight for the sake of a National Home. We fight for our freedom. In our country a foreign power rules.... If we have turned to the gun, it is because we were forced to the gun.

The next day both LEHI assassins were condemned to death. Despite the almost universal horror in Cairo at Lord Moyne's assassination, the bearing and presence of his killers evoked among many Egyptians a grudging respect. There was no doubt that both were idealists as well as fanatics. Neither had hesitated to take responsibility for the deed, and neither seemed to fear death.

On March 22, the eve of the executions, the chief rabbi of Egypt, Nissim Ochana, spent the last night with Hakim and Bet-Zouri. On March 23 they were dressed in the traditional, ill-fitting red burlap suits of condemned men, marched barefoot to the gallows, blindfolded at the scaffold and hanged. They never anticipated less. Hakim said just before he died, looking down at the red burlap, "This is the finest suit of clothes I have ever worn in my life." And many Egyptians understood the appeal of martyrdom.

The impact of the Moyne assassination reinforced many Egyptian assumptions about the nature of politics—the means to act on events. Righteous murder was as legitimate for the Zionists as it had been for Egyptians. For the zealous nationalists and especially the Islamists, long planning and careful organization seldom offered a satisfactory program. The most militant wanted to make an instant impact. They wanted, if not power, then vengeance—wanted to influence the many by the propaganda of the deed. The Zionist assassins had chosen murder because no other means was available and in Egypt many felt that no other means was as potent. The British were enormously powerful. Those who wanted a different Egypt, an Islamic Egypt, could cite as a way of getting there the murder of Lord Moyne.

Two young Jews had made a difference: they had punished the British despite their power. Egyptian patriots might also make a difference. Both those who wanted to construct a nation and those who assumed the future should be determined by Allah accepted that violence could have a future role in Egypt. Most Egyptians retained hope in parties, political pressure, justice recognized, demonstrations and argument, an accommodation with the British. But a few were attracted to the gun.

THREE

THE NEW PHARAOHS: NASSER, SADAT AND MUBARAK, 1945–1982

With the war coming to a close, Prime Minister Ahmed Maher Pasha declared war on the Axis, as prudence demanded and as the British wanted. Ahmed Maher had for some time been seen by Egyptian nationalists as a British instrument. Some Egyptians recognized accommodation with the British as necessary, but many nationalists were resentful: Ahmed Maher was not forced to declare war; he could have shown Egyptian independence in such matters by doing nothing. On February 14, 1945, he was assassinated as a symbol of shame.

By the end of the war, Egypt was in turmoil, the system discredited, the palace corrupt, the government ineffectual, the future in doubt. The police were often creatures of Farouk's palace and the army was riddled with intrigue. There was no unified nationalist movement as there had been under Saad Zagloul in 1918. The British presence in the Suez Canal Zone and power in Cairo were offensive to nearly all. The only maneuvers of the emerging Cold War that were of interest were the anti-imperial struggles.

Those struggles barely reached the masses. In the countryside, in the Delta villages, habits changed little. In the vast complex of the Cairo that lay beyond the famous Khan el-Khalili market, in the shadow of the world's oldest university, al-Azhar, the famous mosques were embedded in some of the world's most wretched slums, where hundreds of thousands of people crowded into ancient districts cut by narrow lanes, two camels wide as the archaic law required. The buildings had no numbers, no water, no ventilation. Some of the desperate were crammed into the Mameluke tombs or lived under the stairs or in huts on the roof of

any available building. Any breeze in the old quarters brought not
relief but the odors of raw sewage, bad cooking oil, petrol fumes
and the eternal gray grit blowing off the Sahara.

In December 1946 there was an assassination attempt on
Mustafa Nahas, which failed when the grenade did not destroy his
car. Mustafa Nahas, one of the old nationalists and so part of the
system, had cooperated with the British. The Egyptian government
requested new talks. The British dispatched a vague response in
January. Then, in a Cairo street in broad daylight, righteous gunmen murdered Amin Othman, another friend of Britain who had
cooperated during the war. The targets were skilled politicians,
administrators, functionaries mostly without charisma whose only
sin was to have been entangled with the British most of their
career.

In February and March of 1946 there were ferocious student
demonstrations. And riots, arrests, arson and strikes, some orches-
trated and most spontaneous, increasingly became the background
music to Egyptian social life. Eventually, in July, the British began
slowly withdrawing troops to bases within the Canal Zone—too
slowly for those who wanted immediate change. The student riots
continued and by the end of the year, guns were being used. The
next year, 1947, was no better, with riots, gelignite attacks, fires set,
grenades tossed, shots fired. The most fervid wanted merely to
drive out the British while the more visionary had begun maneu-
vering to take control of Egypt's future. All were united in the
belief that violence paid.

And then in December 1947, the United Nations voted for
the division of the British Palestine Mandate: there was to be a
Jewish state imposed in an Arab nation. All the Arab states and the
emerging Arab League were absolutely opposed to a Zionist state.
From the first, the palace, the political establishment, the army and
the people of Egypt were committed to war to prevent such a
development. Even while the British were still nominally in charge
of the Mandate, the Arabs began a guerrilla war against the Zionists. The Jews would not withdraw from any settlement, but
reinforced the isolated city of Jerusalem and resisted Arab attacks
that were often disorganized. The Palestinian Arabs could not
defeat the Zionists alone. They needed the help of the regular Arab

armies of Syria, Lebanon, Iraq, the efficient Arab Legion of Trans-jordan, and most of all the Egyptians, the largest and most important Arab nation.

To go to war for the Palestinians in a pan-Arab cause, to oppose the Zionists, to erode British influence was for Egyptians a duty. The palace and the government announced that they were ready, and the generals announced that they were ready too. And so Egypt was prepared for victory over the Jews, a people with no martial tradition, no armed forces, no prospects.

Egypt moved into the partitioned Mandate from Sinai toward Gaza on May 14, 1948, the same day that Israel was proclaimed. The advance was confused, the army ill organized and badly led; it could not defeat the Zionists. One Arab military humiliation followed another. The Arab Legion inflicted heavy casualties but could not cut off Jerusalem. The Egyptians were disgraced, the army was crushed, its corruption and incompetence revealed as the Israelis drove them back into Sinai. Only during the siege at Fallu-jah, where the surrounded Egyptians held out for weeks under heavy attack in the autumn of 1948, did the army earn honor.

For even the most limited *fellahín*, the victory of Israel was the final humiliation: *Nakbah*, "the Catastrophe." The crowds in the streets in Cairo were no longer content with bogus explanations and false victory bulletins. Nearly all Egyptians—the mob, the most conservative Moslem Brothers and the avowed communists—agreed that the system was responsible for the debacle. During the war with Israel, there had been attacks on Jew-ish-, French- and British-owned enterprises, more riots and demonstrations, a bomb in the Jewish quarter of Cairo that killed scores. The real enemy, however, was the British Empire.

In December 1948, Prime Minister Mahmud Fahmi Nuqrashi banned al-Ikhwan. Its branches, offices and publications were closed down and its assets confiscated. Twenty days later a member of al-Ikhwan, dressed as a police officer, shot and killed Nuqrashi. Violence threatened the palace. Those around the king had responded in a similar manner. In February 1949, the supreme guide of the Moslem Brothers, Hasan al-Banna, was murdered at the entrance to the Young Men's Moslem Association headquarters in Cairo. Everyone assumed that the police special branch had killed him in public without fear of prosecution in order to intimidate the others in al-Ikhwan. Even if al-Banna had left little on paper, his ambiguous legacy was ample justification for the militants determined to do political murder.

So intimidation did not work. In March the secretary of the Cairo Court of Appeals was murdered; he had played a part in a trial of al-Ikhwan members two years before. In April there was a dynamite attack on Nahas's residence in Garden City. Everyone suspected al-Ikhwan.

In December 1949, the president of the Young Men's Moslem Association, General Salih Harb, a former minister of defense in Ali Maher's cabinet of 1939, addressed a meeting of a General Islamic Congress at al-Azhar. He waved a revolver in one hand and a Koran in the other: "Brothers, it is these that must speak now." Even if some of the nationalists regarded the Islamic radicals as crude and narrow, bigots in beards, they were sound on the need for change on the national issue. They were useful allies for the time being, not rivals to the radical conspirators. In fact, no one but those involved could readily determine if the murders committed on the streets were done for Allah or for Marx, by a gunman belonging to Young Egypt or by an off-duty Egyptian soldier. The center no longer held.

The British army had withdrawn to the Canal Zone bases; the Egyptian militants' aim was to harass them into full evacuation. After a failure to negotiate a formal British withdrawal, the Egyptian government in October 1951 officially abrogated the Anglo-Egyptian Treaty of 1936—a possibly empty gesture since the British still held the Canal Zone and indicated that they would defend their interests. Egyptian labor boycotted the British and cut off access to the Canal Zone. Crowds demonstrated against their continued illegal presence. Gradually, a largely spontaneous campaign of provocation evolved, including all the radicals, all the nationalist groups, al-Ikhwan and sometimes Egyptian soldiers. The nationalist officers, who had mostly entered the army after the reforms of 1936 opened the Military Academy, responded in their own way. On December 27, 1951, the young officers elected their own slate at the Officers' Club in Cairo—a symbolic defiance of the senior commanders and by extension of the palace.

The British, viewing the *fedayeen* campaign as provocative, reacted with effective anti-insurgency techniques and extended rather than contracted their control of the Canal Zone. They cut off Egyptian units in the Sinai. They were determined not to be intimidated. From November 1951, the British were successfully engaged in an irregular, low-intensity war and by January 1952 were moving relentlessly on Cairo. On January 25, the British commander in Ismailiyya demanded the evacuation of the Egyptian police and authorities. The Egyptians refused, under orders of the minister of the interior, Fuad Serag al-Din. The British promptly deployed overwhelming force and crushed all resistance with dispatch: fifty Egyptian policemen and gendarmes were killed and many more wounded.

At dawn the next day, February 26, 1952, "Black Saturday," the mobs took over the streets of Cairo and burned Western symbols: new car showrooms, Shepheards Hotel, foreign businesses, movie palaces and bars. There was no resistance, no police presence, nothing but howling crowds, clouds of black oily smoke, the sound of falling glass and refugees crowding into embassies, sports clubs and private homes. At twilight, with the fires still burning and the central streets littered with burned-out cars, ash and smashed furniture, the mobs dissipated. They had destroyed 750 establishments, valued at £50,000,000. Thirty people were dead, including ten British citizens.

After Black Saturday the questions were: What came next? Who would benefit from Ismailiyya and the sack of Cairo? The most potent of all the nationalists, the most hidden, were the Free Officers, who had not been directly involved in the *fedayeen* campaign but, under the guidance of Nasser, had wanted to wait until the outcome of their coup was certain. The Free Officers attracted a variety of types: ideologues, military conspirators, soldiers of action; but all shared a sense of purpose.

One of the postwar recruits was Anwar Sadat. The grandson of a Nubian slave, he came from the *fellahín* of the Delta, had gone far and yet was willing to risk all for Egypt. He had a revolutionary history. He had made contact with al-Ikhwan in 1940, had contacts with the Germans in 1942, spent two years in prison, escaped and then became involved in the assassination plots against Prime

Minister Mustafa Nahas Pasha and Finance Minister Amin Othman. Released in August 1948, he had returned to the army in January 1950. There he continued to plot with the other young officers under the leadership of Gamal Abdel Nasser.

If more daring than most of the other officers, Sadat was not alone in the pursuit of a new Egypt. Like some in al-Ikhwan he was willing to kill, and unlike many of his fellow officers, unwilling to wait until conditions were ideal for a coup. For the moment, though, Nasser and caution prevailed: after Black Saturday in February, the officers waited month after month, planning and preparing. Farouk changed prime ministers again and again. Then, on July 20, the king imposed his brother-in-law Ismail Shirin as war minister. The Free Officers feared that his promised investigation would reveal their plots. The time had come to act.

On July 25, the Free Officers took over the nation without opposition. Often first of their social class to rise—Nasser was the son of a postman and Sadat the grandchild of a slave—the officers were dedicated and ambitious, patriots without connections among the rich and famous. They intended to impose honesty and competence on the country. They would decree a revolution if possible and postpone democratic consensus, elections or conventional political activity. They intended to respond to grievance without delay, without need of traditional political allies and within the context of radical, socialist modernization. Their real leader was Lieutenant-Colonel Nasser; but they came to power using an older officer, General Mohammed Neguib, as a front.

Farouk was hustled off into an exile of consumption and dissipation on the Riviera. All the political parties were banned except al-Ikhwan, which was allowed to exist technically because it was an "association," but actually because the officers wanted it to be involved. They offered al-Ikhwan three places on their revolutionary council. The offer was declined. The Moslem Brothers were uncertain of what was to come and decided to wait on events, giving tacit support to the new regime. So the officers had effectively disarmed potentially the most dangerous opponents of the new government.

Al-Ikhwan, unlike the others who had been discarded and disgraced, had never held power or responsibility. The faithful offered a dream, not simply a political alternative or a radical agenda. Egyptians might not be as puritanical as the Saudis, but the vast majority were Islamic as well as Arab. They celebrated the proper feasts and holidays, observed Ramadan, went to the mosque, were socially conservative. They were faithful. Even Sadat had the bump on his forehead earned by kneeling, head to the ground, and facing Mecca to pray five times a day.

From al-Azhar to the villages, most Egyptians were content with the new system. Yet those who followed the laws of the Koran had enormous political potential if the mass of the faithful could be converted to action. The righteous gunmen of al-Ikhwan had already indicated to some the appeal of the gun; and the work of al-Banna had shaped a vast mass organization that, even if damaged by his death, was still in place. So al-Ikhwan had to be treated more cautiously. The new regime first outmaneuvered the politicians of the old establishment, then discarded Neguib before finally beginning to move more openly away from the radical Islamists.

In 1954 al-Ikhwan accepted that with Neguib gone, political parties outlawed and for a time even their own association banned, Nasser and the officers were in full control and their regime's answer to Egypt's problems was not going to be Allah. The new Egypt was to be modern and secular, a praetorian state. Al-Ikhwan faced a military regime that had introduced competency into security and—far worse—that grew more popular daily. Nasser displayed not only the skills of a conspirator and the wiles of a politician but also, increasingly, an enormous public charisma. He could put into words what the masses had always assumed the truth to be. He was becoming the voice of the new Egypt. He was not yet the nation personified, as he would eventually become, but he was effective and dramatic without effort and able to articulate the longings of the everyday people.

If the Egyptians as a whole believed in Nasser's revolutionary Egypt, the religious conspirators, the Islamists, did not. They saw the country led astray again by an emerging pharaoh who still worshipped the ways of the West rather than the laws of Allah. In January and again in September 1954, the militant among them demonstrated in the streets. As in the past, many would advocate organizing and delaying for a better day; but a few always wanted to act right away, to punish. Nasser was their target, an apostate, an affront to the faith, especially because when he spoke, the people listened.

Standing before the crowd in Menshieh Square in Alexandria on October 25, 1954, his simple, crisp uniform just slightly wrinkled, his heavy head erect, Colonel Gamal Abdel Nasser spoke, as always, directly to the people. The radio allowed him to reach out to them all—all of the new Egyptians. He spoke to Egypt of glory to come, a revolution to be made, a nation that would arise as nexus of the Arab world.

As he spoke, more and more of those out in the villages and the dingy rooms in the Cairo slums were caught up in the vision and heard their dreams articulated. And then, above the radio static, they all heard the unmistakable sound of eight shots fired. One determined and dedicated assassin faithful to Islam had acted. Nasser's voice faltered. There was a scuffle as security men closed on the assassin. Every radio in every village and on the shelf of every Cairo shop, from the Delta to Aswan, carried the sounds. Nasser was not hurt. In Alexandria, Nasser stood straight, speaking out again to an Egypt waiting for the future: "Let them kill Nasser. He is one among many and whether he lives or dies the revolution goes on."

The would-be assassin, Mahmud Abd al-Latif from al-Ikhwan, believed he acted for his brothers and for the pious. But his attempt did not inspire the masses who saw no contradiction between the mosque and the revolution, and Nasser grasped the opportunity to transform the attempt on his life into a rationale for destroying his only viable rivals. He announced that al-Ikhwan was a conspiracy in the countryside and even in the army. His regime then eliminated al-Ikhwan. Four thousand Brothers were imprisoned, detained, maltreated and intimidated. Thousands fled into exile. For those in prison, there were trials. Six of those convicted of treason were executed. Al-Ikhwan was shattered and driven underground.

The organization vanished into secrecy; Allah would supply no answers to the state problems in Egypt for a generation. In fact, Nasser could announce a pardon for the imprisoned in 1964 because the threat was over. He himself was the way into the future. He regained the Canal Zone and later the canal, began the great dam at Aswan, seized land for the poor and the means of production for the state, and changed history. Advocating Arab nationalism and Arab socialism as general ideals, Nasser emerged as an enormous historical presence who could impose his perceptions on reality. The Anglo-French attack on Suez in 1956 was perceived as a victory when the expeditionary force withdrew because of American and United Nations pressure. The Egyptian "victory" was thus authenticated by the United Nations and accepted everywhere in the Arab world as humiliation of the West. Nasser was triumphant and Egypt was the center of a new world.

Nasser's only potential opposition came from the narrow fundamentalists, dedicated to a vision of the past. After 1954, these faithful were closely monitored. Some of the most zealous Islamists were suspected of plotting rebellion. On August 30, 1965, Nasser revealed another plot by al-Ikhwan and again arrested the usual suspects. In the Egyptian tradition, there was torture and intimidation, trials and convictions.

The accused ringleader was said to be Sayyid Qutb, who had been jailed after the attempt on Nasser in Alexandria, then reluctantly released, and now was imprisoned again. Sayyid Qutb had begun as a teacher of literature. Then he became a bureaucrat in the Department of Education, urging reform so urgently that in 1948 he was dispatched to professional exile in the United States, where he found not so much modern wonders as a lewd and lascivious society.

In the summer of 1951, Sayyid Qutb returned to Egypt, his Islamic faith revitalized. The next year he was elected to the leadership council of al-Ikhwan. In August 1952, with the Free Officers in power and al-Ikhwan temporarily allowed to function as a legal organization, he was congratulated by both Nasser and Neguib after he had chaired a conference in Cairo on intellectual and emotional emancipation in Islam. By 1954, when the campaign against al-Ikhwan began, Sayyid Qutb had become more committed to Allah as the answer to Egypt's future. He made no secret of his views.

Recognized as a danger to the regime, he was jailed for three months in 1954, released before the attempt on Nasser later in the year, and then re-arrested, tried, convicted and sentenced to twenty-five years. He began his sentence at the Tula concentration camp. Increasingly committed, he began to write a radical analysis of Egyptian society. He was finally released at the end of 1964 and continued writing.

After the al-Ikhwan conspiracy was announced by Nasser on August 25, 1965, Sayyid Qutb was arrested again, tried, convicted and, at dawn on August 29, 1966, hanged. He had been too visible, too persistent, too influential, and so his dissent led to his death sentence—a warning to other Islamists. Not simply another victim of Nasser's praetorian state, he was transmuted by martyrdom into a prophet, and his written word became an Islamic text for resistance to the new pharaoh.

Sayyid Qutb saw all around him a decay of the faith, a world living in barbarism and ignorance of the True Word. It was a flawed society—*jahiliyya*—filled with hypocrisy and deceit. The Islamic establishment only went through the motions of the faith, confusing the people and denying the strictures of the Koran. How would an Islamic resurrection begin? A vanguard must resolve to set it in motion in the midst of the *jahiliyya* that reigned over the entire earth. That vanguard must be able to decide when to withdraw from and when to seek contact with the *jahiliyya*.

In his last work, *Signposts*, written in prison, Sayyid Qutb presented a manifesto to those who wanted to restore the *umma*, the community of believers, and who realized that organizing and preaching were insufficient. The manifesto had the advantage of being dynamic and appealing, but none too exact, and thus open to radical interpretation. Sayyid Qutb wrote that in Egypt as well as in the world of nominal Islam and beyond, there was a powerful and decadent *jahiliyya*. Anyone could recognize this in the new Egypt of Nasser, corrupted by the infidel ideas of the West. The most important task was to free the people from the control of the *jahiliyya* society. The time for words, for politics, for organization had passed. The time of the Book had gone and that of the Sword had arrived. And the quintessential enemy was the new Egyptian regime with its new pharaoh, who had opposed al-Ikhwan, turned away from the Koran and imposed sinfulness on the nation.

Sayyid Qutb offered answers to the three great questions: What is wrong? What is wanted? What is to be done? The evil was secularism; the goal was an Egypt shaped by the *shari'a;* and the only effective means was violence.

After the repression of 1965, the faithful had no way to act on events. They could only persist, frustrated, without capacity but not lacking commitment. The most militant Islamists lost faith in al-Ikhwan as being too large, too accommodating, a failure. Only a few, like the young Sheikh Omar Abdel Rahman, were visible, active and unrepentant. Sheikh Rahman used his sermons in the tiny village of Fedemin to urge action and condemn the new pharaoh, Nasser. He found examples of faith and decadence, offered Koranic interpretations, read Islamic history with a special inner eye. He could cite Ibn Tamimia from the fourteenth century as to the duty to depose Moslem leaders who violated the *shari'a.* His views were noted by the security forces.

At al-Azhar University, Sheikh Rahman was a good but not brilliant student. Provincial, isolated from the secular world, he was not attracted to the conventions of al-Azhar orthodoxy wherein the professors and the pious were content with any Arab ruler and suspicious of any change. Rather, he was an active member of a new generation of fundamentalists who emerged during Nasser's regime. They were impatient. After formal classes, they discussed the proper way to establish an Islamic society, and they kept in touch once they graduated. They circulated letters, messages carried by hand, reports of dramatic events or compelling sermons. When possible, they visited each other. Many of these fundamentalists were Egyptians, but some had come to al-Azhar from elsewhere in the Middle East and had similar views.

What evolved was a group of Islamists who by a careful reading of the Koran had found a rationale for their agenda: an Islamic society achieved at once and, if necessary, by force. They were not an underground, not an organization or a society, not even a conspiracy. Rather, they were individuals who shared a worldview that inspired them to analyze and criticize the West and the secular governments, and to proselytize. Any forum would do, even a village mosque.

The common people of Fedemin had anticipated the arrival of a bright young man from al-Azhar; instead they received a prophet. Every Friday, Sheikh Rahman preached not to them but to Egypt. Few understood his urgency and almost no one could imagine denying the greatness of Nasser, but none disputed his learning, his piety or his eloquence. His fame spread within the circles of the new fundamentalists and so came to the attention of the authorities. The impact of the young sheikh made him a danger to the regime; he was too dedicated, too convincing, too troublesome.

Sheikh Rahman was arrested and locked up in Cairo's ancient Citadel Prison in 1970. His was a classic incarceration in that he was strengthened by it and his reputation among the faithful was enhanced. Rahman's time in prison was served for Allah and thus well invested.

The sheikh from Fedemin who emerged into the unseen daylight after eight months was even more dedicated to an Islamic Egypt. Now a martyr for Islam, he moved on to teach in a girls' school south of Cairo in Assyut, in Upper Egypt, and to offer his pure vision of the future. The *jahiliyya* society of Nasser was to be replaced with one ordered by the *shari'a*. A Koranic society in Egypt and elsewhere would solve all problems, bringing justice, honor, security and respect. The details were not important. What was clear was that a return to Allah would restore pride, reassure those who were adrift in secular societies and eliminate their need to compete by using Western standards. Islam could offer each a role and some a mission. Allah would be the answer to the penalties of modernization and the temptations that weakened Arab society. Sheikh Rahman sought to move back to the future, back to the Islamic basics, the old ways and customs that could assure future salvation.

The sheikh was kept under constant surveillance. There were policemen at the end of the lane, someone taking notes when he spoke, and informers paid to report his movements regularly. He could not work freely or maintain communication with his ideological allies, so he moved into exile in Saudi Arabia. There for three years he taught school and kept in touch with the Islamists.

Meanwhile, back in Egypt, some of the zealots formed special groups, shifting in membership, variously named, often isolated but determined to do something. Sheikh Rahman had contacts with one of these organizations, Gama'a Islamiyya, "the Group" —an underground cell waiting to act. Gama'a was covert, illicit, engaged in plots more than deeds. Even in exile, Sheikh Rahman became a vital asset for Gama'a and for all the Islamists, since his formal education and his prominence allowed him to issue a religious decree, a *fatwa*, that could authorize or rationalize action. When the more conventional, orthodox scholars in al-Azhar disputed his interpretations and his legitimacy, his followers and associates paid no attention.

For the Islamists there was a growing need for Koranic authority to pursue a campaign of violence. The key group among the Islamists was Jama'at al-Muslimin, called "al-Takfir wa al-Hjira" by the police, and founded by Shukri Ahmad Mustafa. Al-Takfir was filled with men determined to destroy the enemies of Islam through violence. These militants worked secretly among the Egyptian people or emigrated to carry on their work abroad. They would offer false allegiance if need be, lie as a duty and use duplicity until the time came to deploy violence.

Al-Takfir thus offered a tactical option to the Islamists looking for a means to act; Gama'a was larger, less coherent, not as focused on tactics, a congregation waiting for the word. No matter the turmoil of the outside world, these small, covert groups remained devoted to revolution in the name of Allah. This was the future of the Moslem mission.

There was little in the outside world to encourage the militants. The masses were still satisfied with the New Egypt. Although there were tangible failures—the desert did not bloom, land reform did not work and the new factories did not change workers' habits or assure capacity—Nasser remained inviolate nonetheless. The catastrophic defeat by Israel in June of 1967 deeply shocked the people: the Egyptian air force ruined one morning, the Egyptian soldiers abandoning their boots and fleeing barefooted from the Sinai, the Egyptian allies Jordan and Syria crushed. But while some Egyptians turned to religion, few turned against Nasser. So he stayed in control until his death in 1970, having guided Egypt through tumultuous times, made the nation count in the outside world, and imposed his dream of the future on the people's consciousness. At his funeral millions of people wept in the streets of Cairo.

Even if the new praetorian system could not generate real power, effective military force or tangible prosperity, the dream remained in Egyptian hearts, kept fresh by the songs of the enormously popular Oom Khaldum, and by the speeches and displays, promises and parades, and the lack of alternatives. Nasser—his voice, his luck, his vision—had retained the loyalty of the masses for the state. For many, Nasser *was* the state, *was* Egypt, *was* the Arab world. Yet his legacy was elusive. The nation that Nasser's successor, Vice-President Anwar Sadat, inherited in 1970 was built from the residue of a generation of Arab revolution, ruined expectations and obsolete policies. There was an experienced administration directed by officers and specialists, an increasingly literate working class (although there was not enough work for them), and more university graduates than could be suitably employed. The old, miserable villages were disappearing, although the slums of Cairo endured. There were roads and television sets and a steel industry. Egypt had a central position in the Middle East, and through leadership of the nonaligned nations played a vital role in Cold War politics.

Sadat also inherited an arid political culture and a limited opposition. The old ideas and the old parties had been neutered, the Islamic establishment was content and even al-Ikhwan was quiescent. The growing and complex extremist Islamic tide inspired by Sheikh Rahman and others was outside the system and invisible. Those in al-Takfir and Gama'a would wait to see how pious the new president, once a friend of al-Ikhwan, turned out to be.

Sadat's major concern was to destroy opposition within the system, in particular the radical left of his colleague Ali Sabri, who advocated Marxism as an answer to Egypt's ills. In this effort the president sought out Islamic allies; he even reached out to Sheikh Abdel Rahman, still in self-imposed exile in Saudi Arabia. The sheikh sidestepped the offer—he had other plans and a different dream for Egypt.

Nonetheless, Sadat's career as a conspirator and an assassin proved useful when he opposed ideologues who, like Ali Sabra, believed that power came from paper and programs, not from a gun. Sadat's military rivals ended up in prison or under house arrest, or simply irrelevant, while he slowly realigned the country with the West.

In many ways Sadat was like most who had ruled the Nile. An obscure vice-president among far more articulate and talented contenders for power, he had proved a highly skilled conspirator who outmaneuvered his military colleagues and concentrated all political power in his own hands. Even as he urged a more open society, he went about purging his rivals. He introduced a free market unrestricted by the state industries and shaped a nation open to new investment. Entrepreneurs rather than socialists were encouraged. There was a new direction: *Infitah,* "the Opening." Sadat believed the new direction to be worth the risk, for the alternative was stagnation and decay.

What evolved was an economy of privilege, investment, inequalities, rebates and monopolies that could barely keep up with an expanding population. The Egypt of Sadat, organized and administered by an elite already in power for a generation, was being expanded by men intimate with the techniques, agenda and advantages of the secular West. They knew how to make money and soon learned how to live ostentatiously. The new bourgeoisie and their colleagues within the praetorian state elite drove new Mercedes cars, kept servants, lived in the high-rise buildings along the Nile, belonged to clubs, wore tailored summer suits. The others who benefited from Sadat's Egypt, the shopkeepers and clerks, the businessmen and the university professors might have fewer assets, less money and more conventional homes, but were still comfortable. Their apartments had several rooms. Their automobiles were inexpensive but clogged the streets of Cairo. They too were content, had high hopes for their children and saved for their month on the beach.

And the employed poor—the tea-boys, the part-time mechanics and the tailor's assistants, the unlicensed tour guides, the doormen who lived on the roof, the sweepers, peddlers and runners in from the slums—all scrambled and subsisted. They raised a family in two rooms, lived from week to week, coped with quiet desperation, persevered on the edge of the abyss. Among those with no work at all, uncertain of each day's dinner, many found no answers in Sadat's expectations or in a new capitalist revolution, but as in the past, they remained passive, vaguely hopeful, potential participants in a riot but not a conspiracy.

The Islamists found Egypt ever riper, not simply because the poor were miserable but rather because even those with meager ambitions were thwarted. The fundamentalists organized schools and clinics and rooms—welfare initiatives not unlike those of al-Ikhwan. The zealots also established mosques where treason was preached as piety. They offered a role and suggested a mission; they had a dream that could be made real only through violence. Most Egyptians merely listened passively. Those most taken by the message—students and workers with skills and spirit, unlike the immobile masses—felt that action could be taken. Some began to organize, insisting on public piety, modesty for women, beards for men, a return to the fundamentals. This religious renaissance had a widening appeal in a seriously flawed state. The conspirators in Cairo and Upper Egypt continued to meet secretly in the shabby rooms, at popular mosques, at university clubs. They formed shifting alliances, small groups often in bitter disagreement with each other, always transient, appearing and disappearing. Some did little, while others distributed cheaply printed exhortations, formed study groups and listened to radical sermons at the popular mosques on Friday. And some within these congregations believed themselves to be the basis of a new holy war.

For the faithful who had found Nasser an affront to Islam, how much more so were Sadat and his cronies—sleek, arrogant men with Western wives and wiles, rich and elegant, symbols of all that was wrong. They were the *jahiliyya*—vile, damned, the enemy. Some of the most militant, as always, sought change through social and political programs, opening clinics, writing letters for the illiterate, providing rooms for the homeless. But as always, a few believed that the key to an Islamic future was violence. Without the protection of Nasser's charisma and with responsibility for both Nasser's failures and his own, Sadat became vulnerable as the years passed.

After delays, promises and false starts, Egyptian troops

crossed the canal in October 1973 and penetrated Israel's Bar Lev Line. For a moment, honor and pride were restored; but for the faithful, the crossing of the canal was mere diversion. Egypt was still not Islamic.

Sadat might be the hero of the crossing, but this illusory victory led only to negotiations with Israel. The Egyptian president flew to Jerusalem to meet with the Israeli prime minister, Menachem Begin, and so began a peace process that led to agreement at Camp David in the United States, a formal treaty, an Israeli ambassador in Cairo, but no state for the Palestinians.

Few Egyptians were enthusiastic about peace with Zionists, and even many of the pragmatists thought Sadat had been outmaneuvered. The West might be delighted and the United States might underwrite the country with billions of dollars in aid, but the near-victory of the canal evolved into a disappointment and for many a betrayal. In June 1974, long before any final Egyptian-Israeli arrangement, a large group of young officers calling itself the Islamic Liberation Group attempted to seize Cairo's Technological Military Academy as a protest against Sadat's policies. They failed. Thirty were killed, but the rising gave Sadat warning that some were willing to revolt under the banner of Islam.

Sadat decided on compromise and accommodation, declaring a general amnesty in 1975. The faithful simply grew more daring. Some ran for parliament, becoming a visible presence, and some prepared for violence, like Shukri Mustafa's al-Takfir. In January 1977, with careful planning, this organization led mobs in ransacking and burning the nightclubs along Cairo's golden strip —symbols of the decadence in Sadat's Egypt. The police arrested sixty members of al-Takfir. In retaliation, al-Takfir militants kidnapped a former minister and demanded a public trial of the accused. When nothing was done, they murdered their hostage.

The state responded with vigor: the security forces investigated nearly 5,000 Islamists, of whom 620 were arrested and 465 tried by military courts. Five were executed, including Mustafa. Sadat also soon announced that sections of the old Napoleonic Code would be replaced with the *shari'a*. The conservative and orthodox, the al-Azhar establishment were pleased by the gesture.

Isolated in the presidential offices from the reality of Egyptian grievances and the appeal of Islam, Sadat was at times outraged
and indignant at the ungrateful people who criticized him, the
Father of Egypt. He remained committed to his vision of Egypt as
part of the West. He was willing to offer concessions to the Islamic
faithful—the hidden enemy—in an effort to corrupt them with
kindness, but he could never turn the country over to narrow
fanatics. In 1977 there were more arrests of zealots. A few were
executed, others received long sentences.

In 1979 the Middle East was in turmoil. At the beginning of the
year, there had been a triumph for the faith in Iran, where another
Western puppet, the shah, had presided over another *jahiliyya*
society. In January the Shi'ite mullahs had driven him into exile in
Egypt, where he died, his presence offensive to the pious. The pious
everywhere, both Shi'ite and Sunni, advocated the Koranic law, the
shari'a, as the basis for a new revolution. Teheran began to fund
and organize militants in Shi'ite communities.

In May, the Islamists in Syria had tried to kill President Hafiz
al-Assad and initiated an armed struggle in the provincial city of
Hama. Al-Assad sent in the army, and for over a month, the Syrian security forces slaughtered the gunmen, murdered the
suspects, killing thirty thousand in all. Hama was ruined and the
survivors were intimidated. The faithful might still despise al-
Assad, but after 1979 they also feared him.

In Afghanistan a communist coup had brought secularists
into control in Kabul in 1978 and engendered lethal rivalries
among the new factions. Then in December 1979, a massive Soviet
intervention began to support the new communist puppet. The
Afghanis and most Moslems saw the presence of the Soviet Union
as an outrage and began a holy war that would attract international brigades of Islamic zealots.

In Saudi Arabia, with a ruling family dedicated to the fundamentalist precepts of Ibn Abdel Wahhab, there was no protection
from the zealots. Many Islamists accepted that the Saudis were not
infidels, but they were obviously decadent, giving alms to Islam
while living in hidden luxury. In November 1979 the zealots seized

the great mosque in Mecca and so held the center of the faith until they were driven out by the Saudi military, aided by the French.

By 1981 Egypt too seethed with discontent. Sadat had full control of the praetorian state but his system could accomplish nothing. It was unable to absorb the literate rural poor, to find positions for the university graduates, to offer hope to the miserable or the ambitious. Frustrated, erratic, emotionally drained, bitter and often on the brink of losing control, Sadat suffered through a dreadful year. In September 1981 he closed down the opposition and arrested all those suspected of dissent, thus alienating still more Egyptians. His interior minister, Nabawi Ismail, and Vice-President Hosni Mohammed Mubarak warned him once again that the country was buzzing with conspirators. Sadat accepted more guards and some American security equipment and advice, but would not greatly alter his habits or his schedule. At rallies he wore no body armor under his suit. He felt that nothing could really be done to satisfy those who wanted an Islamic nation. Resigned, Sadat had spoken repeatedly of leaving office and retiring to his newly built home in his Nile Delta village of Mit Abul-Kum.

October 6 was Sadat's favorite day. In front of the establishment, amid pomp and ceremony, he reviewed the annual parade commemorating the apex of his Egypt—the crossing of the Suez Canal in 1973 to initiate the October war. At this ceremony he was among his own. For several wondrous hours he could relish the victory that had brought Egypt momentary honor. On this October 6, in 1981, he was driven slowly as always through the crowds to the parade grounds and stadium in Nasser City on the northeast of Cairo to inspect his troops, the army that had been his other family.

As his open limousine made its way from his official residence at Eiza, there was the usual crowd on the edge of the street to see the president. There were also special preparations because of the unrest. Police lined the route. Three security guards stood on the running boards on either side of the car and two rode on the back. A heavy security guard cut off easy access to the parade grounds. Spectators had to pass through searches. The media and the foreign guests had to be checked out.

When Sadat arrived at the parade grounds at 11:00, the

stands were packed with two thousand of Egypt's elite, government and military officials, wives and children, along with foreign dignitaries and the media. Everyone who was anyone in Sadat's Egypt was there: his wife, Jihan, his ministers and generals, even his reclusive national security advisor, Osama el-Baz, who seldom attended parades. There was an odd assortment of guests: a few American servicemen in transit; the Irish defense minister, Jim Tully, on his way back from visiting Irish United Nations troops in Lebanon; the Israeli ambassador, Moshe Sasson, symbol of the Camp David peace accords.

Standing before them, clad in his imperial costume of blue jacket, green sash over his shoulder, jodhpurs, glittering knee-high boots, and the Star of Sinai on his chest, Sadat moved to his seat. There he accepted the first salutes of his army. He was flanked by the defense minister, Abdel Halim Abu Ghazala, and Vice-President Mubarak, once chief of staff of the air force—his military allies and political supporters, both nearly as resplendent as Sadat, Hero of the Crossing. To begin the ceremonies, the president walked over to the pyramid arch of the Tomb of the Unknown Soldier and laid a wreath. Then he returned to the pavilion and his first-row seat, separated from the events by a five-foot wall. The parade began: drums and bands, the Camel Corps, American M-60 Main Battle Tanks, and representative regiments—soldiers and sailors, more bands, commandos and mobile artillery. Sadat watched the parade surrounded by dignitaries and uniforms, one hour and then another.

The media grew bored; the television cameras kept generating film of a parade that few producers back in New York or London would want. The parachutists landed as scheduled. The bands played on—two hours under a blazing sun and more to come. Sadat sat joking and applauding, smoking his pipe. With a huge shuddering roar, just after 1:00 in the afternoon, the air force Mirage jets spewing trails of red, green, blue, yellow and gray smoke swept in out of the bright blue sky and then swerved off.

No one took especial notice of a Soviet army truck from an artillery unit towing a South Korean long-range artillery piece, until the driver stopped suddenly, almost directly in front of the reviewing stand, fifteen yards away from the president. Inside the cab, First Lieutenant Khaled Ahmed Shawky il-Islambouli had leaned over from the passenger's side and pulled the hand brake. The driver could do nothing. The other regulars in the vehicle had been replaced with three of the faithful by Lieutenant il-Islambouli. His men had guns with real ammunition, and real grenades. They had come to kill the new pharaoh.

There had been no need of much planning. Il-Islambouli, a member of an al-Jihad revolutionary group in Cairo, had returned to the city in September from a visit to his home in Assyut in Upper Egypt, the center of the new fundamentalism. He was consumed with rage that his brother Mohammed, a member of al-Takfir arrested in 1977, had been arrested again earlier in the year. As the leader of Gama'a Islamiyya in Assyut University's department of commerce, Mohammed had become one of the usual suspects because he was a student of Sheikh Abdel Rahman. So the police had come to the door during the great security sweep and dragged him from his bed in his pajamas. He had been maltreated. The state had defiled the faith. So Lieutenant il-Islambouli, who had chosen the Military Academy over the university, now chose Allah over the army. He returned to Cairo determined to strike at the heart of the state.

In Cairo, il-Islambouli belonged to a faction that followed the ideas of Abd al-Salam Faraj, an electrician turned Islamist, whose book *The Hidden Imperative* was more militant than Sayyid Qutb's *Signposts,* declaring that the only way into the future was through *jihad.* Il-Islambouli brought opportunity as well as resentment from Assyut to his underground associates, who hurriedly put together an operation using his access to the October 6 parade. They would kill Sadat. The faithful in Cairo might rise; those in Assyut surely would.

Il-Islambouli had been sitting next to the unknowing driver as the Soviet-made truck crept toward the reviewing stand. When the six Mirages came back very low and loud, forcing the crowds to flinch and the media technicians to tinker with their sound, few in the stands noticed the soldiers climbing out of the stalled truck; few paid attention even when they rushed toward the five-foot wall.

Then the soldiers began firing their automatic weapons and

tossing grenades. Everyone froze. Lieutenant il-Islambouli leaned over the parapet and shouted to General Abu Ghazala to get away from the president: "I want this dog, this tyrant!" He began firing into Sadat, tipping his assault rifle up, holding it bucking and bouncing as the magazine ran out. Sadat had only time to cry, *mish mahoul,* "not possible," and then died. The other soldiers from the truck continued to fire into the stands. The guards and security people still seemed stunned.

The firing seemed to go on and on. The Belgian ambassador, hit twice, was down in serious condition. The Irish defense minister, James Tully, was nicked in the lip—an unexpected introduction to Middle Eastern politics. Three American servicemen were hit and so was a consultant from Raytheon, but not the American ambassador. The ABC television cameras rolled on, getting the murder live, up close, in color.

The film would be broadcast worldwide within hours. It was quickly pirated and sold as a video, to be run again and again in apartments throughout the Islamic world. The assassination was seen by the curious, the dedicated, the horrified, seen in time by hundreds of millions, watched by some over and over. For many the spectacle was not of an Egyptian president being martyred, but of an evil pharaoh executed—an example for all the righteous.

In the stands, the chaos continued. Some were holding up chairs to ward off the bullets; others clambered up the reviewing stand as the guards and agents finally began firing back at the assassins. In the midst of the turmoil, il-Islambouli was erect, empty gun in hand, reportedly screaming at the crowd: "I am Khalid il-Islambouli! I have killed Pharaoh, and I do not fear death!" He was shot, as were the other attackers. Bloody bodies were scattered before the reviewing stand. At the center, Sadat was crumpled in a heap, soaked in blood. The security people finally carried him away.

There was nothing left but a pile of debris, broken chairs, blood splattered over an oriental carpet, expended cartridges, ruined bodies. The media people were as shocked as those still huddling in the reviewing stands. Then the everyday world returned—film was rushed back to offices, reporters began to report, the parade grounds were sealed off and ambulances arrived. The survivors stood about, dazed and fearful.

Just before three in the afternoon, the news filtered out: Sadat was dead. Egyptian television began to play readings from the Koran, an hour after ABC tape of the assassination was projected worldwide. Shortly after eight, on the evening of October 6, a shattered Vice-President Hosni Mubarak appeared on television offering calm, stability, reassurance. Tomorrow would be like yesterday, he promised: no coup, no al-Ikhwan in power, no mob in the street. Justice would be done and Egypt would move on into a promising future.

Those who murdered Sadat waited for the rising in Cairo and Assyut. They had no remorse, for they were engaged in a *jihad* against the tyrant. The wounded il-Islambouli would say at his trial, "I am guilty of killing Sadat. I am proud of it because the cause of religion was at stake." He had acted to punish the wicked, to destroy the pharaoh and the evil of the *jahiliyya* society. And so vengeance had been achieved, both Allah's and il-Islambouli's. In Teheran a boulevard was named for il-Islambouli. His brother, the cause of Sadat's assassination, was welcomed abroad by the faithful as an honored guest.

There was no general uprising in Cairo on October 6. During the insurrection two days later in Assyut, 130 officers and police were killed and 150 wounded; but the rebellion was crushed. The assassination was, however, the beginning of a sporadic armed struggle in Upper Egypt and in the slums of the big cities that engaged the most militant. Some were hardly known outside the underground, but a few were distinguished. One Dr. Ayman al-Zawahiri, from a well-known and successful Cairo family, had arrived within the underground while at school. He had received a medical degree but put his services to work for Allah, and his interests were far from purely medical. He took leave from an al-Ikhwan clinic in Cairo to visit Afghanistan, where he experienced militant Islam, and returned with the feeling that if a great power like the USSR could be thwarted, then Sadat's Egypt was even more vulnerable. While in Afghanistan, al-Zawahiri had met Osama bin Laden and others who, using the analysis and language of the Islamists, foresaw not just an armed struggle but a holy war, a *jihad*. In their plots against Sadat they had become Egyptian *jihadi*. Dr. al-Zawahiri organized the underground and became leader of Islamic Jihad. Once Sadat was dead, he and the others would continue the *jihad*. The murder of Sadat at the hands of a righteous killer was not merely a symbolic deed, as had been the case so often in the past. Almost without discussion, the new generation of Islamists were committed to widening the struggle. This time there would be a crusade waged by the *jihadi*.

There were widespread arrests and detentions. The prisoners were mistreated and their defense hampered, in the Egyptian tradition. Gama'a and al-Zawahiri's Islamic Jihad were forced to go underground. Many militants fled Egypt or were allowed to go into voluntary exile between 1985 and 1987, and they took with them the new *jihadi* vision. In Egypt those who remained began a low-intensity insurgency. In some of the poorest quarters of Cairo, the Islamists controlled the streets. Those who could initiated operations against the police, Copts, Western targets, the system. Sheikh Rahman had assured the faithful in a *fatwa* that violence could be used—"blood was permissible"—against those Coptic Christians who opposed Islam. At night, unknown gunmen in villages of Upper Egypt shot Christian merchants from ambush and shot at the police. They burned buildings, stole from Coptic shops and created a sense of menace.

For Mubarak in 1981, as for Nasser in 1954, coercive force was the appropriate answer to murder. Security forces immediately arrested 1,536 suspects—not only il-Islambouli and his mentor, Abd al-Salam Faraj, but also famous dissidents like Sheikh Rahman, who was picked up at his home and brought to Cairo. The police had found stolen money and jewelry in his house; he was apparently engaged in laundering *jihadi* money. He was certainly engaged in opposing the regime and in legitimizing attacks on Copts.

Most of the suspects were beaten, tried, found guilty and sentenced to prison terms. On April 15, 1982, twenty-four were executed, including the assassin and Faraj. But for the authorities, not all had gone as planned: Sheikh Rahman had used his trial to attack the system and defend his fundamentalist vision. The prosecutors had allowed him to speak in public. His arguments, his cunning use of quotation, his absolute conviction had been compelling. Censorship had not been effective when the sheikh, blind but imposing, surrounded by his fellow prisoners in a grim courtroom, spoke to all Egypt and all Muslims. He was tried again on similar charges, but could not be convicted. His defense deployed Koranic citations to frustrate his prosecutors in public: "Our duty to God is more binding than our duty to the president of the Republic. We owe to God obedience and no obedience is owed to him who disobeys God."

Photographs of Rahman, caged in court amid the other imprisoned faithful, appeared throughout the Middle East. He then sued the state for torturing him in prison, and received a $10,000 payment for damages. In prison he married for the second time, the eighteen-year-old sister of a fellow prisoner.

Prison was a gift of the new pharaoh, Mubarak. The sheikh was now famous, the voice of the Egyptian faithful, spiritual mentor of the righteous gunmen of the new *jihad*. He moved to Fayoum with his family and resumed his agitation. His Friday sermons were monitored by the police. Still, he persisted for a while, corresponding overtly and secretly with the Islamists, and speaking in public whenever possible.

But Sheikh Rahman could not disguise reality. Both Islamic Jihad and Gama'a Islamiyya had been crushed. He was all but under house arrest and those *jihadi* not in prison had been forced into exile: a generation of amirs dispersed. Still, the dream of the Islamists was untouched by Mubarak's fierce reaction. The faithful might be divided on means but not on ends, and increasingly they felt the attraction of a *jihad*. Many, like Dr. al-Zawahiri, upon release from prison went into exile where they could conspire more freely. Some began going to Afghanistan to volunteer in the struggle against the communist government and the Soviet presence. Others found jobs throughout the Middle East. Some of the wanted managed to flee to Yemen and Saudi Arabia, to the European diaspora, to Pakistan and Afghanistan. In Egypt, others took their place, younger and unknown to the police.

President Mubarak made concessions to Allah in order to erode the power of the conspirators' lethal dream. The government attempted to outflank the *jihadi* by an alliance with the orthodox scholars and imams at al-Azhar University. Public piety became popular. Middle-class women wore veils. Men grew beards. Islamic societies took over university clubs and professional associations.

Nightclubs fell on hard times. Provocative novels and films were banned as sacrilegious. Legal cases were filed against secularists. Al-Ikhwan became almost respectable. The small political class, the few secular intellectuals and artists might protest Islamization, but the masses were enthusiastic for it.

Mubarak's Egypt moved on. The praetorian state was still in charge of events, deploying rewards and penalties, if not in control of history. Over a generation removed from the radical aspirations of Nasser and the Free Officers, Mubarak inherited all its failed promise, all the ruined programs and unpopular initiatives of both Nasser and Sadat, who had taken their luck and charisma with them to the grave.

Mubarak offered more denial, more slums, more tawdry buildings and quick fortunes. New developments—Dreamland and English Village and Golf City—were built over the decayed elegance and seedy grace of the past—Heliopolis, Zamalek and Maadi. The villages had water and lights, schools and small manufacturing plants. Millions had been educated, housed, protected from endemic disease. Cars and televisions proliferated. There were mills in the cities and small firms in the Delta towns. Those who could find no work in the Delta or in Upper Egypt moved on to the cities, especially Cairo, which had become a sprawling metropolis, an enormous gray construct of grim concrete housing estates for the poor, garden cities for the middle class and mud huts spilling down the valley of the Nile, threatening the Pyramids. Dreary new apartment blocks crept into the desert to mingle with a mix of shanty towns and mud slums, far from the famous garden districts and chain hotels of the center.

For some, especially in Upper Egypt, Islam was a rationale to turn on the Christian Copts. For others in Cairo, Islam was a means to express their despair at the country's misery. The West with its glittering prizes was easy to blame. The West supported the Zionists, kept Israel afloat and, most humiliating, also kept Mubarak's Egypt viable through grants and aid. The faithful could offer a wondrous, pure Egypt to those with little or nothing. What Islam could not offer was a practical agenda, a feasible alternative to existing ways of governance; but many didn't care. Any change was better than the status quo.

Because the system had no initiatives and few options, no ideas and no great hope, Egypt after 1981 grew increasingly bleak. What Mubarak administered was not what Nasser had imagined, not what Sadat had sought. The Egypt that Mubarak defended offered a text for righteous gunmen, those who along the Nile in the past had found murder a solution; and increasingly the righteous found allies, converts and advocates elsewhere in an Islam under siege. The Egyptian experience was both example and prologue.

FOUR

THE GLOBAL JIHAD, 1982–1993: ÉMIGRÉS, EXILES AND THE GREAT SATAN

After Sadat's murder in 1981, the Islamists were no longer satisfied with paper concessions. They'd had these since Nasser introduced an all-Koran radio station and religious instruction and permitted classroom segregation between Muslims and Coptic Christians. Such changes had not made Egypt Islamic. The nation was still not ruled by the *shari'a*. Sadat, publicly pious and an old associate of al-Ikhwan, had cooperated with them in crushing Ali Sabri and secular radicals, and had even reached out to Sheikh Rahman in his Saudi exile. He had changed the constitution so that Islamic law was defined as *the* most important inspiration for Egypt's laws. But for the new generation of Islamists, Egypt still had not become Islamic.

Now Mubarak increasingly tolerated the imposition of public piety and Islamic conformity. Power continued to be devolved onto the established clerics and professors of al-Azhar. Piety was more on public display, in women's dress, in the censorship of the secular, and in attacks on intellectuals and artists. Yet Mubarak's Egypt was not Islamic any more than Sadat's or Nasser's had been. There was no concession that could satisfy the Islamists who wanted everything, even a new caliphate, a *Khalifa*. (The old one had been an Ottoman vestige, finally abolished by the secular dictator Atatürk in 1924.) Allah would find an answer. But how? The most zealous were proposing that the only effective means was *jihad*, a religious as well as martial enterprise. Within the constricted world of the Islamists, a tide was running. The cautious, like Sheikh Rahman and the other new amirs, in public legitimized *jihad* indirectly, by carefully selected quotations from the Koran, by indicating without explicitly saying that a holy war was the way and the regime was the first target.

Mubarak's concessions to the zealots began to close further an already restricted society. The Copts had to cope with limited governmental protection and regular attacks—beatings, theft, arson. The established imams and sheikhs and the narrow careerists of Islam were making the daily rules, imposing piety, conformity and the Koran. The excitement and opportunities of the West—the clash of ideas, the creativity and license, the triumphs of science, space exploration and jazz—were not so much unwelcome in Egypt as ignored.

Only a few in the Arab world had ever been deeply concerned with the principles of the Enlightenment, scientific method or innovative art. The great ideas of Marx or Darwin or Einstein were not in the Koran. The new zealots, like their ancestors, opposed skepticism, the life of the mind, curiosity and creativity. Some insisted that Art was Filth and that scholarship beyond the Koran, especially *on* the Koran, was heretical.

The rich now kept to their clubs and apartments overlooking the Nile, out of sight. Those who administered the state, used computer accounting programs, negotiated loans and grants, and kept the Egypt Air planes flying safely and on time caused no trouble by arguing for Western ways and disciplines. The press, academics, television producers and political journals conformed. Resisting the slow creep of Islamization in everyday life increasingly meant placing oneself in jeopardy, and much of the political class refused to take such a risk.

Year after year in the reign of Mubarak, Islam became more visible, intrusive and difficult to oppose. Young women defended their Islamic rights, scorned Western standards, wore scarves and modest dress if not yet the head-to-toe *abaya*, much less the full veil. The fundamentalists could condemn the elegant and successful, and—righteously—punish those clever in the ways of the West by citing the Koran. Lawyers, bankers and administrators accepted the new direction, acted as required, voted as expected. Al-Ikhwan put up candidates, won elections and soon made certain that their opponents were confounded.

For many fundamentalists, each year after Sadat's murder,

each concession, each pretentious Western intellectual shamed or liberal paper closed, each electoral victory for Islam in the professional societies made a *jihad* seem unnecessary. After all, the professors at al-Azhar insisted that the Koran required obedience to Moslem sovereigns such as Mubarak. Who would challenge al-Azhar? So greater modesty and public piety, and a growth in al-Azhar's power and influence tended to isolate the hard-line Islamists.

The zealots focused on local enemies. They first chose the Copts as victims because they were weak and unprotected. The zealots burned cinemas, instigated riots, blackmailed Copt landowners, ransacked Copt stores, and broke arms and legs as punishment. Sometimes the zealots also shot at the police, but there was no general uprising, no real armed struggle, only a decay in order, especially in Upper Egypt. The Moslem masses did not become involved. Yet the assumption remained that the Egyptian *jahiliyya* regime was vulnerable. As the years passed, the Mubarak government stayed in power without sparkle or creative energy, with a persecuted Christian minority and zealots on the loose, but also with ample jails and a huge bureaucracy.

It had its successes. Almost all economic indicators were up, the infrastructure had expanded and population growth was easing. The miserable mud villages of the Delta disappeared. Towns acquired manufacturing plants, public parks, hospitals and new schools. The military received a new generation of weapons. The universities and secondary schools graduated more students with ambitions and expectations. The gray-brown apartment blocks moved out into the desert beyond Cairo to house the poor. But while slowed, the growth in population—doubling to seventy million in twenty years—gobbled up all the undeniable gains. The welfare clinics and additional hospitals increased survival but also the number of Egyptians. The schools generated more of the unemployed. The grim apartments could not keep up with the demands of the poor crammed into slum rooms or shacks on the margins of the cities.

Egypt was crushed not so much by the security forces, harsh legislation and the brutality of everyday life as by lack of hope. Mubarak's Egypt was stolid and sullen. The functionaries of the state, the weight of tradition, the concessions and coercion, past experience and caution restricted the Egyptian *jihad*.

Yet a different *jihad*—a real one, its supporters would say—had begun at the margins of the Islamic world in the shadow of the Hindu Kush mountains of Central Asia. In December 1979, the Soviet Union had intervened with a massive airlift into Kabul to support their communist protégé, but the faithful Afghanis had not been intimidated. The Russians had gradually found their expeditionary force entangled in a complex, cruel and costly guerrilla war. The pious *mujaheddin* had persisted despite the odds and the severe losses. Some Egyptian *jihadi* began looking to Afghanistan as an opportunity, traveling to Pakistan and some crossing the border to help the *mujaheddin*. The war against the atheistic communists slowly became the great Islamic cause.

At nearly the same time, the region had been galvanized by an unexpected and absolute triumph for Islam when the mullahs captured Iran from the shah and the Americans. Unlike most in the Middle East, the Iranians were Persian and spoke Farsi, but they were also Shi'ites and of the faith. The ayatollahs were ruthless and fanatical. And the maximum leader, the ancient, rigid Ayatollah Khomeini, his visage glowering from enormous posters in every Iranian city, cast a long shadow over the world of Islam that not even the war with Iraq could dissipate.

Almost at once, many of the idealists found the Iranian success eroded by zealotry. The revolution had been effective and brutal. Dour revolutionary courts composed of bigots and fanatics in black turbans and long robes condemned the past generation, one culprit at a time, hanging the Marxist radicals from construction cranes and executing the shah's police, his officials, his friends, the successful and prominent. Even the past was adjudicated: the ayatollahs hanged 94-year-old Captain Iraj Matbui, who had led the gendarmes against the mullahs in the Mashad revolt of 1935.

The immediate focus of the new Islamic state had been internal terror, judicial murder and oppression as the mullahs destroyed their rivals. But then, beginning in 1981, the great war with Iraq evolved into a protracted slaughter that killed three hundred thousand Iranians and gobbled up the resources of a generation. The war went on and on, for little gain. Iranian children were sent in waves across minefields with the plastic keys to paradise hanging on a necklace. In an expanding cemetery, the fountain of the Iranian martyrs bubbled water dyed red, a grotesque memorial to a lost generation.

In Baghdad, Saddam Hussein killed his own without remorse or shame, while pouring the nation's oil money into the sands and swamps of the battle. And the Iraqis, too, fought on. Those with no love of Saddam Hussein, the Shi'ites and even the Kurds, often fought for Iraq. As for their leader, his monuments were everywhere—huge and coarse, celebrating the imaginary triumphs and the real power of the dictator. Neither Iran nor Iraq could win, and neither would seek an accommodation. What had seemed a triumph for the faith had dissolved into unending terror and war.

Still, the Islamists could take unambiguous comfort in the struggle in the mountains of Afghanistan, where the enemy was evil and the *mujaheddin* admirable, brave, dedicated, faithful. *Jihad* lived. A few began to volunteer their service there. Saudis, Algerians, Yemenis and Egyptians sought by Mubarak's police made their way to war. Saudi Arabian Airlines gave volunteers a 75 percent discount on their flights. Throughout the Moslem world, the persistent struggle of the *mujaheddin* in the face of incredible hardship continued to attract volunteers. Official grants and programs, individuals gifts and public donations supported the volunteers and the Afghani Arabs. Islamic governments and individuals contributed funds, encouraging the zealous to go into harm's way. Saudi Arabia contributed $3 billion. Pakistan provided a haven for volunteers and a training ground for the battle taking place over the border.

In time even the Americans became involved, shipping ground-to-air missiles into the country through Pakistan to counter the Soviet helicopters: the Cold War fought by proxy in Asia at a cost to the United States of $3.5 billion. Nine hundred American ground-to-air missiles were transferred to Pakistan and many deployed in Afghanistan. The Soviets lost 269 planes and helicopters. The USSR not only was made to pay dearly for the war, but also, eventually, would be forced to accept that the cost was far too high.

The Pakistan ISI, the Inter-Services Intelligence Agency,

intent on constructing a radical Islamic presence in Afghanistan, controlled the missiles and much of the aid. The ISI made sure that the most radical of the fundamentalists got the weapons. Some became clients, like Gulbuddin Hekmatyar, a brutal, primitive Islamic warlord who received an estimated $600 million. Hekmatyar and all the others fought to accumulate power and destroy their enemies. They accepted the money and the missiles, accommodated a generation of volunteers, kept the Pakistanis as friends and fought on—the nation a ruin, the population scattered, the future mortgaged. Over the next twenty years Afghanistan would generate more refugees than any other country.

The war dragged on and on, funded from abroad for the purposes of others, funded locally by the sale of narcotics, and fought no matter the cost. Prisoners were tortured, villages bombed, suspects routinely murdered. It was a cruel and bloody war of attrition; but unlike the internecine Iran-Iraq conflict, this war had a proper imperialist enemy, the atheist, communist infidels, and so it was fought under the banner of Islam. In Cairo and Yemen, in Algiers and Riyadh, the struggle was compelling, the cause just. Islam was committed to *jihad*. Thus, frustrated along the Nile, the Egyptian underground found new hope in Afghanistan—a luminous crusade, a dream in action.

In a way, the Afghan war came at the right moment. Elsewhere the Islamists were in disarray: badly governed, fractious, inept. Few Arab regimes were legitimate, none democratic. There were coups, tribal rebellions, conspiracies, internecine wars fought with Cold War discards. And the war against Israel, the war that mattered most, had become a litany of defeat. The unpalatable triumphs of the Jews remained an unbearable humiliation, especially since Israel prospered and flourished while development in the Islamic world was uneven and industrialization a disappointment. Self-pity, spite, envy and rage were common for Arab individuals, for governments, for all who saw history passing them by.

The poor had no hope. Everything was imported—films, carpenters, ideas, computer engineers, Mirage jets, hotel managers. Indeed, entire hotels were shipped in, assembled by foreigners, opened by the amir and managed by Swiss accountants, swept out by Asians and maintained by Koreans.

Something had gone wrong. Even the vast oil reserves brought not prosperity but corruption, consumer trinkets, plastic fountains for the foyer and warplanes that no one knew how to deploy. Moreover, someone else was always responsible for this malaise—someone in the palace or in power, someone in Washington or London, someone in the pay of the Zionists, someone who denied respect to the faithful.

The Arab world had not found a way into the future. Secularization, sold by the intellectuals, had been a mixed benefit and mostly for the small political class. Democracy was given lip service or simply declared by the rulers to be inapplicable to their specific needs and the customs of the Moslem world. In politics there were no checks and balances, no creative competition, no place for opposition or dissent. Arab nationalism always failed and often led to lethal rivalries. Prosperity was elusive. When oil and gas were subtracted, the exports of the entire Middle East had the same value as those of Finland. Capitalism did not work in the Persian Gulf and socialism did not work anywhere. Development fell into the hands of bureaucrats. In the *suq,* the bazaar, merchants tapped out their sums on a Japanese calculator while the pious urged an end to usury—no interest to be paid amid an era of global capitalism.

Two generations of al-Ikhwan had failed. Islam had never had a chance to be the solution. In Saudi Arabia, where the puritanical Wahhabi ruled, the royal family prayed five times a day. Women could not drive; graven images could not appear in public; tourists could not come to the kingdom. Yet in private, both the princes and the everyday people enjoyed Western diversions. Everyone knew this; the fanatics who seized Mecca knew that the Saudis were corrupt. The special nonusurious banks, the decapitation of criminals, the isolation of women and the religious police roaming the streets could not hide that corruption. For the Saudis, Mecca had become a state asset and the old Bedouin virtues were forgotten. The rich sons still frolicked on the Riviera, the thousands in the royal family prospered on vice and the rest of the people watched *Dallas* reruns behind the walls of houses purchased with state aid.

The people consumed Western products and so enraged the fundamentalists. The Arab poor wore Fanta T-shirts, watched soap operas, listened to The Police or U2. The rich sent their children to UCLA and vacationed in Switzerland. The clever recycled the ideas heard at Parisian café tables or American MBA programs. And amid the decay of Islam, the Arab regimes intrigued, plotted, warred against each other. In Lebanon beginning in April 1975, the warlords slaughtered one another, killing entire families of their rivals and leaving the riddled bodies on living room floors. Beirut was a ruin, the great hotels burned out, the city center rubble, and Arab unity a farce. The Palestinians quarreled among themselves and often employed terror, but did little to destroy the great enemy, Zionist Israel.

The West was dismayed with the chaos of the Middle East. An entire region, rich in oil, filled with decent and deserving people, could not be left to ruin. Washington felt that it ought to encourage enterprise even if stability could not be imposed. Israel and Egypt were funded in order to prevent war. Oil was shipped out of the Gulf and glass high-rise offices went up. English and German salesmen filled their order books—more mobile phones, more Mercedes stretch limousines, more Airbus jets, more computer terminals. The zealots were outraged at the success of such Western temptations. America, the Great Satan, was at fault, not those who succumbed to the lures of modernity. The fundamentalists wanted an end to temptation; they wanted a pure society immune to rock-and-roll and women's rights. If there was a return to the golden past, to the *shari'a*, to the former sureties and the promise of paradise, then the triumphs of the West would turn to ashes. The Arabs would not have to compete with the infidels or be judged by their standards.

Most Egyptians simply wanted a congenial, traditional, pious Egypt—and they also wanted Egypt to matter. They wanted respect. They did not want an Israeli ambassador in Cairo or Israeli tourists at the great Pyramids, but they had no time for the Islamists' golden age. They had seen that an Islamic revolution apparently guaranteed only violence, terror and misery.

Still, the Islamists kept working. When the Egyptian People's Assembly, on May 4, 1985, rejected a motion demanding the immediate application of the *shari'a*, there was immediate anger. The Islamists didn't want to hear about the Christian minority or the cost of imposing the seventh century on the twentieth. In June, Sheikh Hafiz Salama threatened to lead a giant protest, what he called a "Green March," if the *shari'a* was not enforced. As a result, in July the popular mosques of the fundamentalists were put under state control. When there were Islamic demonstrations in Fayoum and Alexandria, Sheikhs Salama and Rahman were arrested.

In August 1985, Sheikh Rahman was paroled so he could make the pilgrimage to Mecca—a concession. He was re-interned when he arrived back in Egypt from Saudi Arabia and kept in prison until October. After that he was again maintained under constant surveillance. He might be a provincial, a pedestrian scholar, his vision narrow and his harsh interpretation of the Koran contrived, but he was famous and he had a following.

On October 5, 1985, an Egyptian soldier shot and killed five Israeli tourists in the Sinai. This was the same day that the regime, confident that the Islamic threat had been moderated as always by concession and repression, had released Sheikh Rahman. He promptly resumed his agitation, cunningly using ambiguous phrasing in his *fatwas* and Friday sermons so that the zealots knew his intention but the state could not prosecute him. His *fatwa* on Copts meant for the *jihadi* that he had legitimized the murder of Christians. The sheikh's words could as well be taken as authorization to kill tourists, to pursue the enemies of Islam everywhere.

The *jihadi* along the Nile were fascinated by events in Afghanistan: a holy war against a traditional enemy, not just guerrilla resistance. Frustrated in their dream of power in Egypt, the zealots became more entangled in Asia. In so doing, they, like many Arabs, entered a new underground, a complex shadow world of conspiracy with global reach. Once they found hope for victory in Afghanistan, Egypt mattered much less.

There had always been secret international conduits and contacts for the fundamentalists. Al-Ikhwan could be found in various forms, usually secret, in various states. Traveling imams were common, but now on each trip within the covert world of the fundamentalists, the Islamists spread the *jihadi* doctrine. They met not only potential converts but also agents and patrons, contributors and spies. After 1979 their work became easier because of Ayatollah Khomeini in Teheran. Not only had Iran become an Islamic state, but the Teheran government and the Shi'ite elite believed that the triumph of the faith should be exported.

Regional clandestine action was comparatively easy in the Middle East because national identity was weak, and agents, subversives, terrorists and state operatives found a familiar environment. In the Arab Middle East nearly everyone spoke the same language, had been shaped by Islam, shared similar attitudes and assumptions. This was also true within the expanding diaspora—mosques in London, Iraqi exiles in California, Egyptian students in Germany. An Arab Islamist might not feel at home in the West but could almost surely find others from home with whom he could discuss the *jihadi* dream.

Nasser's Egypt, the new Algeria, the Baathists in Damascus and Baghdad had found friends and agents with ease—and with promises, money or threats. Every ambitious Middle Eastern state sponsored a Palestinian guerrilla group, and many supported revolutionary groups elsewhere in the Third World. The operation of this growing secret world was everywhere facilitated by the trends and technology of globalization: inexpensive air flight, instant communications, migrant labor, the uniformity of popular culture. Even those without a formal flag—parties, exiled factions, secret private armies, Sheikh Rahman, the Palestine Liberation Organization—suddenly had international dimensions.

In the Middle East, sponsor states had always grasped advantage in this shady world, seeking cheap, swift gains by acting through a proxy, a puppet or a secret ally. After 1967, a dozen Arab states had sponsored Palestinian organizations. After 1979, most Arab states became interested in the fundamentalists as allies, as threat or as proxy. So the zealots reached out across national borders to the faithful, not only evading repression in their home states but also becoming useful to the ambitions and fears of others.

The Iranians gained the respect of the zealots because they too wanted to eliminate the enemies of Islam and punish the infidels. The ayatollahs abhorred the secularists, the arrogance of the West, the ignorant power of America, and most especially the existence of the Zionists. Their enemies list was shared by fundamentalists and many secular Arabs; they reached out to each other. After 1979 Iran became deeply involved in Islamic militancy and the new wave of *jihad*. This new transnational underground differed from many contemporary revolutionary organizations, not only because the zealots pursued global goals by a global holy war but because they had no central command.

The emerging *jihadi* underground shaped the will of the faithful into an effective attack on global power without recourse to traditional structures: no secret army or covert party, no high command or guerrilla columns. Many undergrounds, like the Stern Gang in the Palestine Mandate, were composed of a few cells and a small command structure (three men in LEHI) engaged in an armed struggle through recourse to terror or display. Such small groups are controlled either by charisma or by consensus—the organizing power of an individual or the requirements of an agreed-upon, revealed truth defined by the leadership. Everyone knows either the leader or what the truth requires, or both. Each underground relies on the ideal and gains advantages from the tangible grievances of the volunteers. The larger the group, the more the tangible assets, but also the more difficult are communications, command and control, and the more important is structure. Charisma is difficult to deploy as an organizing principle in a large and diverse underground.

The IRA, for example, evolved out of the Irish Republican Brotherhood, founded in 1858 to promote an Irish Republic—all but established in the hearts of all the Irish—by physical force. The IRB was a conspiracy with local branches and a central command in Ireland, but in the United States it operated almost openly. When physical force failed, the IRB created a national militia, the Irish Volunteers, and ordered the Easter Rising of 1916, a conventional insurrection. When this failed, the IRB and Irish republicans persevered, organized a counterstate and a secret army, the Irish Republican Army (IRA) and waged a partially successful guerrilla campaign that led to the Irish Free State. Those who persisted evolved into a covert nationalist revolutionary conspiracy, illicit but claiming legitimacy, and when possible engaging in armed struggle.

Thus after 1969, the IRA underworld remained organized as an army that democratically elected a leadership with power concentrated in the seven-man Army Council. To broaden the struggle, the movement had a political party, Sinn Fein, overt publications, committees and support groups, but relied on consensus and military structure to pursue a well-defined goal: the withdrawal of the British from Ireland and the establishment of an Irish Republic. The IRA had contacts abroad, within and without the Irish diaspora, and conducted military operations in England and on the continent, but was essentially a national liberation movement.

In fact, for fifty years most undergrounds, no matter the ideology or agenda, acted almost exclusively on a national stage. In Italy, the new generation of the sixties responded to the flaws of society, the corruption and incompetence, by recourse to a terror campaign formally directed against the imperialist state of the multinationals, the capitalist West. For a time there were dozens of groups acting independently and sporadically—soon rivaled by neofascist cells—to create turmoil. As time passed, the key groups of the Red Brigades remained classic in form, a series of cells in the major cities of strength, tied to a central command committee that could not risk giving general orders that might be disobeyed. Thus each urban arena had considerable freedom of action, each group an agreed ideology and agenda, and often a charismatic leader. The cells did not grow bigger but reproduced, maintaining the advantages of size, control and independence.

If the IRA was a secret army shaped by consensus and the Red Brigades a classic covert ideological conspiracy, there were a variety of other organizational forms for revolution. Latin America was an arena for dozens of *focos*, small cells of the dedicated seeking to expand by revolutionary conversion and persistence on the Cuban model. There were states with formal guerrilla armies, as in Africa. After Mao there were only a few examples of rural guerrilla revolution, as in Malaya and the Philippines, the conventional underground guerrilla armies dominated by the party. The urban guerrillas everywhere closely resembled the Stern Gang.

In the case of Palestine, all militants had exile bases. The leaders might profess crucial ideological differences, but all groups were structured around a dominant individual and a radical strategy—usually terror. Most restricted operations to the national arena and those who extended the struggle, as did the Palestinians, chose targets related to the specific national struggle against Israelis and their American and European allies.

The *jihadi* that developed out of frustration in Egypt, out of success in Iran, and in the struggle in Afghanistan were not organized into counterstates like the Palestine Liberation Organization; they had no national base like the IRA or the Red Brigades, no central command and control, no agreed agenda beyond slogans —"Allah is the Answer"—and no consensus except on the need to punish the decadent West and pursue Islam's interests.

What shaped the operations of these organizations was perceived vulnerabilities. The existence of opportunity inspired the faithful to form an action-group, similar to most underground action-groups. The conspirators needed what everyone needed: money, arms, intelligence, martial skills and cover. What they had first was a target: a poorly guarded Western embassy, an airport lacking security, an underground garage with no gate, a business executive or a visiting Arab dignitary with too few bodyguards. If the vulnerability attracted a few potential *jihadi*, they might seek funding, advice, aid and comfort. They might coalesce into an action-unit, but once the operation was complete—the bomb detonated, the executive kidnapped, perhaps the conspirators arrested—the survivors would then drift back into the general population.

The *jihadi* underground was not there until required—a potential suddenly transformed into reality by opportunity. The *jihadi* underground, devoted to a vast global dream where Islam would triumph over all as Allah intended, was both insubstantial and enormously resilient, and quite unlike anything familiar to the authorities since the revolutionary anarchist threat had evaporated at the onset of the World War in 1914. Since then, few global revolutionary ideologies had produced global undergrounds. (The communists were apt to be an extension of Russian interests, and the fascists local variants with a local agenda.) The *jihadi* were different: their underground benefited because it was novel, elusive, transient, difficult to counter with conventional means, and self-replicating.

The basic American assumption was that all people were much the same, or at least were becoming more so. Cultural differences were superficial and American values were applicable to all. Why else would so many Arabs want to emigrate to the United States? The "looney-tunes," as President Reagan once called the *jihadi*, were the exception. Safe and secure in the Middle East's Hilton archipelago, where they could speak English, meet bankers or journalists, and drink imported water, Americans believed that the Arabs, no less than any Westerner, were part of an emerging global society.

Everyone could deploy American skills and assumptions, establish open societies and prosper, and in time, everyone would do so. There would be free elections, profit and investment, civil liberties and democratic societies. Then there would be no need of provocation, terrorism or hostages. International conflict could be resolved by good faith and common sense.

Americans did not understand that many Arabs saw their country not as a mentor but as greedy and self-interested, maintaining Israel as a crusader state, an insult imposed on Islam. Arab editors and officials and scholars, so sensible when they were in Berkeley or Cambridge, went home and there propagated the notion that the Mossad ran the world for the CIA, that the *Protocols of the Elders of Zion* were authentic, and that a Western conspiracy prevented Arab development. Every American—the kidnapped teachers in Beirut, the oil engineers in Saudi Arabia, the tourists along the Nile—was now a provocation, not only to the ultranationalists but also to the fundamentalists. America became awash in an ocean of venom without ever knowing it. For most Americans, it scarcely mattered. The Middle East was simply an irritant, the more so because the Arabs and the Persians seemed beyond reason. All of this was best left to the specialists. That many of those specialists seldom left Washington and almost none strayed far from the embassy and the Hilton did not matter. Who could make sense of the "looney-tunes" anyway?

This had been true in Lebanon after April 1975, when the country had collapsed into turmoil. The Lebanese menu of the year included ethnic murder, wanton car bombs, political revenge, and killers waiting at roadblocks for the day's prey. The Druze attacked the Moslems who attacked the Christians. Beirut burned, the great hotels were soon ruins and the city a heap of rubble filled with faction fighters. Syria became increasingly involved, seeking not peace but advantage. By 1982, already in control of a protective zone in the south, the Israelis drove their tanks north into Beirut and expelled the Palestinians. In time the Israelis withdrew to the south, attracting Shi'ite guerrillas, suicide bombers and protests. The Syrians stayed. There was neither peace nor prospects.

The Reagan administration agreed that American interests—and those of the Lebanese people—would be best served with Western involvement. If something were not done, there might be another Israeli war and spreading regional instability. And so in 1982, a Western force arrived to accommodate the rivals and keep the elusive peace. The Islamic militants, the Palestinians and many Arabs all perceived this as a new crusade: the West had come to help the Christian Arabs. Many of the locals, watching the Marines move into position and set up headquarters at the international airport, felt humiliated and bitter. The result was a rare meeting of militant minds, a unity of purpose. The Islamists and the radicals wanted action, as did the Syrians and the Iranians. Operations congenial to the Shi'ites could be funded, and organized in a way that assured plausible denial. The multinational force was a tempting target.

The Ayatollah Khamanei in Tehran publicly urged the Shi'ites to "put an end to the shameful occupation of Lebanon." The anti-Western forces and regimes almost at once began to organize covert operations to punish the West. A key Shi'ite figure in Lebanon was Imad Mugniyah, born in 1962 near Tyre in south Lebanon. He had briefly attended the American University of Beirut, for generations a font of revolutionaries and radicals. He had joined Yasser Arafat's al-Fatah, and when the Palestinians had been driven out of Lebanon by the Israelis in 1982, had joined a variety of radical Shi'ite groups and secured the support of Iran. Competent, elusive, energetic, well connected and charismatic, he maintained contacts with both the Shi'ite Iranians and the secular Syrians. He had become a player in the dark world of terror, anti-American ideologues, Islamists and resentful regimes. He soon had patrons who supplied resources, technological skills, operational material, suggestions and enthusiasm.

Mugniyah, his zealots, the officers of the Syrian intelligence services and various agents of the Iranians put together an ambitious operation. A terrorist suicide mission against the American Marine barracks needed only to reach the target, not worry about withdrawal. And local intelligence indicated that the Marines sent by Washington to Beirut were unprepared. (Later, it would be revealed that their rifles were not even loaded.) On October 23, 1983, a truck bomb with a suicide driver would be dispatched to penetrate the limited security at the Marine base to the south of the city at the international airport. Only minimum skill, explosives and a detonator, a pickup truck and one martyr were needed.

Just after dawn, Hassan Ali Talbakaran, the chosen one, drove a yellow Mercedes truck past Marines standing guard with empty weapons. They shouted. He paid no attention; he was driving to heaven in a yellow truck. He accelerated past open gates and banged through a barbed-wire fence. The truck stopped. It was very quiet. He had arrived at ground zero inside the giant concrete structure. For a moment, Hassan Ali Talbakaran, a young man of special merit, nearly twenty years old, sat in place, a small smile flickering on his face. He was blessed, fulfilled.

At 6:22 A.M. he flicked a switch and a white glare lit up the barracks as the 1,200-pound bomb detonated in a huge roar. The explosion generated a vast roiling cloud of black and brown smoke, spiraling up in the bright Lebanese sky, visible for miles. Talbakaran and the yellow truck had been vaporized, but he had also killed 241 United States Marines. Mugniyah's operation was vindicated, his associates and sponsors content, the faithful delighted.

For the Shi'ites organized into Hezbollah, there would be more bombs and murders, more aid and comfort from patrons —the various Syrian intelligence agencies, the Iranian Ministry of Intelligence and Security, and the radical Iranian Revolutionary

Guards Corps. In the Lebanese debacle, Western enemies of Islam would be targeted. Gunmen seized, imprisoned, tortured and killed William Buckley, the American CIA station chief in Beirut. Kidnapping soon became a cottage industry in a country that already held the record for airliner hijacking.

In time there was a truce to local terror, but Imad Mugniyah, who had found his vocation, remained active and committed—as did the Syrians and the Iranians. He established his own underground of the unrequited, the Islamic Jihad Organization. His *jihad* focused on the power of the West and especially on American targets. He followed the injunction of the Koran: "You should prepare whatever is within our reach in terms of power and horses to terrorize..."

As *jihad* faltered along the Nile, Egyptians increasingly decided to stay abroad. They were joined by Algerians and Yemenis. Pakistan became a haven where they established an infrastructure to support the Arab Afghanis. New Koranic schools were established, along with newspapers and journals. Rest houses and indoctrination centers for volunteers were opened and hospitals staffed. In one hospital was a special Egyptian, Dr. Ayman al-Zawahiri, who in exile had brought his medical vocation to the service of the *jihadi,* just as he once had done at the al-Ikhwan clinic in Cairo.

Ayman al-Zawahiri had begun to evolve into one of the amirs of the *jihad* very early during his conventional studies. He had joined al-Ikhwan at fifteen, almost immediately coming to the attention of the authorities during a demonstration. Since his family was distinguished and his dissent relatively tame, he was allowed to continue his studies. As a student he became more and more alienated from the state and attracted to the most fundamentalist ideals. In 1973, while still a medical student at the University of Cairo, where his father had been professor of pharmacology, al-Zawahiri, along with an electrical engineer and an army officer, founded the underground Islamic Jihad. The organization sought to focus the armed struggle specifically against the state—government offices and buildings, government employees. The authorities promptly banned it.

Al-Zawahiri was quiet, English-speaking, intelligent and from a good family. One grandfather had been a diplomat; the other was Rabiaa al-Zawahiri, the grand imam at al-Azhar. His great uncle Abdel Rahman Azzam was the first secretary-general of the Arab League. Al-Zawahiri graduated from the University of Cairo in 1974 and received a master's degree in surgery four years later. He specialized in pediatrics. He didn't look like a revolutionary conspirator; although he had a full beard and wore a white turban, he also peered out through heavy glasses with the look of a benign family physician. He offered his medical service to al-Ikhwan, but so did many middle-class Egyptians. He attracted little attention, gave no speeches and signed no petitions; but he wrote books. The most famous, *The Bitter Harvest*, was a study of al-Ikhwan. As the journalist Peter Bergen later noted, "When you meet him you do not think that he has anything to do with violence."

Soon after the Sadat assassination, the police had penetrated an Islamic Jihad training camp. They found arms manuals, intelligence data, bomb technology classes and extensive planning. Dr. al-Zawahiri was taken into custody, questioned, tried, convicted of sedition and sentenced to three years in prison. On his release he reorganized Islamic Jihad under the cover name "Vanguards of Conquest." He had long since lost his anonymity. He was placed under intense surveillance, allowed to practice medicine but not to pursue *jihad* without risk of arrest. Like so many others, he slipped out of Egypt and appeared in Pakistan—where his grandfather Abdul Wahab had been Egyptian ambassador—and then went on to Afghanistan to help the *mujaheddin*.

Once he had left Egypt as an exile, al-Zawahiri entered the new global underground. For him, as for all the fundamentalists and for many Arabs, the new Afghan war became the great cause, a true *jihad*.

Many came to Afghanistan to observe the struggle. Some volunteered their services. Some returned to their homes elsewhere in the Middle East to spread the news of the *jihad*. One of the most imposing of all these *jihadi* leaders was Abdullah Azzam, who as much as anyone had given shape to the new Islamic underground. He was born in 1941 near Jenin in the Palestine Mandate. By the time he earned a degree in Damascus in 1966, he already hated Israelis and fought against them in 1967. Instead of guerrilla revolution or conventional war, he had from the first argued for *jihad*. After the 1967 war, he went to Cairo, as did so many of the pious, to study at al-Azhar, earning both a master's degree and a doctorate in Islamic jurisprudence. More important, he met others who had similar views, befriending the family of Sayyid Qutb, author of the crucial *Signposts*, who by then had become the great martyr of the Egyptian Islamists through his execution for treason. Azzam also met Sheikh Omar Abdel Rahman and they shared their visions of Islamic triumph by *jihad*. Exposed to the Egyptian theorists of *jihad* in the land of al-Ikhwan, where militant fundamentalism had evolved over two generations, Azzam had learned about the Egyptians' analysis of the dangers of modernism, the power of the Zionists, and the corruption of secular Arab authority.

After getting his advanced degrees, he joined the faculty of the University of Jordan in Amman. He taught Islamic law, making no secret of his opinion that the staff and management of the university were unworthy secularists. He was dismissed and moved on to Saudi Arabia to teach. The Saudis might be uneasy about his radical Islamic views, but what could they do? They were fundamentalists too, guardians of the holy places. From his new post, Azzam began traveling to keep old contacts and make new ones, encouraging the Islamists. His message, backed by Koranic quotations, was simple: what was wrong with the Islamic world was Western secularism and corruption; what was wanted was an Islamic society ruled by the *shari'a;* and how to achieve this was through *jihad*. Azzam turned himself into a one-man lecture agency, an information bureau and a conduit for all Islamists. He knew everyone and everyone soon knew him.

Large, charismatic and eloquent, Azzam appeared in Kuwait, Yemen, Bahrain, even the United States. Virtually unnoticed was the fact that a steady stream of Arab immigrants had created a new diaspora in America. Arabs were settling not just in the well-know neighborhood off Atlantic Avenue in Brooklyn, but now also in Houston and Los Angeles and Detroit. Azzam moved across the country from one popular mosque to the next, meeting in upstairs rooms and hired halls, spreading word of a future Islamic revolution, the confusion of the West and the coming defeat of Israel—without the authorities even noticing.

At his Saudi base he gathered and spread news, raised money, produced videotapes, delivered sermons and diatribes. He used the mail and fax machines, computers, al-Azhar contacts, personal meetings, wires and telephones and secret agents to create an international community of conspirators. Then in 1980 he met Afghan *mujaheddin* fighting the Red Army and decided to devote himself wholly to *jihad.*

Leaving Saudi Arabia for Pakistan, Azzam first took a position as lecturer at the Islamic University in Islamabad and then moved on to Peshawar. He was highly visible, an imposing figure with a long, gray beard and a gift for the hard word. He wanted everything and wanted it now. He wanted to restore the *Khalifa,* the caliphate, by "*jihad* and the rifle alone, no negotiations, no conferences and no dialogues." He traveled through Afghanistan encouraging resistance and making contacts. Azzam appeared wherever there were *mujaheddin:* in Lujer, Kandahar, the valley of Binjistr, Kabul, Jalabad. But *jihad* in Afghanistan was merely the beginning. He also urged his contacts in Palestine, Bokhara, Lebanon, Chad, Eritrea, Somalia, the Philippines, Burma, southern Yemen, Tashkent and Andalusia to act. Azzam established the Services Office—Mekhtab al-Khadama—in Peshawar, gathering in one place a community of the faithful attracted to the war.

At Peshawar, the Pakistan-Afghanistan border had become a bizarre place with border guards and regular Pakistani troops and operatives from the ISI, *mujaheddin* on a visit, Soviet spies. It was easy to find Afghani Arab training facilities and summer camps for the young and arms factories in tents and sheds. Rocket launchers and AK-47s could be bought with ease. There were jerrybuilt mosques, refugees in tent cities, American agents and arms dealers, observers reporting to Moscow, journalists, and soon Stinger ground-to-air missiles on the way to the *mujaheddin.* There was tuberculosis, measles, polio, sometimes cholera, and always malnutrition, privation and crippled beggars in the gutter. Gunsmiths made automatic weapons by hand in the back of sheds. Shoppers could find Japanese video games, English marmalade, opium or canned tomato soup. The faithful opened *madrassas* to teach children only the Koran and *jihad.* The war across the border dominated everything.

Even blind Sheikh Omar Abdel Rahman appeared in Peshawar in 1985 to experience the *jihad.* He visited Afghanistan under the aegis of the ultra-Islamist Gulbuddin Hekmatyar, one of the most zealous of the *mujaheddin* and also one of the bloodiest and most uncompromising. The sheikh made his way across the country, led by guides through minefields and across mountain passes so he could feel the reality of the struggle. He wept at the sound of the artillery in the distance, because now he could hear the echo of *jihad.* He returned to Peshawar, where he had met with many of his old friends and with new converts, and then went back to Cairo. When times grew too confining in Egypt, he would return again to Peshawar to establish a guesthouse for the volunteers. Joining *jihad* were young men of all sorts, including two of his sons who had followed him from Fayoum. The sheikh also made contact with a new generation of *jihadi,* among them a Saudi eager to help who also had control of a fortune: Osama bin Laden.

Like other converts to *jihad,* the young Saudi had turned his back on the contemporary secular world after traveling as a reluctant playboy to Europe. The world of secular modernism did not appeal to him. He had studied under Azzam, had grown more militant and in 1984 set up a guest lodge, Beit al-Ansark, "House of the Supporters," in Peshawar. Because of the fortune he had inherited, his lodge became a way station into Afghanistan. In 1987 the sheikh stayed there and found bin Laden's instincts to be sound. Tall and slender, with a scraggly beard and a confident manner, bin Laden had dedicated his inheritance to militant Islamic causes.

Sheikh Rahman was enthusiastic at the dedication and sacrifice of a new generation. Many of those involved were Egyptians who had fled arrest and repression. Some were simple gunmen, but there were also the new amirs. One of these leaders in exile who attracted the sheikh's interest was Dr. al-Zawahiri, whom he had known in Egypt because of his Islamic Jihad organization. In Afghanistan, al-Zawahiri was creating an Islamic Jihad in exile. For help he had turned to bin Laden, whose views he found congenial. The single most divisive issue for the *jihadi* was where to focus the struggle.

Al-Zawahiri was operationally far more experienced than bin Laden, but like Sheikh Rahman, he was still focused on events along the Nile. Bin Laden, on the other hand, increasingly offered a worldview. The key ideological difference between them was bin Laden's growing conviction that a global defense of Islam against Western intrusion took precedence over the destruction of corrupt Moslem rulers. For bin Laden, the true enemy of the moment was not Mubarak, but the crusaders, the communists, the Jews, the Great Satan.

Bin Laden had come from a rich Yemeni family from the tiny village of al-Rubat in the Hadramaut, south of the Arabian empty quarter, a vast desert and one of the most isolated and devout areas of the peninsula. When the family left al-Rubatin and moved into Saudi Arabia, it entered a society still shaped by ancient imperatives. Ibn Saud had led his tribe in a liberation campaign against the Turkish Empire. When the Turks were defeated in 1918, he turned on his Arab rivals, deploying an army staffed by his sons and a people composed of the puritanical Wahhabi sect. (When the triumphant Wahhabi entered Mecca in 1924, they smashed all the mirrors, the first they had ever seen.) For some time Saudi Arabia remained in many ways a Bedouin kingdom. By 1960, 85 percent of the population was still illiterate, and six years later a significant Saudi religious leader could condemn the Copernican heresy—for him and his followers, the sun circled the earth, the Koran was ample guide, and all change was suspect.

By the 1970s, Saudi Arabia had been flooded with oil money and so with foreign workers, agents, banks, new technologies and new ideas. The royal family could keep out tourists and visitors and maintain a special religious police, but it could not ban all novelty, the appeal of popular culture or new temptations. Amid the inevitable construction of a modern state on oil money, the conventions of the past eroded.

Osama bin Laden's father's construction firm had made a fortune in Saudi Arabia. In a Wahhabi society, an obsession with the flaws of the *jahiliyya* had not dominated Osama's life as the impact of the new pharaohs had done with the blind sheikh, al-Zawahiri and the other Egyptian *jihadi*. It was the intervention in Afghanistan by the Russians that engaged bin Laden's concern and ended his drifting existence. He went immediately to offer aid to the *mujaheddin*. He opened his Beit al-Ansark guesthouse for volunteers; eventually two of Sheikh Rahman's sons would work there. Bin Laden gradually collected his own *jihadi*, moved into Afghanistan, took part in military operations occasionally and reached out to others in Pakistan.

Bin Laden made a tour through the Gulf in 1986 to raise more money. By then he had met al-Zawahiri. Each contact in the elusive Islamic underground that bin Laden made widened his perspective on the global battlefield.

In 1987 bin Laden, along with two or three others, formally founded his own *jihad* group: al-Qaeda. This was soon merged with al-Zawahiri's exiled Islamic Jihad. In time the daughter of the Egyptian Muhammad Alef, Dr. al-Zawahiri's deputy, married bin Laden's son and so created a traditional Arab alliance.

In February 1989 the Soviet Union began to withdraw from Afghanistan. For the *jihadi* this was a momentous victory that proved the inherent weakness of secular power. The fundamentalists, taking major credit for the defeat of the Russians, had prospered throughout the Middle East and in the Islamic diaspora, and so offered a cover for the exiled *jihadi*. Both bin Laden and al-Zawahiri had contacts throughout this secret Islamic world. The years invested by Azzam and the others might have put an underground of the zealous in place to take advantage of the Afghan victory, but had not offered an action agenda. This bin Laden intended to do by continuing to draw on his own capital from his family's business. The mission was uncertain, yet al-Qaeda, unlike any secret army or conspiracy of cells, was ready. What bin Laden and al-Zawahiri constructed in this organization was an infrastructure with an international reach: intelligence, contacts, loans and grants, advice and experts.

On Friday, November 14, 1989, the emerging global conspiracy suffered an unexpected and unexplained loss in Peshawar. Abdullah Azzam was murdered at the gate to the Saba-e-Leit mosque when a bomb detonated under his car. The professor and both his sons, Muhammad, 23, and Ibrahim, 14, were killed. Some suspected Islamic rivals, some the Pakistanis, others the Russians or Mossad; but no one really knew. Azzam left behind a tangible, if invisible legacy: a covert structure of ideological Islamists, potential activists, aspirant martyrs, sympathizers and supporters. The underground was not a party or a faction, not a matter of cells, not a secret army; it was an environment for those who awaited a mission. Its assets were immediately picked up by al-Qaeda.

When the Russians were defeated, the Pakistanis, like the Afghanis, wanted the volunteers dispersed. The Afghani fighters had never felt the need for the Arab volunteers and the Pakistanis had used them for strategic purposes. This was not a disaster for the *jihadi*. There were other wars—in Algeria and in Yemen, soon in the Balkans and the Caucasus; and the armed struggle was about to be renewed in Egypt. Yet the *jihadi* temporarily lacked a specific mission and their only patron was a new regime in Sudan.

There, in a swift and bloodless coup on June 30, 1989, the fundamentalists had seized power. The new president was Brigadier Omar Hassan Ahmad al-Bashir, but the dominant figure in Khartoum was his mentor, Hassan al-Turabi, even though his small National Islamic Front had won only 6 percent of the vote in the 1986 elections. Al-Turabi, a Sorbonne graduate, mature in years, mild in manner, erudite and reasonable in discourse, was fanatically dedicated to a pure Islamic state. And so, for the first time, the Islamists had a state base, although it was torn by a costly and unending war against anti-Islamic rebels in the south and hampered by ancient quarrels, limited talent and a stunted infrastructure.

Then on August 2, 1990, Iraq seized Kuwait and the West responded. Western, especially American, troops began moving into Saudi Arabia. Bin Laden, who had no sympathy with Iraq's Saddam Hussein, was horrified at the appearance of Western forces in the Holy Land, but al-Qaeda no longer had a secure base because Afghanistan was in turmoil and the Arab Afghanis had been dispersed. Only Sudan offered a base for any campaign against the Western presence. In December 1991, bin Laden flew out of Peshawar for Khartoum. He was committed to a *jihad* against the West, especially the Americans, but the time was not ripe and al-Qaeda's assets were still limited.

In Egypt too, *jihad* was frustrated. There had been an Islamic mobilization in the universities in April 1986, after a riot in which a Gama'a Islamiyya student was killed by the police. Sheikh Rahman was arrested again on April 29 and remained in jail until May 8. The next year was little different. In April, al-Ikhwan won thirty-seven seats in the Egyptian legislative elections, indicating the potential and power of organization and conventional politics rather than armed struggle. In 1986 an assassination attempt on a former minister of justice failed. As always the state responded with repression. In June five hundred Islamists were arrested.

On October 6, Hosni Mubarak was reelected president. Because the pharaoh was still in power, the sheikh was still active. In 1988, back from his travels in Afghanistan, he denounced the most famous Egyptian writer, Nobelist Naguib Mahfouz, as an apostate of Islam. Five years later, one of the zealots attempted to kill the elderly writer, who was gravely injured but survived. The sheikh was seen as having inspired the fanatic by issuing a *fatwa* that authorized murder; but the regime could not act, for fear of provoking disorders. Sheikh Rahman preached at his mosque in Fayoum under informal house arrest. Each Friday, guided by his son, he made his way to prayers down a narrow street lined with shoddy houses draped in laundry hanging from lines, while children kicked a soccer ball in a vacant lot. The two were followed by two police cars creeping down the lane behind them. From their balconies the locals could see the mosque's barred windows, the wooden door, the parade of the police and the pious. When finished, again on the arm of his son, the sheikh returned home, followed by the same two police cars. A nod to the sheikh and your name went on file.

Rahman was finally arrested again at Fayoum along with thirty-five suspected members of Gama'a Islamiyya. The government was engaged in repression and concession as usual, so on August 10, 1989, the sheikh was released but hundreds of Islamist militants were arrested. Rahman found normal life with his family and at the mosque almost impossible. The police were everywhere, anyone he touched was contaminated and he could do less and less. Like others before him, he decided to withdraw from Egypt, and in April 1990 he traveled to Khartoum, a safe fundamentalist haven.

The sheikh continued to intervene in Egyptian affairs from afar, galvanizing the surviving *jihadi*, who finally launched a serious armed struggle along the Nile. On October 12, 1990, Rifat al-Muhjub, the president of parliament, was assassinated, as were various infidels—tourists, Christian Copts. Arson and ambush spread along the Nile, especially in Upper Egypt. There were 30 fatalities in 1991 and 93 the next year. The numbers would continue to escalate until 1997, when 1,200 died. Yet the more were killed, the less likely victory appeared and the more ordinary people were alienated from the zealots.

For the Egyptian *jihadi*, buoyed by the slogan "Allah is the Answer," murder was increasingly all that mattered. Those underground would kill and everyone else would follow. And they still had ideological allies, even a few among the orthodox of al-Azhar. One of them, Sheikh Muhammad al-Ghazali of al-Azhar's Islamic Research Academy, declared that anyone who did not advocate implementation of the *shari'a* was an apostate or a non-Muslim, and those killing such people were not liable for any punishment. Two weeks after al-Ghazali's *fatwa*, on April 8, 1992, members of al-Gama'a, Sheikh Rahman's group, killed the writer Farag Foda, one of the most provocative and irritating of the intellectuals. No significant religious figure condemned the murder.

On October 12, 1992, an earthquake hit Cairo, leaving 552 dead and 9,000 injured. While the government responded slowly, the fundamentalists rushed into the ruined slums with aid and comfort. The Islamists took the event as a sign from God. Who needed detailed programs or philosophical justification? God had spoken. The earth had moved. The struggle had been validated.

There was also comforting news for the zealots from elsewhere: The Afghani Arabs were at work or at war in Yemen and Bosnia and the Caucasus. Sudan was secure for Islam. In Algeria in 1992, the Islamic party had been so sure to win the election that the military regime canceled it. In response, the Groupe Armée Islamique began a rebellion: vicious, intense, composed of ambush and murder, with enormous civilian casualties and no certain outcome. Villages were wiped out overnight—as a lesson, by mistake, in retaliation.

Even the Gulf War alliance, the Americans in Arabia, the

collapse of Saddam Hussein's Kuwait adventure—all of which could have been cause for pessimism—were interpreted as encouraging signs. And the rising chaos in Somalia offered an opportunity to oppose America directly. In Sudan, al-Qaeda dispatched agents to help any anti-American resistance. In Egypt itself, the *jihadi* remained confident and assured. The Americans were, indeed, fearful for Egyptian stability and so continued to send money. Mubarak assumed that in time the *jihadi* would simply run out of gunmen. Those gunmen assumed that what they perceived as having worked in Afghanistan would work also in Egypt.

Early in 1993, the United Nations intervention force in Somalia became entangled with warlords. The United Nations and especially the Americans had brought food and medical supplies, doctors and distributors, and sought to keep the peace and rebuild the nation, but the soldiers were treated by some of the clans not as saviors but as enemies. Americans were killed. Osama bin Laden was delighted that some of his agents had found their way to the struggle. In 1994 the United Nations withdrew—another victory for Islam, another success for *jihad,* no matter that it left Somalia ravished and partitioned, with roving warlords in charge, the cities ruined, children hungry, roads unsafe, no government and no future.

The *jihadi,* like all underground fighters, saw what they chose to see. Increasingly they saw a new target, not the *jahiliyya* societies in the corrupt Arab world, but the global system established by infidel power. Islam must be defended and intervention—in Bosnia and Somalia and especially Palestine—must be repulsed. Then, the corrupt national governments would collapse. Thus the local struggles in Egypt or Algeria became battles in the great struggle, the confrontation between the faithful and the infidel. And for the global *jihadi,* the key enemy remained—as Ayatollah Ruhollah Khomeini had declared in Teheran—the Great Satan: the United States.

━━━   ━━━

The new *jihad* first struck out at America in one of the most isolated Middle Eastern countries, Yemen, where politics were tribal and the governments relied on bribes, betrayal, foreign funds, terror and—if needed—a public display of piety or fashionable ideology. Ruling Yemen had never been easy. The old reactionary Imam Ahmed, who came to power in 1948, was finally assassinated in 1962. The civil war that followed involved Egyptian troops supporting the republicans and Saudi support for the royalists. The war cost 150,000 Yemenis their lives by the time the fighting ended in 1970. South Yemen had become independent in 1967 as a neo-Marxist state, many of whose citizens feared for their lives. Three hundred thousand refugees fled to the north and assured a generation of tension, border war and conspiracy. Over the years, many of those involved in Yemeni politics were driven into exile or imprisoned, often dangling in chains from the wall of a dungeon with little chance for pardon.

Yemen became one country on May 21, 1990, and stayed that way until 1994, when the south tried to secede, thus provoking a civil war. The Sana'a regime in the north raised an army with tribal levies and also used as shock troops those who had served in Afghanistan. The victory over the rebels in July 1994, at a cost of ten thousand lives, meant that Yemen was again united.

Yemen had been a key source of Afghani Arabs. General Ali Mosen al-Ahmar, a player in the power structure, had met with bin Laden and arranged the recruiting of volunteers for Afghanistan. Some three thousand Yemenis had then served and returned, still militant, still seeking a mission. They found allies. Tariq Nasr al-Fadhi, not just a veteran but an influential tribal leader, son of a southern sultan and a member of the presidential council, emerged as leader of an active Islamist group. With Saudi sponsorship—soon withdrawn—he had already led a campaign against the communists in Aden. Like many Yemenis, he was a fundamentalist by experience and conviction, and had become a *jihadi*. There was, as well, the highly visible and very influential Abdel Meguid al-Zindani, virulently anti-American and anti-Jewish and a public supporter of the *jihad* in his sermons. With his long beard dyed red with henna and his commanding presence, he was a force to be considered. The victory in Afghanistan by no means ended the commitment of such Yemeni zealots.

In Yemen there had always been a constant din of low-level

violence. There had been small bombs, something thrown on the roof of the Italian embassy in February 1991, and then explosions at the British embassy in March and at the American embassy in September. This time the *jihadi* wanted more serious results.

So in December 1992 the Islamists prepared a truck bomb; informers later said that those involved belonged to Tariq Nasser al-Fadhi's group. In Aden they had found an ideal target in the two best hotels, where alcohol was sold. More important, the hotels catered to hundreds of American Marines on their way to Somalia for Operation Restore Hope. A small group of *jihadi* loaded two trucks with explosives. The detonators were fixed and the truck bombs driven into central Aden. The first truck bomb exploded near the Goldmohur Hotel, killing a hotel employee and an Austrian tourist. In the car park of the Aden Mövenpick Hotel, a faulty detonator caused an explosion that injured two of the terrorists but did no other damage. Six arrests were made, but all the suspects escaped from jail. The incident was added to the chronology of Yemeni terror, filed and forgotten.

No one in the West saw much significance in another bombing in an odd corner of Arabia. Yemen was inclined to be violent at any time; kidnapping was a tradition and bombs were a means of political communication as well as intimidation. What relevance could a pair of botched truck bombs near a couple of seedy hotels have? Who could even find Yemen on a four-color map?

Yet the detonations of the bombs in Aden were heard around the Islamic world. The Islamists increasingly accepted that there were only two parties in the world, the Party of God and the Party of the Devil. Already there had been violence in Egypt and Algeria. Islam had been defended in the Balkans and the Caucasus. Now, a global *jihad* had begun at the end of the world, in the heartland of the faith in Yemen.

More significantly, in the Arab diasporas of Brooklyn and Jersey City, the faith had also arrived again in an especially virulent form in the person of Sheikh Omar Abdel Rahman. In July 1990 he got off a plane at Kennedy International Airport in New York with a visa granted in Khartoum, Sudan. His name had been on the State Department terror-warning list, but the list was often incomplete and the local consular officials less than conscientious. His visa had actually been granted by a CIA officer working with consulate cover who had been too busy to check his credentials thoroughly.

Led through the airport, the sheikh was quite visible in long robes, red turban, full beard and dark glasses, a substantial middle-aged man in the midst of crowds. He was met, as always, by colleagues and fundamentalist friends. He was taken first to a house rented for him in Bay Ridge in Brooklyn. He then began to visit the faithful in the small mosques to prepare their minds. He gave sermons on Fridays. He met with the interested, talked, admonished, encouraged. He traveled about America speaking on the faith, and never making any secret of the apocalypse that awaited the world. He then flew off to England and Denmark to preach.

Sheikh Rahman returned to America, again through JFK Airport, his visa still accepted. On January 31, 1991, he applied for a permanent residence visa. It was granted two months later. He continued his American sermons but kept a close watch on Egyptian affairs. He had brought with him to America his understanding of the Egyptian example: the righteous murders, the ideals of al-Ikhwan, the worldview of fundamentalism, and a commitment to broaden *jihad* beyond the Nile. The voice of the past speaking of the future, he preached Friday nights in the shabby rooms of popular mosques in Jersey City and Brooklyn. His sermons became famous. He spoke in storefront offices and upstairs rooms. He could not see these dingy rooms but only a luminous vision: *Jihad.*

FIVE

THE JIHAD IN NEW YORK, 1992–1993

At home in Fayoum, among his own, the blind Sheikh Rahman had been able to speak from his frantic heart. In New York he rarely talked to an American or to anyone other than the faithful. He didn't know America at all. He could not see the skyline of the city, the Empire State Building or the World Trade Center. He could not see the inside of the seedy apartments and the local walkup mosques, Abu Bakr Elseddique in Brooklyn and Masjid al-Salam in Jersey City, a few mean rooms with strip lighting and folding chairs.

Those who followed Middle Eastern matters knew him by reputation. In time, journalists sought to interview the notorious Egyptian fundamentalist who had come to America. They were apt to argue, provoking him rather than exploring his thoughts. And he seldom found such encounters useful. Who cared what the infidel Americans, declared enemies of the Truth, thought or read? As the sheikh told one journalist who had climbed up a narrow staircase in Jersey City to find him in a bare room stacked with boxes along the wall, holding copies of his sermons and speeches, "It may be that my presence in the belly of the Great Satan could show it the way to the right path." But in fact Rahman knew, if the journalists did not, that the Great Satan was beyond redemption, arrogant, powerful, ignorant.

It seemed unlikely that a real threat to America could arise from a blind bigot living in rented rooms on the outskirts of a great city, at the edge of real events. Everyday Americans would have found his sermons to be the ravings of a fanatic, his language bizarre, and the threats he uttered risible. In his robe and skull cap, he was dressed for a sideshow and spoke like a villain in a badly translated film. How could anyone take Sheikh Rahman or his message about crushing Americans seriously?

Destroy them thoroughly and erase them from the face of the earth. Ruin their economies, set their companies on fire, turn their conspiracies to powder and dust. Sink their ships, bring their planes down. Slay them in air, on land, on water. By the command of Allah, kill them wherever you find them. Catch them and put them in prison. Lie in wait for them and kill these infidels. They will surely get great oppression from you. God will make you the means of wreaking a terrible revenge upon them. He will support you against them. He will cure the afflicted hearts of the faithful and take all anger from their hearts.

His was a strange voice, but Rahman made no secret of his intentions; revolutionaries seldom do, just as their targets rarely pay attention to their threats. In his Friday sermons in New York, he was the voice of zeal, purity and righteousness, untouched by the outer world.

He was also an Egyptian, coming from a village where he had preached to the poor and argued with the skeptical. He had married first Aisha and had children—two of his sons were volunteers in Afghanistan; and then he married again while in prison in Cairo. His world was almost as circumscribed as that of the *fellahín*. Beyond the Koran, which he used to transform the contemporary world into an arena for the great battle between truth and darkness, he knew little and cared about less. Literature was suspect. Music, novelty, sensation and pleasure held no interest. He was denied access to the visual arts. Science was a mystery. The Koran contained all that need be known. His analysis was coarse, constructed from stereotypes and ignorance, based on the needs of a village fanatic who had learned by rote. His time at al-Azhar had not made him a scholar; his research was only to find justification for his convictions in the Koran. His mind formed by repetition and revelation, the sheikh possessed cunning but lacked sophistication and often common sense.

He came to New York not as a pilgrim but as a harbinger. His sponsor on the first trip in 1990 was Mustafa Shalabi, a former chemist in Egypt with an electrical contracting business in exile.

Shalabi had become the director of the Alkhifa center in Brooklyn, which had moved a few doors down from the al-Farouq mosque to a small apartment at 566 Atlantic Avenue. The center was sparsely furnished: a few chairs, a desk, a fax, a telephone. The walls were lined with stacks of pamphlets, cassettes, printed sermons. Militants moved in and out, attending meetings, leaving messages, exchanging money. It was an archetypical office for political exiles, no different from that of a radical anarchist faction in Hamburg or republican Sinn Fein in Dublin, with unread flyers and old posters, take-out food and dirty cups, and the faithful few.

From the apartment on Atlantic Avenue, Shalabi had directed Afghani recruitment with contacts in twenty-six states and collected money for *jihad*. The sheikh's presence and speaking tours had increased contributions, but Shalabi was focused on Afghanistan and did not always share Rahman's interest in Egyptian events. Then on March 1, 1991, someone entered Shalabi's gated community in Brooklyn, got into his apartment and killed him. Some suspected the sheikh himself was behind this murder, since with Shalabi out of the way he would now be able to control the New York diaspora. The police could find nothing, however, and cared little for ideological quarrels in immigrant ghettos.

By this time, the *jihad* in Afghanistan was over, so the zealous in America sought other ways to serve. Some in the New York area had organized a training camp in the backwoods of Pennsylvania near Harrisburg, found instructors and practiced marksmanship, firing live rounds, wearing camouflage uniforms and waiting for direction.

The sheikh's former driver and guide reappeared, back from the Afghan wars. Mahmud Abu Halima, an Egyptian, was also a taxi driver with a suspended license and a record of violations. He was like most of the Egyptian Afghani who had been attracted by the dreams of the new amirs and fought in the war. He was born in 1959 in Kafr Dawar, a drab Delta town that had evolved into a bleak suburb fifteen miles south of Alexandria. The town was typical: a collection of rough concrete bungalows for workers, the usual narrow unpaved lanes, uncollected trash, a few tattered palms, a few shops, a barber, the mosque, the state school—and dust.

In time his lack of prospects soured Abu Halima on the government, the system and Egypt itself. He quit school early and emigrated to Munich, arriving just before Sadat was murdered. In Germany he lived only among his own, all poor, resentful, isolated, rootless and without intellectual or emotional resources. They had Arabic in common, useless on the streets, and Islam, which gave them a temporary place in religious centers and mosques on the edge of German society. Abu Halima found a job first as a dish-washer and then in the meat department of a grocery store. He didn't like the Germans—they drank too much, spent too lavishly, and seemed emotionally cold; but in order to stay in the country, he married one. When the first German wife did not work out, he married another. He faced expulsion when his visa expired in 1986. Without telling anyone, Abu Halima and his new wife, Marianne Weber, a convert to Islam, left for America.

In New York he found work as a taxi driver. He filled his cab with Korans and religious books and played cassettes of sermons, so he could live within his own special Islamic world inside the taxi. He despised the pedestrians, often the customers, and the Americans in mass—they were too rich, too materialistic. He drove his taxi without a license or registration. He often ran red lights and his chauffeur license was suspended ten times for repeated traffic violations.

Abu Halima and Marianne lived in isolation in Brooklyn with their four children in a cheap, badly furnished apartment, where they ate off the floor for lack of a table. His German in-laws visited and were appalled. After returning to Germany, they sent money and sweaters for the grandchildren. They didn't understand that he had created his own pure world not only in his taxi and in his apartment, but in his mind.

Abu Halima was like the others who had emigrated to the West: the take-out delivery men from Yemen and Shi'ite messenger boys in north London, and the Algerians in the concrete high-rise slums of France. Young and inexperienced in everything but Islam, they had no certificates or skills, only appetites and a confused and shallow understanding of the Western world. They were surrounded with temptations and denied opportunity. They usually proved inept and awkward in the presence of other values. They didn't fit in. Even if they were married to Americans or

Germans, they did not feel Western. Years might pass and they could find comfort only among others equally alienated. They could not go back to the village in Egypt or Algeria, but neither could they find fulfillment in their new world. Drifting between two cultures, they were alienated, marginal, filled with resentment.

Without old friends or intellectual resources, such migrants sought out the familiar comfort of Islam. They could glory in the assurance of a paradise denied the capitalists, the getters and spenders, the chic women who waved down the taxi or the rich marching across the television screen. They were possessed both by specific grievances and by the imperatives of the Truth.

Like the others, Abu Halima placed himself in an Islamic cocoon. His habits and experience, his lack of education and his inability to mold his own character to his new prospects circumscribed his life. What made him an Arab—what was comfortable, congenial, shaped by the expectations and rewards of Islam —insured that he could not integrate into the West. He could have a job like everyone else, dress as they did and watch the same television shows, but he would always remain different and ineffectual because of what he believed.

Many of the other Arab emigrants in Brooklyn, and many others in the slums of Cairo or the mountain villages of Yemen, had been exhilarated by their experience in Afghanistan. In *jihad* they had a home for the first time. They were respected; they mattered. From New York, Abu Halima had made his way to Peshawar and then across the Pakistani border to the war against the Soviets in Afghanistan. He had returned a proud veteran, a man with a mission and a role. And he was proud once again in Brooklyn, guiding the sheikh's steps, driving his car and applauding his words.

Sheikh Omar Abdel Rahman had brought with him to America not only the universals of *jihad* but also the disheartening Egyptian experience with armed struggle. Mubarak and the other new pharaohs had proved intractable. The new capitalists had distributed their wares, collected their money and ignored the truth.

Everywhere the effort to impose the Koran was opposed by the *jahiliyya*, the corrupt society. Now, in Jersey City, the sheikh believed the challenge to Islam was assumed to be global: *jahiliyya* could only be defeated in a universal *jihad*. As Abdullah Azzam insisted, "*Jihad* and the rifle alone: no negotiations, no conferences and no dialogue."

It was a war that offered the prospect of vindication and martyrdom. Taqi al-Din Ibn Taymiyya, a medieval scholar often quoted by the Islamists, said, "Death of the martyrs for the unification of all the people in the cause of God and His word is the happiest, best, easiest and most virtuous of deaths." A *jihad* would defend Islam, restore lost lands like Andalusia, humiliate the infidels and permit the restoration of the caliphate, thus creating a single Islamic society from Spain to South Asia.

These expansive ambitions, the language of *jihad*, the perceptions of the Islamists would have seemed irrational to most Americans. The public statements were rants, anti-Jewish and anti-American tirades out of time and experience: "Hit hard and kill the enemies of God in every spot to rid it of the descendants of apes and fed at the tables of Zionism, Communism and Imperialism. . . . There is no truce in *jihad* against the enemies of Allah."

Americans did not understand the faithful who soaked up the ideals of *jihad* in Egypt and brought them along when they moved elsewhere—often pursued by Egyptian arrest warrants. They might settle in one of the Pakistani *madrassas*, a coldwater flat in Manchester, a classroom in Florida, a seedy hotel room in Hamburg. For the sheikh it was two storefront, walkup mosques: the Masjid al-Salam in Jersey City and Farouq Majid at 554 Atlantic Avenue, above the Chinese Fu King restaurant, in Brooklyn. There, in small rooms thousands of miles from the Nile, he could use his inner eye to see the future even more clearly than he had in Fayoum.

In America the Great Satan was vulnerable and innocent. Little terror had been experienced here beyond the actions of presidential assassins, a few Puerto Rican nationalists, the residue of the radical left bombers of the 1970s, the survivalist militias and a few other lethal sects. The media had a short attention span. Those responsible for defending the nation against terror had no real constituency, no continuity of purpose, no effective government presence. There were committees, panels, secretariats, but no central strategic control. Responsibility for a response became only an additional mission for the intelligence community, the State and Defense departments, law enforcement and fragments of the national security system. There was no coherence, no effort to coordinate agendas or to change attitudes and processes, and most of all, no sense of urgency. Terror spectaculars created immediate outrage and indignation, soon superseded by other events and priorities. Nothing—not even the crash of Pan Am 103 or the explosion at the Marine barracks in Beirut—had changed American priorities.

In New York, a crucial event was the murder of Rabbi Meir Kahane, leader of a small but highly visible and provocative Zionist faction: the paramilitary Jewish Defense League. Kahane had begun his career at fifteen, in 1947, throwing stones at the limousine of the British foreign secretary when he visited New York. He had shaped a career as a hard-line provocateur in Israel and in the United States, where he was repeatedly arrested. He had few followers and many critics, including most Zionists. His rants and threats, his unbending opposition to any accommodation, his convictions in New York of conspiring to make explosives—all made him a highly recognized figure, a new zealot for Zionism.

In 1984 Kahane founded Kach in Israel and called for the expulsion of all Arabs from the country as well as the occupied territories. He was elected to the Knesset in 1984 and then expelled for advocating racist positions. Kach was banned in 1988. In the autumn of 1990, Kahane returned to America on an organizational tour, speaking regularly before audiences of his followers.

Kahane had long been a monster in the minds of most Arabs in the American diaspora. He was what they believed every Zionist was at heart: a racist bigot dedicated to force. But the arrogant and insolent Kahane was also the perfect target. And el-Sayyid Nosair, the Arab militant who decided to act against him, was in many ways typical of the new generation of migrant militants. Born in the Canal Zone in 1955, Nosair received a degree in industrial design engineering from the College of Applied Arts in Cairo in 1978, left Egypt after his mother's unexpected death, and in

1981 came to America, living in Pittsburgh. For a time, he was charmed and delighted with the country, its zoos and museums, nightclubs, fast food, and especially its young women. In 1982, having overstayed his visa, he married an American. He ran into trouble at work because he focused his attention on other young women there. He didn't fit in.

Coming to New York, he was attracted to the congregation at the Masjid al-Salam in Jersey City. He was seriously injured in an industrial accident, and sued the Port Authority in 1988. By then his life was entangled with the militants in the Masjid al-Salam community. Suddenly, el-Sayyid Nosair decided to resolve all his ambiguities by killing Meir Kahane.

On November 5, 1990, the rabbi would attend an organizational rally in a New York hotel. Security would be limited; Kahane would suspect nothing. Nosair's operation, planned in haste, unfolded in a series of blunders. The idea was that Nosair would walk into a room filled with militant Zionists, stand around unnoticed, and then try to get close to Kahane. There he would wait for an opportunity, shoot Kahane and run out through the crowd to a waiting car. On the evening of November 5, Nosair appeared at the hotel. He waited until Kahane had finished speaking and then mingled with the crowd of supporters asking the rabbi questions. Just as he hoped, nobody noticed him. In front of more than a dozen eyewitnesses, Nosair suddenly pulled out his gun and fired on Kahane, who collapsed and died immediately. Nosair tried to flee in the turmoil, scuffled with the crowd, shot an elderly man who attempted to stop him, and ran outside. His getaway car was not there—his driver was parked in the wrong spot.

At gunpoint Nosair commandeered a taxi. The terrified driver was caught in a traffic jam only seventy-five feet down the street. Nosair leaped out, and a federal postal inspector passing on the street tried to stop him. Nosair shot him in the chest. Only lightly wounded because of the bulletproof vest he happened to be wearing, the inspector then shot Nosair in the throat.

Rushed to Bellevue Hospital, Nosair survived. On November 7 he was arraigned as he lay in intensive care with monitors, dangling IV tubes and an oxygen mask. The result of the trial seemed a foregone conclusion. No one bothered much about the material found in his apartment; no one translated the guerrilla manuals or noted the photographs of potential targets in New York: the Empire State Building, the World Trade Center. There was no need: the murder had been done in a room full of people. The postal inspector identified Nosair. The gun that killed Kahane was lying beside Nosair after he was shot.

Defended by the notorious radical lawyer William Kunstler, Nosair saw the certain case against him dissolve. He claimed to be innocent. Sixteen witnesses had seen Kahane shot, but none had actually seen Nosair shoot him. The jury convicted him only of assault and on a weapons charge. The verdict was unexpected and, according to presiding Judge Alvin Schlesinger, "devoid of common sense and logic."

So on January 29, 1992, Nosair was sentenced to the maximum possible sentence, 7-1/3 to 22 years, and moved to Attica Prison. He did not consider himself fortunate to have escaped the murder charge, for he did not feel guilty; he had acted for Islam. There was no justice. He had no intention of serving his time. His efforts to gain his freedom generated intrigues and conspiracies within the Arab diaspora in New York. Consumed with urgency, Nosair hoped that some of his enemies, like Judge Schlesinger, could be killed with pipe bombs. In the spring of 1993 he suggested to the local Islamists, who admired him and wanted to help, that Henry Kissinger and Richard Nixon might be kidnapped and used to barter his way out of Attica. This was an exercise far beyond the capacities of his radical friends, but Nosair wanted *something* done.

About the time Sheikh Rahman returned to America for his second stay, Nosair's militant friends were seeking an operation. All the militants looked to the sheikh. They knew he had advocated *jihad,* offering rationales to kill President Mubarak or infidels. After Mustafa Shalabi had been found murdered 1991, Sheikh Rahman had no rival in the United States and many followers. Everyone was exhilarated and encouraged by his sermons, although they offered no specifics. Some of the militants had gone off to the makeshift paramilitary training camp near Harrisburg. Some merely listened to the sheikh, donated to the cause, and went home to their small apartments and pious wives.

None had spent time underground. They had no useful skills: one was a conventional industrial chemist and the others were limousine drivers, street peddlers and delivery men. They could, however, hire space to work; order, buy and store bomb materials; construct a device and place it in a vehicle; choose a target and decide on the right time to detonate the bomb. All of this required minimal skills, access to the internet, the purchase of a chemistry text or a guerrilla manual, along with some care and planning.

These men had allies-in-waiting among America's many enemies: Iranians and Iraqis, Syrians and Libyans, Hezbollah in Lebanon, Afghani Arabs, dedicated and experienced Palestinian terrorists. They found the right contact to these groups in a new Palestinian associate, Muhammad Salameh, who had entered the United States in 1988 on a Jordanian passport. He had applied for legal residence and was turned down. Like so many Arab immigrants, he stayed anyway and no one came looking for him. He gravitated to the Islamists, and now, at age twenty-six, he was the one among them with the right family connections back in Palestine, who could help to turn their desire into a professional operation.

One of six children of a Jordanian warrant officer with a small pension, Muhammad Salameh came from a nationalist family. His maternal grandfather had participated in the famous 1936–1939 Arab Revolt in the Palestine Mandate. As an old man, he had joined the Palestine Liberation Organization and had been jailed by the Israelis. Salameh's maternal uncle Kadri Abu Bakr had been arrested in 1968 for terrorism and served eighteen years in an Israeli prison before being deported; he ended in Baghdad as second in command of the PLO Western Sector, a Palestinian branch office under Iraqi influence. Salameh himself had been neither radical nor especially pious. He had dropped out of the only university course that would accept him—Islamic law—and came to America with high hopes.

Finding no steady employment, Salameh attached himself to the Islamists, loitered in their meeting rooms and made friends.

They convinced him to do something for Nosair, so he began making international calls to his uncle Kadri Abu Bakr in Baghdad. In six weeks, Salameh ran up a bill of over four thousand dollars before his telephone service was cut off. By then, something had been arranged.

For the faithful in New York, Nosair had become transformed into a cause, an honored volunteer in a great war, not merely a resentful and bumbling gunman. What the loose group of conspirators needed was an expert operation leader, and Muhammad Salameh had finally provided such a man through his uncle.

The man who finally appeared in America to help them was an impressive young zealot, Ramzi Ahmed Yousef. He was known to the Iraqis and to the *jihadi*. His background was unclear; he had gone to school in Pakistan and probably came from a Baluchi family in southeast Afghanistan. Like so many, he had been involved in the struggle against the Soviets, in a *mujaheddin* unit organized by Abdul Rasul Sayyaf and funded by the Pakistani ISI as well as by Osama bin Laden. After the war Yousef had attended Sayyaf's new Dawaa al-Jihad University, the "Convert and Struggle University," but known more popularly in Afghanistan as the school for terrorism.

At the end of the Afghan struggle, some of Sayyaf's *mujaheddin* comrades had enrolled in his new university, but others had moved out to new battlefields. Some, including Arabs, organized the Abu Sayyaf terrorist organization in the Philippines. Others sought a mission that would allow them to attack the Great Satan more directly. Such a mission emerged for Yousef when the appeal from New York, transmitted through an old Palestinian in Iraq, circulated in *jihadi* circles. Ramzi seemed ideal for the job. He was eager, experienced, talented. He spoke Arabic, English and Urdu, dressed with elegance and radiated assurance. He also spoke the language of the Islamists, had the proper friends and would be taken on trust.

There would be no firm control either by the Iraqis or by the *jihadi* in Pakistan. Ramzi Yousef would travel to New York with another volunteer who knew the country, a somewhat less promising recruit named Ahmad Muhammad Ajaj, a Palestinian then in Pakistan. Ajaj was a petty forger who at times had produced counterfeit documents for the underground as well as for his own profit. He had been arrested for counterfeiting in 1987 in Israel, for forgery in 1988 in Jordan, and there again in 1991 for smuggling arms, a more serious matter. He was deported from Israel to Jordan. In September 1991 he had managed to emigrate to America, applied for political asylum and stayed with his uncle in Houston. He worked delivering Domino's pizza until April 1992, when he flew back to Peshawar. There he worked at the famous center for Afghani Arabs founded in 1984 by Professor Abdullah Azzam. He soon found that he liked Houston far better than Peshawar, but could not return to Texas because he had left the country without notification while his asylum application was pending. He was then introduced to Ramzi Ahmed Yousef.

Documents were arranged and adjusted. Ahmad Ajaj boarded at Islamabad with Yousef and the two arrived at JFK International Airport on September 1, 1992. Ajaj offered the immigration official a clumsily doctored Swedish passport with his photograph crudely stuck on the page. Questioned at the immigration counter, he became agitated and aggressive. He began to shout. Immigration officials then examined his luggage and found his three bags packed with guerrilla manuals, videos of suicide bombings and two false passports. No one noted that his manual on operating abroad was like the one found at Nosair's apartment during the Kahane murder investigation. Ajaj was detained and soon jailed for illegal entry.

During all the commotion, Yousef had kept his distance, standing quietly in line at passport control with his one carry-on bag. He did not present the stolen British passport that he had used to board the plane in Pakistan, but instead an Iraqi passport without an American visa. He immediately appealed for political asylum, claiming to have been brutalized by Saddam Hussein's regime. He was fingerprinted and briefly detained before being released while his appeal was investigated. By then Ajaj was in custody and on his way to prison for immigration violations. Ramzi Yousef had no such problems.

Yousef did not go to Houston, as he claimed that he would, but to an apartment of an Iraqi living at 34 Kensington Avenue in Jersey City. He was in the same building as Muhammad

Salameh, whose Palestinian uncle had been his original contact point in Baghdad. The two apartments were soon filled with Arab militants making plans. Some wanted to kill Jews and others to bomb tunnels. Yousef, who spoke the language of militancy, was soon accepted by all. He and Salameh moved to share another apartment in Jersey City. In November 1992, Yousef and some of the others began to prepare a list of specific targets. New York City offered plenty of possibilities: the Statue of Liberty, the Empire State Building, the United Nations, the embassies of Islam's enemies, the New York Stock Exchange. There were federal buildings, subway tunnels, famous bridges, power grids and telephone facilities. But the World Trade Center was at the top of Yousef's list. The towers were famous. More importantly, the twin towers had very limited security with a parking garage open to the public. It would be easy to drive in, walk out, then blow up. All that was needed was a car bomb, a conventional terrorist device from Belfast to Beirut. Port Authority security offered no real deterrence. An Office for Special Planning had been formed in 1984 in response to the executive director's concern about the vulnerability of the Trade Center to terrorist attack. The report was made and the dangers noted, including the fact that the parking facilities offered an enormous opportunity for terrorists to bring in an explosive-filled vehicle. Apparently all that happened as a result was a hardening of the structure of the executive offices.

As the years passed, building security became a matter of bored guards working by rote. Even in 1992, after a new generation of terrorist spectaculars abroad, Americans found it difficult to imagine anyone taking terrible revenge on them for imaginary crimes. Terror had been deployed against Americans, but not *within* America. Nobody feared to go to the movies or fly to Las Vegas. There were no human bombs at the pizza place or snipers on the roof. That these new terrorists might try to kill as many infidels as possible, rather than kill a few to influence the many in the manner of the Palestinians, worried only the specialists.

The men that Ramzi Yousef met in America wanted to say no to the direction of history by striking at the heart of the imperial state and doing all the harm possible given their limited resources.

They recognized that violence is cheap yet its impact can be enormous. On January 25, 1993, one man, a Pakistani name Mir Amal Kansi, murdered two CIA employees in a car waiting in traffic at the CIA headquarters in Langley, Virginia. He then, somehow, fled the country. Although he had acted almost alone, his background was not unlike that of the *jihadi* in New York. Kansi had entered the United States in 1990 using a visa issued in Karachi, where he had participated in anti-American demonstrations. Once in America, in 1992, he applied for political asylum and was routinely processed just like Ramzi Yousef, and then given a work permit. He had purchased his AK-47 assault rifle legally in Virginia. After his deed, he escaped to Pakistan. As a result of information supplied by two Afghani informers, four FBI agents appeared in Pakistan and on June 15, 1997, took Kansi into custody. Tried in Fairfax, Virginia, he was convicted on November 10, 1997, after his crime had been forgotten. Kansi was a harbinger of the operations of the global *jihad* in the United States.

In 1992, what those near Sheikh Rahman had wanted was a target more symbolic than a couple of government employees. And what better target than the huge, world-famous towers overshadowing Wall Street, sign and symbol of the Great Satan's arrogance? With luck, one huge tower might even crash into the other, resulting in tens of thousands dead and leaving the Great Satan confounded, the *jihad* triumphant.

Aside from the more sophisticated Yousef, the conspirators were a sampling of Arab immigrants, often ambitious, some with degrees and high hopes, many resentful, and all increasingly attracted to the vision of the blind sheikh. Yousef's traveling companion on the flight to America, Ahmad Muhammad Ajaj, fit the pattern, but he had been sentenced to six months for his passport violation and would not be released until February 24. Mahmud Abu Halima was a key conspirator. He had always been at the sheikh's right hand, his guide and driver. Nidal Ayyad, a Palestinian, was a friend of Salameh who had made the contact in Baghdad. Unlike the others, he had American credentials. In January 1991 he graduated in biochemical engineering from Rutgers University and then took a good job at Allied-Signal, a New Jersey chemical concern. In 1992 his mother went to Jordan to find him a suitably religious wife. In 1993 he was married in Amman, and back in America, his wife was soon pregnant.

Another Egyptian, Ibrahim el-Gabrowny, originally from Port Said, was a construction contractor and president of the Abu Bakr mosque in Brooklyn, who had gone on welfare so he could dedicate himself to his cousin el-Sayyid Nosair's cause. He had immersed himself in the legalities of the case and supplied drivers and money for the defense, maintaining his intense interest in the case even when Nosair had been sent off to serve his sentence in Attica. And there was a new immigrant, an Iraqi named Abdul Rahman Yasin who was born in Bloomington, where his father was working on a Ph.D. at the University of Indiana. Taken to Iraq as a child, he grew up in Baghdad, and returned to America in 1992 for medical treatment. He was willing to help out.

Once Ramzi Yousef had settled in, met the others and was accepted, the plot could move forward. He had a driving sense of purpose and a grasp of the operational necessities. In January 1993, the first telephone calls to chemical companies began. The bomb had to be made from scratch. They needed everything: a place, storage lockers, tools, chemicals, plastic tubs, the basic fertilizer, rubber gloves from surgical supply companies, lengths of rubber tubing. Salameh rented a locker where the bomb-making equipment would be stored. He bankrolled the project out of a joint account with Ayyad. The money was of uncertain origin and limited, but not a great deal was required. Ayyad ordered chemicals and hydrogen tanks delivered to Salameh's storage locker. For their bomb factory, they rented a room in a drab, crudely painted building on Pamrappo Avenue in Jersey City, near their self-storage center.

The construction of bombs is not an especially romantic undertaking. What the conspirators typically produce is a heap of plastic bags filled with gritty powder. There is a small device—a radio, an electronic timer, a wrist watch—along with a few bits of cord and a vial of murky liquid or a bag of commercial explosives. The acquisition of the basic ingredient, often sugar bought in bulk or fertilizer in hundred-weight sacks, attracts no notice unless there is a visible and ongoing bombing campaign like that of the IRA. Fertilizer can be turned into a lifting explosive with the aid of plastic tubs and tubes. The process is difficult and dirty, requiring cheap masks, persistence, stooped labor, and often a certain degree of innocence concerning the risks involved. When the bomb is finished, the back of the van appears to hold nothing more than plastic bags.

The final requirement is a device that will set off the inert chemical mass with a sharp explosion. Construction of the detonator is a more complex and delicate matter, requiring very volatile materials. For the timer there are many options. It is possible to use a mercury-tilt switch that goes off when a car hits a bump. An expert can make a timer that will detonate the basic charge after the second or third change in air pressure; thus a jetliner may land and then take off before reaching a prescribed altitude that triggers the timer. A small electronic clock can be set for months or even years ahead. The bomb and clock timer in the Grand Hotel in Brighton intended to kill Prime Minister Margaret Thatcher that exploded on Friday, October 12, 1982, and almost brought down the building had been plastered into the wall a month earlier.

The bombs can be small and cunningly hidden, or huge and moved by truck. They have been put in telephones and attaché cases, placed under beds and in airline seats, wrapped as Christmas presents, molded into pots or religious statues, and rolled into a hotel basement as milk tins. A few actually look like bombs—a bundle of dynamite sticks and an electronic timer running on with the numbers clicking—but most do not. The giant ones are usually moved by car or truck, often over a distance that seems enormous to the driver, with a thousand pounds of volatile explosives and a detonator clicking just behind his head. The large bombs that are intended to bring down buildings, destroy a street or blow away a passing car are not very prepossessing—a pile of plastic garbage bags, a few wires, the small timer hidden away near a packet of commercial explosive or a bottle of nitroglycerine.

When all goes well (as it often does not), the detonation will create a massive, rapidly expanding, lifting explosion. Such an explosion can bring down the concrete Marine barracks in Beirut or blow out all the windows over a square mile of the City of London—or as the vehicle detonates and sprays outward, fill a street with debris and death, smashing every window and killing every pedestrian. The terrorist bomb does not cut out support points and bring down buildings into a neat heap as do conventional devices used by demolition specialists, but relies on the blast wave of a lifting explosion to batter down any obstacle. The larger the bomb, the greater the lifting explosion and the more devastating the result.

The men in Jersey City were constructing a device that would produce a velocity at detonation of between 14,000 and 15,500 feet per second, ample for their purpose. They wanted something that would fit in a pickup truck they could park near a wall under the target. That way the tower supports could be blown away, causing the entire building to collapse, perhaps into the other tower.

The hard part was the detonator. They made their own using nitroglycerine as the crucial initiator, attached by two 20-minute lengths of fusing surrounded by boosters of magnesium, lead azide and ferric oxide. The nitroglycerine, the most volatile element, was apt to detonate at any prompting—a sharp change in temperature or pressure because of some contingency: a slight jar, a bump in the road. To reduce the chance of a premature explosion, the bomb makers suspended the nitroglycerine in water. The basic explosive, once refined, was distributed to plastic garbage bags. The dirty brown liquid nitroglycerine was suspended in a Mason jar of water without incident and stood ready to be lowered into a nest in the midst of the plastic garbage bags when the time came.

There were certain additions to the basic bomb. One consisted of three 126-pound metal cylinders of compressed hydrogen gas. The other was sodium cyanide, capable of being vaporized into cyanide gas that would be sucked into the north tower's air-conditioning system. The bomb makers continued to hope that the lifting power of a half-ton of explosive detonating in the basement garage would destroy the foundations of the tower, toppling one into the other; but if not, the cyanide gas might at least kill the occupants of the building. All that was needed now was to hire transport sturdy enough to take the device into the Trade Center garage.

On February 23, Salameh went to the Ryder Rental Agency in Jersey City to pick up a van, a one-ton Ford F350 Econoline that would carry the bomb. On the morning of February 26, he and Yousef drove the van to a Shell service station to fill the gas tank and managed to attract the attention of the attendant, Willie

Hernandez Moosh, who later remembered that the conspirators looked peculiar because they tried too hard to look ordinary. Their tradecraft was negligible—they had already left a trail of documents, rental agreements, addresses, notes and receipts, and had failed to tidy up the bomb factory. Yousef might be charismatic and cunning, but he had never directed a covert operation in the West. The conspirators focused only on getting the job done, finishing the device and getting on the road.

On the morning of February 26, Salameh drove the Ryder van into Manhattan's financial district. The conspirators had already undertaken two dry runs, testing access to the garage, and there had been no problems. The operation was a go. There would be a massive attack on the heart of America: the World Trade Center towering over Wall Street.

It would not be the first diabolical device brought into the financial district. On September 5, 1920, a bomb in a horse cart outside J. P. Morgan and Company had detonated, smashing into the bank and the stock exchange, killing thirty people and injuring hundreds. Little was left of the cart or horse, and no one took responsibility. There had been other New York bombs since then: George Metesky, the Mad Bomber, had set 37 pipe bombs over 17 years because of a grudge against Con Edison. Puerto Rican nationalists had set bombs, including one at Fraunces Tavern in the financial district that killed four people. Someone had left a bomb in a locker at La Guardia Airport that killed 11 and injured 75. And in 1970, a premature explosion at a townhouse at 18 West Eleventh Street had killed three members of the Weather Underground. But until February 1993, New York had never been a target of *foreign* bombers.

No one noticed the yellow Ryder rental van entering the World Trade Center parking garage at midday. Anyone could drive in to park without question. With the bomb's timer set, the driver needed only to move—carefully—on down the ramp, turn and park. Salameh stopped in a no-parking zone that put him close to a wall. Even if someone noticed the infraction, the tow truck would not come for hours. The Ryder van had come to a halt about eight feet from the south wall near the support column K31/8, below the Vista Hotel. Two men got out, shut the doors carefully, and walked out into lower Manhattan.

At 12:18 P.M. there was a muted blast, a heavy concussion heard near the base of the Trade Center. Lower Manhattan is filled with everyday thumps and bangs, manhole covers trembling, subway trains passing under the street and trucks backfiring. This time it was a bomb: the force of the explosion was driven down into the lower levels and also burst into the cafeteria next to the wall, where four people eating lunch were killed. A man getting out of his car in the garage was killed instantly and his body was not found until a day later, at the bottom of the bomb crater.

Almost at once, in the middle of lunch, the first word of an explosion came into the Manhattan central office of the fire department from a street alarm box at the corner of West and Liberty Streets. There was no great concern. At the same time, a call came from Engine Company Ten across from the World Trade Center to report what appeared to be a transformer vault—an explosion—on West Street. Then, Engine Company Ten advised headquarters that there was a fire inside the Trade Center.

Soon telephone calls began to come in from both towers and from the Vista Hotel. There was smoke, people were trapped, help was needed. As the calls began to cascade, the other borough fire officers took on the flow. More operators were brought into the response. For the first time in fifteen years, a borough call was made for more units. The bomb had ripped out a huge, L-shaped interior crater under the northeast corner of the Vista Hotel. At Level B-2, it was 130 feet wide, 150 feet long and 7 stories deep. Some 6,800 tons of material was displaced by the explosion.

In the shattered garage were the twisted and blackened ruins of 124 parked cars and the anguish of more than one thousand injured survivors. Some were still trapped in the wreckage and others were lost amid the blinding smoke and debris. Many could not see in the smoke and haze. Many could not hear because their eardrums had been shattered and they had no idea what had happened to them. It was nearly four hours before the last survivors emerged from the dark, smoky, poorly marked stairwells. Some people were trapped in elevators for ten hours. The rescue efforts produced more injuries: 88 firefighters, 35 police officers and an emergency medical worker.

As the acrid smoke began drifting into the shafts and ventilating devices, evacuation continued. The power plant for the entire complex had been knocked out. The elevators didn't work. The lights didn't work. All the television channels with their transmitters on Tower One were off the air. Only CBS 2 and the cable stations could operate. There was no heat on a chilly February day. There were over fifty thousand people in the building and none knew what had happened. And there was the constant thickening of the sooty smoke drifting up through the building, but no visible flames.

The two conspirators had waited in vain for an enormous explosion that would collapse the north tower into the south tower. Instead there had been only a muffled thud—no great white-hot flash, no blast wave. One was on his way back to New Jersey and saw nothing. The other was standing at the second floor of the J&R Music World watching the basement garage from across Broadway, but could see only the rising column of smoke and the ongoing arrival of fire units and emergency workers.

The reeking smoke crept into the stairwells and corridors and filled the lobby, while the coughing office workers without evacuation instructions managed to stumble out of the building into the crowd of firemen and police filling the streets near the complex. Inside, the sprinklers were off. Emergency lighting went off when the water-cooled generator overheated. The office workers kept coming down the stairs, across the lobby and out into the street, passing the firemen on the way up. It would take eleven hours to search the two 110-story buildings and the 99 elevators for strays. The last victims were released from the last elevator at 11:25 that night. The fires were contained. There was still anxiety about the stability of the structure, so emergency repairs were begun immediately.

All this turmoil was caused by a device put together by a few marginal zealots at a cost of a few thousand dollars. Their bomb might not have had a catastrophic effect, but the damage was extensive and dangerous, if largely invisible. The loss of life was incredibly small, but the cost of reconstruction would be enormous: hundreds of millions of dollars. The experts and specialists knew all too well that matters could have been much worse. The basement retaining wall could have ruptured. The underground structures of the subways, trains and major conduits could have been breached. The entire building could have been put at irreparable structural risk. There could have been many more casualties. America had been lucky.

The conspirators had taken limited precautions because of their urgency to punish the Great Satan. In the crater on February 28, during the collection of explosive residue for analysis by forensic chemists, a bomb technician found a 300-pound fragment from a van that carried a dot matrix number of a vehicle reported stolen the day before the bombing. This allowed the FBI to track down the Ryder van, and soon afterward, all those conspirators who had not yet bothered to flee the country.

Ramzi Yousef had apparently prepared for his withdrawal after the operation during a series of international telephone calls. On the evening of February 26, he was driven to the JFK Airport by Muhammad Salameh and took a flight to Pakistan using forged documents. He reached Karachi, took a local flight to Quetta and disappeared into the Islamic underground. Salameh drove back to the apartment.

Mahmud Abu Halima flew to Jiddah in Saudi Arabia and then on to Egypt the day after the bombing. Security there was tight because of the escalating armed struggle of the *jihadi*. Halima should not have expected to walk through customs in Cairo and home again, but then he had little practice at being a fugitive. The Egyptians were waiting for him. He was arrested in March, soon after he arrived, then brutalized as was the custom. His brother was arrested and also mistreated. Abu Halima confessed to the Egyptian interrogators, as was expected, and was extradited to the United States.

Salameh had personally left a highly visible trail by using his own name and his old driver's license to rent the van. Once the bomb exploded, he too wanted to get out of America. While the FBI agents were present in Jersey City, Salameh telephoned in to the Ryder agency trying again to get a refund on the van that he had reported stolen. He needed the money. He had a ticket dated for March 5 to Amsterdam on Royal Jordanian Flight 262, which would continue on to Amman; but it was a child's ticket costing only $65. While he had been able to use this ticket to get himself a Dutch visa, he could not actually fly until he could pay for an adult fare, and to do this he needed his refund. He was arrested on March 4.

Two suspects managed to talk their way out of the conspiracy. One of these, Bilal al-Qayai, was a suspect because of his friendship with both Nidal Ayyad and Salameh. He went to stay with friends in Carbondale, Illinois, after the bombing and gave himself up on March 24. Questioning produced limited evidence of any role in the conspiracy. The authorities had no witnesses. So Bilal al-Qayai was found guilty only of lying to immigration authorities and sentenced to twenty months, to be followed by deportation.

The other suspect, Abdul Rahman Yasin, was arrested during a sweep of sites involving Salameh. At the FBI's Newark office, Yasin proved to be very cooperative, revealing all the safe houses and the location of the bomb factory—and so he was somehow assumed to be an innocent who had accidentally become entangled with the others, even though he admitted mixing chemicals and coaching Salameh on how to drive the van. Still, he was so forthcoming, so pleasant, so unlike a dedicated terrorist that the FBI released him. The next day he flew to Jordan and then on to Iraq. He was finally indicted in New York on August 4, 1993, but he did not return for a trial.

In the meantime, the authorities found the storage locker with 300 pounds of urea, 250 pounds of sulfuric acid, nitric acid in gallon containers, two 50-foot lengths of hobby fuse, a bilge pump, trash cans smeared with chemicals, gallon containers—all the residue of a bomb factory—and a two-quart bottle of nitroglycerine in very unstable condition. No one had bothered to tidy up after the bomb was made and put in the van. No one bothered to clean up after the explosion.

The authorities were running through the list of contacts that each arrest produced. At one of the addresses Salameh used for his driver's license, they questioned the tenant, Ibrahim el-Gabrowny, known to the authorities because of his support of his cousin Nosair. Although they did not assume him to be part of the

conspiracy, el-Gabrowny reacted badly to being questioned. He
became belligerent, refused to be searched, struggled and resisted.
When he was searched after his arrest, he was found to have on his
person five Nicaraguan passports, five birth certificates to go with
the passports, and two driver's licenses. His clothing had chemical
stains consistent with the urea and nitric acid used in the bomb. He
ended up in jail as a co-conspirator.

Nidal Ayyad—Rutgers University degree or not—also left a
trail of evidence: documents, receipts, a computer filled with
incriminating data, and records of telephone calls. The communiqué to the *New York Times* claiming responsibility for the bomb
in the name of Allah revealed a match with his computer. A DNA
Q Alpha test on the flap of the envelope was a match with his
saliva sample. Other evidence began to pile up against him—as in
the case of the others, because of ignorance and naïveté, precautions not taken, common sense not used.

The authorities had four key conspirators: Muhammad
Salameh, Mahmud Abu Halima, Nidal Ayyad and Ahmad Ajaj,
who had been in prison since landing at JFK. The key figure, Ramzi
Yousef, was gone, and Abdul Rahman Yasin was living with his
family in Baghdad. There were no eyewitnesses to the bombing
and no clear evidence concerning the direct involvement of others, especially not Sheikh Rahman, who was the most visible New
York militant. From the first, the incident was perceived as a law
enforcement matter, not a national security concern or an arena for
the intelligence community. No one in the Justice Department
wanted to become involved in proving that Sheikh Rahman, a
Moslem cleric, was entangled in the bombing or that an external
patron like Iraq might have been involved. Four men had committed a crime and were formally charged. The few in the FBI, the
New York police or the CIA who wanted to pursue matters found
no encouragement.

Federal district attorney Mary Jo White decided to prosecute
the four on the basis of the enormous amount of evidence collected: telephone records, airplane tickets, parking stubs, rental
contracts, videotapes, the plastic trash cans stained with chemicals,
boarding passes, computer disks, DNA tests, fingerprint analysis,
chemical traces on the Ryder truck, evidence from the detonated

explosives, forensic analysis from the bomb-making factory, from clothing and from apartments.

To prove that Ajaj, the driver Salameh, the chemical engineer Ayyad, and Mahmud Abu Halima were guilty, the government presented 207 witnesses and 1,003 exhibits. The defense lawyers had little to offer in return. After five months of testimony, the four were convicted on all counts on March 4, 1994. Speaking of the detailed evidence presented at enormous length by the prosecution, one juror commented to the *New York Times*, "We saw so many visual IDs, so much evidence, so much paper trail.... These guys never thought for a moment about the fact that they had paper trails and it choked them to death."

On hearing the jury's decision, Ayyad began to shout: "Victory to Allah!" Others joined in with "Allah is great!" Muhammad Salameh shook his fist at the jurors: "You unjust people, you did us injustice." He then ran toward the judge screaming out in English, "Cheap government!" Everyone was hustled out of the courtroom as the trial ended in turmoil. Each of the conspirators would receive a sentence of 240 years. They were then dispatched to prison.

These convictions, however, did not answer many questions irrelevant to successful prosecution but important nonetheless: Was there a wider plot? Who else had been involved? Were foreign agents involved?

Even if questions remained unanswered, everyone in the police, the New York office of the FBI, law enforcement officials and security firms began to pay attention to the threat of the *jihadi*. The FBI recruited an informer named Emad Salem, an Egyptian, perhaps pursuing Cairo's interests but certainly his own. Charismatic, sly, arrogant, short of temper and greedy, he was untrustworthy but accepted by the Islamists. He appeared at the fundamentalist mosques, talked with the zealots, listened, did favors, picked up gossip. Soon he was wearing a bug, taping hour after hour of the conspirators' conversations. His evidence did not always convince the FBI, but he was on the inside and reporting back.

Salem's intelligence revealed little about the February 1993 bomb, but his reports indicated a further conspiracy in the New

York area involving new names and former suspects. The government kept up payments for his evidence. It would be reported that he ultimately collected a million dollars.

Surveillance in the spring of 1993 indicated that the zealots did not seem to be especially wary. They had not learned about the costs of leaving a paper trail. They did not focus on the need for planning or the obstacles faced by the February conspirators, but instead on new prospects. New York was still an ideal target, a city filled with symbols like the United Nations—House of the Devil—and the Empire State Building. There had been talk among the *jihadi* about killing President Mubarak of Egypt if he visited the city. Almost from the moment the bomb detonated, the *jihadi* in New York began to conspire for the next deed. This time they wanted a devastating attack. A few men in a rented room had already shown what could be done.

The ongoing conspiracy proceeded with a singular lack of craft or concealment. Sheikh Rahman, for one, hardly made any secret of his views. Anyone could hear him speak—in Arabic—at the al-Salam mosque any morning at four. He lived in America but his mind was still shaped by his Egyptian experience. He still detested President Mubarak, a pharaoh who was now overseeing the execution of twenty-two Islamists involved in the escalating armed struggle of the *jihadi*. From Jersey City, the sheikh threatened the Cairo regime with counterviolence. On June 17, 1993, in the al-Salam mosque, for example, he warned that there would be a bloodbath in Egypt: "The first people who will drown are Mubarak and his regime. They have to understand, they will have to bear the consequences of their actions." He was not planning to act but only predicting the future. He chose his words carefully so that he would not be held responsible for any violence—a tactic that had worked in Egypt. In private, however, among the *jihadi*, he was becoming more specific.

In the meantime, during the spring of 1993, the authorities were accumulating and weighing data other than the reports of their informer Emad Salem. Documents found after the World Trade Center bombing and sermon transcripts in Arabic calling for the destruction of targets in the West had been discovered, but alone were not sufficient proof that the sheikh was involved. Statements made by the sheikh, who appeared regularly at al-Salam and at al-Farouq and Abu Bakr mosques in Brooklyn, were themselves proof of nothing. But the FBI learned of the paramilitary camps and the web of *jihadi* contacts, as its agents followed the meetings and the paper trail. Agents crisscrossed the metropolitan area accumulating extensive files of documents, cassettes, stacks of pamphlets, printed sermons, fiscal records, bits and pieces that fit together. A conspiracy that involved dozens who met together and worshipped together emerged.

By June 1993, the New York City Joint Terrorism Task Force felt that it had a case against many of the conspirators, perhaps even the sly sheikh. The authorities could prove that there was a plot linking everyone and everything from el-Sayyid Nosair's murder of Rabbi Kahane, to a new conspiracy to bomb the Lincoln Tunnel, the United Nations and the Federal Building in lower Manhattan that housed the FBI headquarters, and then to assassinate President Mubarak when he visited New York in October 1993. More important, there was tangible evidence that a bomb was being made.

One of the most active in the conspirators was Siddig Ibrahim Siddig Ali, age thirty-two, from Sudan. In his seven years in the United States, he had a sporadic career as a security officer—once at the Federal Home Owners Bank in the World Trade Center. He had ended up as a street peddler. But whatever his job, his real life was elsewhere. He acted as the sheikh's interpreter and he was regularly at the mosque, while renting a small, one-bedroom apartment at 112 Brunswick Avenue in Jersey City, cluttered with Koran tapes, pamphlets, the local newspapers and pious tracts. He boasted that he had recruited a pilot to bomb Mubarak's presidential home on the Nile from the air. More practically, he claimed he could get access to the United Nations parking lot.

His fellow conspirators had similar profiles. They were immigrants, often in the country on expired documents, unemployed or underemployed as sometime taxi drivers, delivery men, supermarket clerks—all of them isolated from everyday America. Traditionally, revolutionary conspiracies have middle-class leaders who write proclamations and plan operations. The *jihadi* in New York looked to no operational leader. The sheikh supplied rationalizations and encouragement, but had no experience in waging an armed struggle, only in aiding those who did. In Egypt he had laundered money, hidden papers, passed messages, delivered sermons, but never used a gun or made a bomb or planned an operation. The other conspirators were not soldiers or guerrillas. They knew nothing of war and little about the underground. They lived in small apartments in Jersey City, in Brooklyn and the Lower East Side of Manhattan. None were very young, but only one was middle-aged: Mohammed Salah, 40, was married with three children and owned a gas station in Yonkers.

Fares Kallafal, 31, worked for a company that delivered medical supplies and lived in a few rooms at 926 West Side Avenue in Jersey City. There were a few chairs and a table. In one bedroom, there were two unmade, mismatched beds and a night table with a small television, a photograph and a pile of books. One of the books was *Electronic Devices and Circuit Theory*. There was a wall tapestry with the words "Save Jerusalem" over one of the beds. Later, when the police came to Siddig Ibrahim Siddig Ali's apartment, they found the floor covered with scrap paper, printed sermons, local newspapers and trash. In the kitchen an abandoned, hungry cat walked back and forth across the worn floor in front of the open refrigerator door.

By May 1993, the conspirators had narrowed the focus for their next target to the tunnels, the FBI Building and the United Nations. They planned on using three bombs. They had rented a workspace at 139-01 90th Avenue, Jamaica, Queens, in a Guyanan and Hispanic working-class district of one- and two-family homes. "I Love New York" was scrawled on the outside wall. They paid $1,700 a month for the space, about three times the going rate. Cars and vans drove up and drove away, sometimes with women driving. No one in the workshop wanted to talk with the neighbors. The workers were there at all hours. Packages were carried inside at night and vats unloaded. Their actions were so obviously mysterious that the neighbors decided they must be a drug squad engaged in surveillance. So no one bothered them—or called the police.

Test runs were made in the tunnels and practice bombs were constructed. Two were set off in wasteland off the New Jersey Turnpike and a third in the woods in Connecticut on June 20. Three days later, vans and cars pulled up in front of 139-01 90th

Avenue. Canisters filled with diesel oil were unloaded and the vehicles drove away.

After five months of surveillance, the Joint Terrorism Task Force decided that the time had come to act. On Thursday, June 24, the FBI moved in and picked up eight men, all Arab immigrants, five of them mixing explosive nitrates and diesel fuel in 55-gallon plastic vats. They were arrested so quickly that they didn't realize what was happening until the handcuffs went on.

Within days there were more arrests. Those charged would include not only men involved in the new bombing plot, but also participants in the prior World Trade Center bombing and el-Sayyid Nosair, although he was still in prison. Several suspects were Sudanese. Two were not Arabs at all, but members of the faith: Clement R. Hampton-El, 51, who lived in the New Vaderveer and had offered to supply firearms and grenades for the assassination of Mubarak; and Victor Alvarez, 32, a former supermarket clerk, born in Puerto Rico, who worshipped in the Jersey City mosque and had offered guns to protect the bombers and the Queens bomb factory.

In a few days, Sheikh Rahman was also arrested. After his driver tried to evade police cars, he gave himself up at the firehouse of Engine Company 250 near the Abu Bakr mosque on Foster Avenue in Brooklyn—a five-minute walk from where Rabbi Kahane had lived during his days at the Jewish Defense League. The sheikh had talked too much, too often, and to too many people about the wonders of *jihad* and the Islamic duty to wage war against the Great Satan. He was not simply an imam but a co-conspirator who had become involved in plans that included not only bomb attacks but also the assassination of Mubarak and of the United Nations secretary-general, Boutros Boutros-Ghali, another Egyptian, whose ancestor was the Boutros Pasha Ghali who had been assassinated by a Moslem zealot in 1910. They had also targeted Senator Alfonse D'Amato and Assemblyman Dov Hikind, both supporters of Israel. The prosecution had an enormous amount of tangible evidence, enhanced by evidence gathered during the arrests at the bomb factory and the revelations of the FBI informer Salem concerning the sheikh's personal involvement in planning the attacks.

In many ways, the trial that opened in June 1995 was a replay of the first World Trade Center bombing conspiracy trial. No one was officially interested in global plots, state sponsors, or the complexities of the dark world of the Islamic underground. The prosecutors were certain that the evidence would convince any jury.

In February 1995, Siddig Ibrahim Siddig Ali had changed his plea and implicated all but one of the other eleven suspects. His evidence was damning and he included the sheikh in the assassination and bombing plot. The content of the sheikh's statements, the articles and tapes, the evidence of Siddig Ali left little room for doubt: Sheikh Rahman from the first had been a conspirator, not simply a clerical mentor.

Defense lawyer William Kunstler faced an even more daunting task than he had when defending Nosair for killing Rabbi Kahane. He concentrated on the informer Emad Salem and insisted that the Egyptian had planned the whole operation: "He signified what the targets were gong to be, he rented places, he spent $30 on the drums, then he got those poor slobs to mix the stuff." The argument was not compelling.

After the jury had been out for thirty-seven hours of deliberation, the ten were convicted. The sheikh, who was at the center of the conspiracy, and Nosair, who had killed Kahane, received life sentences. The eight other defendants were handed prison terms of 25 to 57 years.

Islamists in Egypt were outraged that their cleric Sheikh Rahman had been convicted by the infidels. "If America does not respect Islamic scholars, it does not respect Islam. And everyone will fight for Islam, for its dignity and sanctity." The verdict would be appealed, but by then the sheikh was in a high-security cell in the mountains of Colorado, a neighbor of Theodore J. Kaczynski, the Unabomber. He was isolated from Islam, restricted in movement and rarely allowed telephone calls. His attorney could visit him but no one else. Yet his influence remained and so, too, the global *jihad* he inspired.

One World Trade Center terrorist who continued to evade apprehension was Ramzi Ahmed Yousef. He had matured into the new-model transnational operator: deft, ingenious, anonymous, with no home base. After his flight out of New York, he had disappeared into the Islamic underground. He had, however, continued to pursue his career in terror. In fact, his career ran like a thread through the escalating confrontation between the *jihadi* and the West. Over time the search for Ramzi Yousef would help to untangle the nature of the new global conspiracy.

Once he was safe within the Islamic underground, Yousef looked for a secure base from which to strike at the West again. He had the right contact in the Philippines in Khalid Saikkh Mohammed, 38, whom he had known previously in Afghanistan, where both had been associated with Osama bin Laden. The advantage of the Philippines for Yousef was that he had a potential ally in the radical Islamist movement Abu Sayyaf, founded by former Afghani volunteers in 1991 to fight for an Islamic state. The group had been partially funded with money from Muhammad Jamal Khalifi, bin Laden's son-in-law. In the Philippines it remained small and primarily involved in an armed struggle in the islands in the far south. Still, for Yousef their cadres could provide useful contacts in Manila. Khalid Sheikh Mohammed, 30, who had close ties with bin Laden's al-Qaeda and other groups in the *jihadi* underground, arrived to help with both money and advice. Yousef sent for an old high school friend, Abdul Hakim Murad, 28, as someone he could trust to assist him in a strange land.

Ramzi Yousef began to build a cover, arranging false papers, finding a secure apartment, acquiring a girlfriend. Khalid Saikkh Mohammed stayed with him the apartment. As in the attack on the World Trade Center, local talent was limited. Although Yousef trained some members of Abu Sayyaf in explosives, he thought he would need very few assets in Manila to make a major impact. His ambitious wish list of terror spectaculars included bombing several airplanes at once, assassinating Pope John Paul II and the president of the United States, and ramming hijacked planes into CIA headquarters.

In Manila, Yousef made himself into a master bomb maker. Unlike the crude truck bomb he had constructed in New York in 1993, the sophisticated devices he learned to construct could be easily smuggled past guards and through inspections, then onto airplanes, to be reassembled in the toilet and left to detonate later. He modified a digital watch to use as a timer, worn on the wrist, and adjusted before being inserted into the explosive. He used plastic contact-lens solution bottles filled with liquid components for nitroglycerine. In Manila, on December 1, 1994, using his newest methods, he successfully detonated a practice bomb in the Greenbelt movie theater.

For a final test, he concealed a device on Philippine Airlines Flight 434 from Manila to Tokyo ten days later. Using a ticket in the name of Arnaldo Forlani, he took the bomb components on board himself, assembled the device, activated the timer, left the device under seat 26K, then got off at the next stop at Cebu before Flight 434 flew on to Japan. Once the plane was in the air again, the device exploded, but the detonation was too small and contained. The muffled explosion killed the Japanese passenger in seat 26K, Haruki Ikegami, and injured ten others; but the pilot managed to land the damaged Boeing 747 safely in Okinawa.

For Yousef it was a failed lab experiment from which he learned exactly what he needed to know. The next time, he intended to explode more powerful bombs on twelve jetliners over a two-day period—a superspectacular.. He had been painstakingly scientific in testing his devices but less so in covering his tracks. He didn't know that one of the Philippine Abu Sayyaf terrorist guerrillas, Edwin Angeles, had surrendered to the authorities and begun cooperating with the police. He informed them that Yousef was in Manila and that the bomb at the Greenbelt theater had been a test of his new method for constructing nitroglycerine-based bombs. So Yousef had been on the police wanted list in Manila even as he was perfecting his devices. By the time the bomb exploded on Flight 434, the authorities knew they had a cunning and determined terrorist at work in the city and were trying frantically to locate him.

Using the name Naji Owaida Haddad and working with his friend Abdul Hakim Murad, Yousef was staying with his Filipina girlfriend, Carla Santiago, in Room 603 at the Josaefa Apartments late in 1994. He had specifically requested a view on the highway side, not the more popular seaside view—a curious preference, except that the highway was part of the Pope's planned route through the city on January 12, 1995. Yousef didn't want maid service. He didn't want visitors. He wanted to be left alone.

On January 6, while working on his devices, he started a fire in the apartment that began to spread. He could not douse the flame and the smoke poured out into the corridor. At 10:45 P.M., security guard Roman Mariano pushed his way into the apartment to see what was happening. Mariano quickly telephoned the alarm to the fire department and the police. He and the tenant Naji Owaida Haddad went downstairs. The tenant kept going. Mariano stood at the lobby door and watched him walk down the street speaking into his mobile phone.

After Ramzi Yousef had disappeared once again into the underground, authorities searched his rooms in the Josaefa Apartments and found explosives, chemicals, timing devices, sulfuric acid and evidence of plots. The police learned of his plans to bomb a dozen airliners and assassinate Pope John Paul II six days later. There were even clerical robes to be used as a disguise. Yousef's fingerprints were on a laptop computer. And there were erased computer discs that still contained retrievable details of the airliner operation.

The authorities quickly arrested Yousef's friend Murad, who immediately informed on him and gave details of the various plots and plans. Other arrests in Manila followed, but Ramzi Yousef was gone. There was now a $2 million reward for information leading to his arrest, advertised throughout the Pacific area on video, television, posters and matchbooks. Yousef was wanted not only for the World Trade Center bomb but also for the bombs in the Philippines, for the planned attacks on a dozen airliners over a weekend and for the plot to kill the Pope.

Yousef fled to Bangkok. At the beginning of February 1995, with the Americans and others closing in, he moved on to Islamabad in Pakistan. He then took a local flight to Peshawar, still a haven for the Islamists and the last stop before the security offered by the Afghan *mujaheddin* of the radical Taliban faction across the border. Using the name Ali Mohammed, he signed into Room 16 of the two-story Su Casa Guest House.

He was back from service in *jihad*, back in Peshawar,

unshaven. Confident that he was in a friendly environment, he carried his two suitcases up the stairs to a rented room. He was unaware that his old friend had already betrayed him in Manila or that the Americans had deciphered his abandoned computer disc. He didn't seriously consider that the huge reward now on his head might tempt anyone; but it did. And so the Pakistani author-ities quickly learned that he had arrived in Peshawar. Even the Americans knew of his arrival and feared that he still might dis-appear across the border into Afghanistan. At 4:30 in the afternoon of February 7, 1995, the police came for him at the Su Casa Guest House. Bundled up, barefooted and shrieking his innocence, Yousef was carried away into custody. He was questioned about every-thing: about two small toy cars packed with explosives found in his luggage, about the news clippings detailing his exploits that he had kept, about his manuals and devices and chemicals, and about the bombs and the flight schedules found in his two bags. He was questioned about his past, his plans and his contacts until the Pak-istani police and intelligence service had all they felt they could get from him.

In the meantime, the U.S. national coordinator for counter-terrorism at the White House, Richard A. Clarke, had hurriedly telephoned John P. O'Neill, the newly appointed head of the FBI's counterterror office in Washington. Clarke feared that Yousef would somehow get away from the Pakistanis and escape into Afghanistan. Someone had to make sure he was turned over to the Americans and extradited, and that was O'Neill. He had to make do with one agent in Pakistan and work for three days himself to coordinate the effort. In Pakistan the American ambassador hur-riedly collected the one FBI agent, several DEA agents, and one State Department diplomatic security official—the ragtag arrest team—and rushed them over to the local head of Pakistani mili-tary intelligence to insure that Yousef would be kept in custody. As it worked out, the Pakistanis were delighted to be rid of him. He was turned over to the Americans and flown back to the United States in a military 707 jet.

In custody, on the way across the Pacific, Yousef defended his operations. He bragged about planning a suicide air attack on the CIA headquarters at Langley. He admitted that he had planned to kill Pope John Paul II. He also had planned to kill President Clinton with phosgene gas during his upcoming Philippine visit. He explained that he had already specifically targeted the twelve American jetliners, scheduled to fly in January 1995, that would be bombed in his terrorist spectacular. He was confident that his new devices would not be detected. He left no doubt that he had hoped to cause as much havoc and kill as many Americans as possible—as much as could be accomplished by one man dedicated to the faith.

His *jihad* was like that of the New York followers of Sheikh Rahman, like that of the gunmen along the Nile—a campaign to punish and leave the future to Allah. He may have failed but he was not a failure. His deeds were righteous. He had no apologies, no regrets. As he later said, "If 'terrorist' means that I regain my land and fight whoever assaults me and my people, then I have no objection to being called a terrorist."

The military jet carrying Yousef landed at Stewart Airport in Newburgh, New York, and he was moved into Manhattan on a Port Authority Sikorsky S-76A to stand trial. At twenty-eight, he was a master terrorist carrying a $2 million reward. In 1996, he was tried and convicted on charges arising out of his plot to bomb American commercial airliners. He joined the sheikh and the Unabomber in the high-security prison—Super Max—in Florence, Colorado.

On his way to prison in handcuffs, sitting on the airliner next to a federal official charged with his transport, Ramzi Yousef looked out the window as they flew over the two towers of the World Trade Center. The agent pointed them out to him: "See, they are still there." Ramzi Ahmed Yousef replied: "They would not be if I had enough money and time."

PART TWO

SIX

THE WAR AGAINST TERROR, 1993–2001

T he *jihadi* conspiracies in New York revealed new American
enemies and put terror on the national political agenda.
That agenda was a complex and shifting list of priorities
involving domestic legislation, national security issues, emerging
crises, political considerations and personal predilections. American
foreign affairs did not run smoothly. There seemed always to be
trouble and crisis. Counterterror often had to wait in line for attention—and as FBI man John O'Neill discovered in Washington
during the rush to extradite Ramzi Yousef, other priorities sometimes came first, which meant that those charged with responding
to the *jihadi* had to make do.

When President Bill Clinton took office in January 1993, a
month before the World Trade Center bombing, he had to cope
with matters quite unrelated to his primary legislative concerns
and goals, which were domestic in nature. America became
involved in small wars in Haiti and Somalia. The administration
had to respond to genocide in central Africa, to larger and more
dangerous wars in the Balkans, to the continual vibrations coming
from the collapse of the Soviet Union, and as always to the ongoing Israel-Arab confrontation.

Terror became only one more item on a long list of concerns,
and then mainly because the bomb in New York had been very visible. Yet one bomb hardly seemed a strategic threat, no matter how
grandiose the ambitions of the zealots. In the past terrorists had
made their point by choreographing spectacular operations that

didn't need to kill a great many people; their aim was propaganda of the deed. But in time, hijacking and airport massacres, bombs and urban terror became the dissonant muzak of the modern world.

There was concern in Washington about state-sponsored terrorism, especially coming from the Libyans or the Iranian ayatollahs. In 1993, President Clinton, responding to evidence that the zealots involved in the assassination attempt against former President Bush in Kuwait in April of that year had been sponsored by Saddam Hussein, ordered six retaliatory missile strikes. This was similar to President Reagan's response when he lost patience with Qaddafi in 1976. But while such events had become part of normal statecraft, the menace of a terrorist underground simply did not seem very great to Washington unless the zealots acquired weapons of mass destruction.

Counterterror required a shift in priorities, as well as time and money and commitment. Only some within the government found the new threat sufficiently real, and although they had gained in visibility as a result of the 1993 World Trade Center bombing, they were still on the back burner. Most in authority preferred to make only adjustments rather than real changes to deal with the reality of *jihad*. The Treasury Department did not want to monitor money transfers outside the formal banking system, including the Arab *hawala* network, and opposed covert attacks on *jihadi* fiscal entities and funding by a proposed National Terrorist Asset Tracking Center. The State Department found the terror issue intrusive. The office of the assistant secretary in charge of drugs, organized crime and terrorism, often referred to as "Drugs and Thugs," had limited influence. The Department of Defense, never comfortable with unconventional tasking, particularly assignments within the country, thought that any response should come from the CIA or the Justice Department. The intelligence community was focused more on analysis and satellite surveillance and so lacked effective agents in the field and the willingness to risk contamination by unsavory sources. The CIA had cut back on foreign operatives, increased Washington-based analysis and relied more heavily on technological information gathering. The FBI not only had other priorities but also had little experience in monitoring internal subversion beyond responding to murders by the Ku Klux Klan or threats by the militia movement. The Justice Department was focused on pursuing perpetrators rather than organizing a defense against terrorist penetration. The Federal Aviation Administration left airport security largely in the hands of the airline industry.

In fact, only a few within the national government could see an antiterror mission as a necessity. Many officials perceived only the complexities and the cost of responding to what had not yet happened and—a few *jihadi* conspirators notwithstanding—what might never happen.

There was no central national control, no contingency plan for a major episode of terror, much less a series of assaults. While the experts and specialists might warn of weapons of mass destruction, these weapons had never been used by terrorists, which created an assumption that they never would be used. Any variant of terror was hard to visualize, hard to fit into organizational priorities, hard to take seriously. Within the bureaucracy, those involved in counterterror were often orphans, members of ineffectual committees, working with a limited budget. Even after the World Trade Center bombing put terror on the administration's agenda, when Clinton and his diplomats held talks with two key countries, Pakistan and Saudi Arabia, the subject never rose above third on the topic list. In fact, many in and out of government had anticipated a decline in violence once the new, post–Cold War world order was established. The prospects of globalization, free trade, an end to major war, the spread of open societies and democracy seemed to be the wave of the future, rather than a new era of gunmen and assassins. Still, despite the bureaucratic inertia, Clinton's classified Presidential Decision Directive 35 of March 2, 1995, listed terrorism on his intelligence priorities, although it came after support for ongoing military operations and the analysis of potential enemies in Russia, China, Iraq and Iran. Ten days later the first of two dramatic events began to transform the way government viewed the terrorist threat.

The first incident occurred in Japan on Monday morning, March 20, 1995, amid the heaving crowds and jam of the rush hour on the Tokyo subway. The Chiyoda Line underground cars entered the Shin Ochanomizu Station. On board one of the cars was Dr. Ikuo Hayashi, a middle-aged cardiovascular surgeon and a medical graduate of the prestigious Kei University, who was commuting to destiny. As the car slowed, he leaned over and placed three plastic pouches of clear liquid wrapped in newspaper under his seat, then stood up with his umbrella in one hand and the folded newspaper at his feet. He was not just another commuter or even just another doctor. He was a dedicated member and head of the Home Affairs Ministry of the Aum Shinri Kyo.

The leader of this bizarre religious sect, Shoko Asahara, held all the members in a firm grip. Born Chizuo Matsumoto in 1955, into an impoverished family on the southern island of Kyushu, he had recreated himself as Shoko Asahara, prophet. Nearly blind, but claiming to have attained Nirvana, Asahara had created his own world, in which he could levitate, impose his will on new recruits and prepare for the final catastrophe. He sold his vision on television, in person, to those with skills and assets. In time he and all those in the new sect of Aum Shinri Kyo anticipated a great Armageddon, the end of time.

Increasingly, Asahara focused on accelerating history and ways of provoking a cataclysmic event. March 20 of 1995 was chosen as the day when he would make history through a nerve gas attack on the Tokyo subway, creating panic and disarray. It would also distract attention from a murder investigation involving Asahara himself. Dr. Hayashi and four other followers had been ordered to take the newspaper-wrapped pouches at great risk onto the subway. Each double plastic pouch continued Sarin nerve gas. When their train arrived at the designated station, the five were to puncture the plastic, release the lethal gas and bring Armageddon closer.

As the subway train came into the Shin Ochanomizu Station, Dr. Hayashi looked down between his feet at his packet and paused. Still holding his umbrella with the carefully sharpened tip, he glanced up. "When I looked around, the sight of many commuters leaped to my eyes." he later said. "I am a doctor and in theory I've been working to save people's lives...many people could die at once." Orders were orders, however. The Holy Emperor Shoko

Asahara had given him responsibility. Hayashi was home affairs minister for the Aum organization. What else could he do?

At 7:45 A.M., Dr. Hayashi looked down, away from the commuters, and stabbed the sharpened tip of his umbrella into the newspaper, puncturing the plastic pouch. The lethal gas was slowly released into the car. Each of the others on the team followed suit. When the doors opened, the invisible gas began to drift out into the Tokyo subway system.

The Sarin had been hastily made under pressure from Asahara, who wanted an instant action. The umbrellas had all been purchased at the same time in a small store at two in the morning, on a day without prospect of rain. Because of their anti-Sarin antidote, pyridine aldozime methioxide, the five umbrella-carrying Aum members were able to move away in safety once they had carried out their job.

As the gas spread within the subway system, nobody knew a chemical attack was occurring. Individual telephone reports from various stations simply informed the subway authorities and the police that people were ill, staggering into the street, coughing and fainting. There was no coordination in the response, no feel for the scope of the disaster. Ambulances and medical personnel arrived, and victims were taken off to the hospital. And then there were more victims, more alarms, more reports. Gradually, authorities began to understand the extent of the attack. The toll for the day was twelve dead and over five thousand injured.

Even so, the impact was not at all what Asahara had hoped for. He wanted tens of thousands dead, the country in chaos, a massive Japanese disaster. But the Sarin—isopropyl methylphosphono fluoridate—had been a weakened strain, less than full strength because of a lab error and Asahara's insistence on haste. The gas had not been effectively dispersed throughout the subway system. If the results disappointed the organization's founder and guru, however, the attack galvanized the world media. Terrorists using weapons of mass destruction became the topic of the moment. The Japanese cult had placed all nations in jeopardy: Sarin, anthrax, smallpox, nuclear devices and poisoned reservoirs, all gained new credence as terror weapons. In the future, losses could be enormous. A barrier had been broken.

The Japanese authorities soon realized that the subway attack was not Aum's first attempt to create an apocalypse; Shoko Asahara had been working to disrupt society for some time. With extensive property and financing, and highly disciplined and obedient members eager to obey, his sect had recruited skilled technical and scientific talent, opened laboratories in Japan and in Australia, established contacts in Russia, and so for years been preparing for a spectacular collapse of society. Even with elaborate facilities, the cult could not make or deploy a weapon of mass destruction until the covert labs had made the Sarin: colorless, odorless, lethal when dispersed in the air, one of the oldest and most effective chemical weapons. Just as Ramzi Yousef had tested his bomb in a Manila cinema, so in June 1994, Asahara had ordered a test for the Sarin. The targets were several judges on his enemies list—those investigating the sect who were working in the district court building in the center of Matsumoto, a city northwest of Tokyo.

On June 27, 1994, a six-man action team set out to gas the judges. The Sarin, contained in three tanks, was to be sprayed out of a newly designed atomizing and nozzle system. But Asahara was so anxious to create mass death that no one had a chance to try out the spray. The poison was rushed through production. The new dispensing device was quickly loaded into a two-ton white refrigerator truck and the containers attached. The Aum team rented a black station wagon as a lookout car, leaving a paper trail just as the *jihadi* had in New York. Then the Aum team arrived too late to proceed as planned because they had stopped to alter the license tags with spray paint and then to buy worker uniforms as disguises. By then, the judges had gone home.

The leader of the team was Hideo Murai, who had risen to leadership in the cult and was determined to carry out the test no matter what. So he switched the target from the empty courthouse to buildings nearby. Dressed in their newly purchased work suits, his group stood around the truck waiting for the wind to change. Time was passing. A following wind was vital; the spray needed just the right weather conditions. When Murai decided the conditions were about right, he ordered the team to put on white protective suits and newly designed breathing apparatus. They took their PAM anti-Sarin pills. Murai adjusted the heating unit to bring the Sarin up to a proper temperature, turned on the computer and watched the spray activate. The mist was cobalt blue, not colorless as expected, because in their haste the technicians had added too much isopropyl alcohol to the mix, thereby creating hydrogen fluoride. Murai ignored the problem. The wind shifted and the spray no longer drifted toward the target. The mix unexpectedly turned into a heavy white mist around the truck.

Residents in the middle-class neighborhood soon noticed a strange vehicle and people in white space suits spraying a chemical into the air. The truck was shrouded in a white mist. Suddenly the cloud of the lethal Sarin began to blow back toward the Aum team. They panicked and pushed back into the truck. The driver pulled away and sped off down the street. The startled driver of the observation vehicle, the black station wagon, screeched out of the parking lot after the truck. In fright he slammed into a concrete pillar on the side of the street, bounced and kept going. Ahead, the white truck was tearing along with the atomizer nozzle still dangling, spraying the last of the Sarin. The team had forgotten to turn off the device.

Where the lethal spray had settled, the first victims were coughing and writhing in pain. People began telephoning for medical help. The city of Matsumoto had a crisis. The attack killed 7 people and injured over 500, hospitalizing 59. It could have been much worse if the Sarin had been properly made, if the attack team had arrived on time and the attack had gone as planned. Experts detected the Sarin, but what had actually occurred took months to piece together. By that time, the attack on the Tokyo subways had riveted world attention.

Then, on April 19, 1995—less than a month after the Tokyo subway attack—a former American soldier named Timothy McVeigh parked a rental truck containing a huge explosive device in the center of Oklahoma City in front of the Alfred P. Murrah Federal Building. McVeigh had none of the skills available to the Aum Shinri Kyo cult, no laboratories or facilities, very little money. Yet his bomb would finally bring the reality of terror to America.

With the help of one man, Terry Nichols, McVeigh intended

to attack a federal government target, a government he believed guilty of destroying the utopian community of the Branch Davidians outside Waco, Texas. In Kansas, where he had served in the army at Fort Riley, McVeigh and Nichols intended to make their bomb with a base of ammonium nitrate fertilizer and racing fuel that would turn into a mix of bright pink balls. On the eve of the attack, McVeigh's ancient Pontiac station wagon finally collapsed. He traded it and $300 for a 1977 yellow Mercury Grand Marquis with 97,204 miles on the odometer. He screwed an Arizona plate on the car, drove to the Ryder rental agency in Junction City on Interstate 70 and made arrangements to rent a van for $231.31, using cash. He told the rental clerk, "I need a truck that will hold five thousand pounds."

He drove off and parked the van beside a secondary road, where he and Nichols loaded the 4,000-pound bomb made of bright pink balls in plastic barrels. The basic mix would be set off with dynamite and blasting caps. His getaway car was already in place to the south in Oklahoma City. Nichols then went home and McVeigh spent another night at the Dreamland Motel where he had charmed the clerk into lowering the $28-a-night rental to $20.

On April 19, McVeigh got up before dawn and stopped for gas at the Cimarron Travel Plaza truck stop on Interstate 35, just over the Oklahoma border. He then drove on to Oklahoma City and came to a stop in front of the downtown Alfred P. Murrah Federal Building, stepped out of his yellow Ryder van and walked away.

The Alfred P. Murrah Federal Building at Fifth and Harvey Streets was one more large, clunky pile of offices with glass curtain walls in a middle-American city, not a World Trade Center or even the central Tokyo subway system. Yet it was a perfect symbol for McVeigh. On the morning of April 19, the building filled with workers, early visitors, children in the day care center on the second floor, people arriving at the Social Security Office—the usual cross section of the working city. At two minutes after nine, the rental truck detonated with a huge roar that went on and on.

A bright, white flash splattered across the north facade of the building at 8,000 feet per second. The whole building buckled and twisted. In the street, automobiles were reduced to gnarled black hulks, tossed about, set on fire. The glass was blown in by an enormous wave of superheated gases and then the air in the building was sucked out, creating a lethal vacuum. The inside of the building facing the street was shattered. The outer walls had been torn away, ceilings jumbled with the floors. All of this collapsed: the twisted beams, broken concrete, office furniture, plywood panels, pipes, mortar and victims. A jumble of ruins was heaped in the streets and in the huge crater, 30 feet wide and nearly 9 feet deep. More debris continued to fall, more panels, desks, sections of the floor, and more pipes. The entire front of the building was gone, leaving dangling cables, skewed girders, blackened retaining walls, pipes spurting water and, somehow, many of the lights still on.

The people inside near the north face had been smashed by the blast, cut by the glass, killed or trapped: 168 dead, including 19 children, and over 500 injured in a white flash and a roar. Spectacular terror had come to middle America.

He had paid in cash and attracted attention by his behavior, written his real name on the motel register and used the valid Arizona plate number as identification. He was recognized in Fort Riley by those who had known him when he was stationed there. He had appeared on a MacDonald's television security camera. The authorities followed his trail. His prompt arrest put an end to early speculation about global conspiracies, especially another *jihadi* attack. McVeigh fit the pattern of American presidential assassins more than holy warriors: marginal strays in a complex society, usually men, young, medium height, without credentials, perhaps military service but mostly a record of failure. They formed no firm personal relationships, had no real prospects, never kept jobs long, were isolated and remained resentful adolescents in an adult world. These were people who would prefer to be wanted for murder than not wanted at all. Most offered a fashionable political reason to give meaning to a gesture that was meaningless.

McVeigh had a tenuous connection with the radical American right—survivalists, those who believed in various conspiracy theories, families living in small colonies of dissent and disenchantment. He had been a visitor at the siege outside Waco. He had been exposed to the revolutionary tactics of the day through media coverage. Everyone knew about car bombs: IRA car bombs in London, Islamic car bombs in Beirut, and at the World Trade Center in New York. The technical construction of such bombs could be found in guerrilla guides, on websites, in military experience or through conversation at gun fairs. The basic chemicals were easy to acquire and so were the dynamite and blasting caps to set off the mix.

The details of what happened once the mix detonated didn't matter greatly to McVeigh. He had set his bomb, made his mark. The people in the shattered office building were merely collateral damage. The world outside his own resentments was hardly real. He acted not in the name of Allah or even the guru of a cult, but on account of his own warped agenda.

For the authorities, what mattered was that one man with a grievance against the federal government and with very little money had done horrific damage to innocent people, destroyed a huge building and shattered the nation's complacency. If the Aum sect's act in Japan indicated the tangible dangers of certain kinds of weapons, Timothy McVeigh's bomb showed that anyone could strike at the heart of America.

The only recent government experience with a threat that cut across bureaucratic and geographical lines had been the impact of drugs, largely cocaine, mainly originating in Latin America. The public had backed a declaration of war on drugs, but there was no easy way to mesh all the relevant agencies: local and national law enforcement, intelligence, immigration, public health and education, along with the new bureaucracy. The czar of the new antidrug bureaucracy found that public and administration support, the reality of the threat and firm budget prospects did not change old institutions. The inclination of the intelligence community to seek information without indicting informers, for example, remained in conflict with law enforcement's mission to secure convictions. Everyone opposed the drug trade but nearly everyone had other responsibilities and agendas and answered to a special constituency. In the case of terror, although the threat seemed more awesome, most of the same problems existed. Still, even if those involved in all these attacks were strange—a guru who could levitate, a lone killer inspired by a Texas cult, and a blind sheikh who had called on the young men of Islam to free Egypt from "the grandsons of monkeys and pigs who have been fed at the tables of the Zionists, Communists, and colonialists"—such people had shown they could slaughter the innocent; so something would have to be done.

The American response to terror was hampered by national attitudes that shaped the responsible institutions and by the traditional inertia of bureaucracy, but most immediately by the difficulty in organizing command and control. There was no equivalent of a drug czar, no antiterrorist commander appointed by the president. Each agency involved in counterterror thus responded independently within special traditions, habits and experience.

The police, city forces, state troopers and federal authorities—the FBI, the DEA, or Alcohol, Tobacco and Firearms in the Treasury Department—were all concerned with enforcement of the laws. They sought to acquire sufficient evidence to allow arrest and prosecution. They lacked both mission and capacity to focus clearly on preventing terrorism. And local police lacked the skills and resources to do so.

The FBI had been involved after 1941 in the surveillance of potential foreign enemies, first the Axis or their sympathizers and then communists during the Cold War. But despite extensive domestic surveillance and files on suspects, the FBI continued to focus on traditional federal crimes: kidnapping, organized crime, labor rackets. The FBI agents concerned with the *jihadi* conspiracy in New York had responded as a law enforcement agency, not a counterterror agency. There was little FBI experience in defending against such subversive penetration from abroad. Aside from a handful of agents assigned to U.S. embassies, the FBI barely operated abroad, and so had to depend on other federal agencies for foreign intelligence.

For most of American history there was no real intelligence service because an open society did not seem to need such an organization. There was no apparent need for a domestic police force charged with a defense against subversion because there was no subversion. And most Americans assumed that threats from abroad would be conventional, calling for a response by the military or the diplomats. The idea of American agents operating pragmatically in a covert world filled with the vicious, cruel and criminal was not part of the national self-image. Even CIA special operations when revealed seemed like adventures beyond the rules—rash, inane and counterproductive.

During the sixties, the CIA became for radicals a symbol of American repression, dirty tricks and the subversion of liberalism. In 1975, an investigating committee chaired by Senator Frank Church found that the agency had conducted domestic surveillance and been involved in assassination plots and coups, such as the one that deposed the elected government of President Salvador Allende in Chile. Congress imposed more restrictive guidelines.

Abroad, the agency was often assumed to be all-seeing, all-powerful, routinely manipulating governments and markets, and funding secret armies. This was hardly the case, as the failed invasion at the Bay of Pigs in Cuba in 1961 had revealed. Decade by decade, more blunders emerged; but the CIA had become a symbol, a subject of thrillers and films. The real CIA was much like other government agencies, filled with administrators, accountants and clerks, computer specialists, scholars, analysts and retired military officers. Most of the data that poured into the American agencies came from technical collection or open sources. There were very few spymasters and only limited special operations capacity.

By the late 1970s, careers were more likely to be made, programs funded and policies undertaken that did not require unsavory contacts, secrecy or duplicity. Technical means of information gathering were preferred over personal contacts, analysis over the collection of field data, and administration in Washington over the running of sources by reporting agents in obscure places. The movement of a Soviet missile launcher could be tracked, but not an Arab terrorist operating in Yemen.

President Jimmy Carter was suspicious of the special operators. President Reagan had used them in the struggle against the Evil Empire, but discovered that they had enormous and unexpected political costs. With the arrival of the Clinton administration in 1993, new officials came into the intelligence community who were dedicated to liberal values and civil liberties.

They disliked the culture of the covert. In fact, with the end of the Cold War some liberals in Congress, like Senator Daniel Patrick Moynihan, doubted the need for a covert intelligence service of any kind.

So in 1993, when the bomb went off in New York, very few at the CIA cared about the Egyptian zealots or the Afghani guerrillas. American intelligence knew little of the Middle Eastern arenas—not to mention the Islamic underground. The idealists appointed by Clinton did not trust the agency or intelligence, did not want to understand the secret world, did not want the country entangled with despots, bigots, warlords or agents of drug cartels. The data that unsavory sources might offer did not seem to be worth the cost to American civility.

For different reasons the Department of Defense did not perceive terror as a major threat either. The Pentagon, like the new CIA, was suspicious of the unconventional, preferring advanced technical capability and the concentration of great power—real wars fought with massed forces and impressive weapons. The admirals and generals had chosen their lessons from Vietnam and so shaped the military to pursue only those wars that could be fought with advanced weapons systems to a specific, predetermined end, with limited cost in lives and a clear exit strategy—and with full popular and political support. This became the Powell Doctrine, named after General Colin Powell. The generals and admirals were preparing not so much for the last war, as for the war they preferred to fight.

For years there was a series of small wars and limited missions, as one administration after another deployed limited force in peripheral areas: Grenada, Panama, Lebanon. After the Pentagon's dream war in the Persian Gulf, "Desert Storm," it was back to small wars like Haiti and Somalia and Bosnia. In such conflicts, the mission was often not clear, the exit strategy unrelated to military needs, and—most disorienting of all—combat was unconventional. The enemy was often irregular and elusive, able to evade American power. And that power might be limited by our allies or the United Nations. In the nineties, the record with these irregular campaigns was spotty. The intervention in Haiti led to humiliation: the first expeditionary force had to be withdrawn without landing because of a ragged mob that stood on shore ready to riot. Somalia evolved into a debacle after the U.S. Rangers suffered eighteen fatal casualties in an effort to bring a local warlord to justice. The military and the president feared that the American people would not tolerate more battle losses. At least in the Bosnian peacekeeping mission and later during the Kosovo crisis, the Americans avoided any ground fighting.

If there had to be wars, they should be congenial to American attitudes and virtues. Deploying a conventional army against a global terrorist conspiracy was not an appealing prospect, while deploying conventional force against a tiny group of elusive gunmen within the *jihadi* underground was all but impossible. This seemed to the Pentagon to be a law-enforcement task, a paramilitary responsibility outside of the American military's basic responsibilities.

No one in the military, in the intelligence community, or in government generally saw counterterror as a compelling mission. There could, however, be no denying the potential cost of weapons of mass destruction, if not the operations of assassins or conspirators like those rallied by Sheikh Rahman. The problem seemed to have no solution: a response to the terrorist threat and weapons of mass destruction required special commitments and capacities across the entire spectrum of governance—local police, customs agents, airport security, legal access to fiscal records, new small-unit military tactics, and new intelligence sources. There would be new missions for the Coast Guard, for the Centers for Disease Control in Atlanta, for the Department of Energy's emergency response NEST groups which were ready to act against a nuclear threat. There would have to be more authority for the Federal Emergency Management Agency (FEMA), long a Washington orphan. And every investigation of American antiterrorist capacity had focused on the single greatest need: a central command structure that would really work in a crisis.

As terror gradually became a line item on President Clinton's agenda, various officials and advisors took steps, set out procedures, built control centers and trained agents. In Washington, Richard

Clarke at the National Security Council began to tie the policy responses together. In New York City, Mayor Rudolph W. Giuliani took steps to prevent a repetition of the 1993 bombing, along with other local officials, sometimes with the aid of the federal government programs and sometimes independently. The mayor appointed antiterrorist advisors and initiated antiterrorist programs, including a New York City Joint Terrorism Task Force. And there were, as well, reminders that Islamic terror had not gone away.

In March 1994, Rashad Baz, an immigrant from Lebanon, and two Jordanian immigrants fired into a van full of Hasidic students on the Brooklyn Bridge, wounding four. The Arabs belonged to no organization and had acted alone. The next year, on March 8, the city was again reminded of the long-distance fallout from the World Trade Center bombing when terrorists armed with automatic rifles murdered two American consular officials in Karachi, Pakistan, apparently in retaliation for Ramzi Yousef's extradition.

In February 1997, Ali Hassan Abu Kamal, a Palestinian teacher on a tourist visa, suddenly produced a 14-shot semiautomatic pistol while standing on the observation deck of the Empire State Building. He opened fire on the tourists around him and killed seven before killing himself. In a strange letter left behind, Abu Kamal wrote that he was taking vengeance against enemies of the Palestinian people. He was obviously disturbed, and not a member of a terrorist group; but he had operated just as did the zealots, using flaws in immigration procedures to stay in Amerìca, and purchasing a gun in Florida despite a federal law prohibiting sales to aliens who do not have at least ninety days of residency.

On July 31 the same year, Abdel Rahman Mosabbah, 29, who had spent the previous twelve days after arriving from Egypt in an apartment in Park Slope in Brooklyn, managed to meet with two police officers at a subway station. His English was too poor to use the telephone. He told them that two Palestinian Arabs staying in the same apartment were planning violence. Early the next morning, the New York Police Department Emergency Service Unit broke into the apartment and, fearful that the two men were about to detonate their bombs, opened fire, wounding both: Gazi Ibrahim Abu Mezer, 23, and Lafi Khali, 22.

The police found pipe bombs and soon evidence of a plot to bomb targets in New York City. Abu Mezer admitted that in 1996 he had planned to kill President Clinton in Seattle but had been arrested on an immigration violation, imprisoned for six months, and then released on bail. Abu Mezer denied that his bombs were intended to be used on the subway, but rather insisted that he was planning to be a martyr-bomber and kill as many Jews as possible. Abu Mezer and Lafi Khali were tried and convicted. Not only did the arrests keep terror as an issue alive in New York, but also, once again, revealed that a potential terrorist could still evade interdiction at the border and deportation if residence was denied.

When the United Nations celebrated its fiftieth anniversary on October 22, 1995, President Clinton stressed the threat of terrorism—especially by those who had "plotted to destroy the very hall we gather in today"—as well as the dangers within the new world order: organized crime, drug cartels, weapons of mass destruction. Globalization had encouraged global terror at the very time that the *jihad,* for ideological and practical reasons, had embarked on their global holy war.

At the same time that the United Nations was meeting, across town at the Warwick Hotel on West 54th Street, Richard Clarke was briefing reporters on terrorism. He was becoming recognized as the key player in counterterror. Clarke was in many ways the ultimate Washington official, a member of the Senior Executive Service who had attended the University of Pennsylvania and MIT and then in 1973 taken a position in the Department of Defense analyzing nuclear weapons and European security issues. In 1979 he moved to State as a senior analyst focused on the issue of the day: theater nuclear weapons and cruise missiles and European security. He was deputy assistant secretary of state for intelligence in the Reagan administration and assistant secretary of state for political-military affairs for George Bush.

Over the course of his career, Clarke had been involved in the core issue of national security policy at higher and higher levels. By the time he moved to the National Security Council in the Clinton administration, he had become the ultimate insider, largely known only to specialists and colleagues. If his career had been spectacular, Clarke's analytical concerns had been conventional; he even looked conventional, his well-cut suit and glasses projecting an aura of competence whatever the assignment: peacekeeping, Haitian democracy, Persian Gulf security, international crime. In 1992 he had become chairman of the interagency counterterrorism committee—not a major arena, but one that he soon dominated.

In effect, he created a central command in his office in the Old Executive Office Building across from the White House. The FBI and Justice were listed in the president's guiding directive as lead agencies, but Clarke was at the real center of the action. From the National Security Council, he could reach out across bureaucratic boundaries to respond to the terrorist threat without institutional restraint. The interagency task forces, the committees and panels, the CIA's counterterror unit and even the FBI had not put together a national policy, but Clarke could. He knew how the bureaucracy worked. Clarke could rely on organizational skill, persuasion, persistence and presidential power.

By the end of 1995, the administration realized that terror was a strategic and not just a tactical threat, not merely a problem of law enforcement solved by putting Timothy McVeigh or Sheikh Rahman or Ramzi Yousef in prison. Clarke had been given the backing of Sandy Berger, the national security advisor, to impose antiterrorism as a priority. And although still unknown to the public, he became in effect the antiterror czar, involved in programming and personnel decisions, urging immediate action despite bureaucratic inertia and competing agendas in the bureaucracy, which was split between those concerned with foreign threats and those protecting domestic security, between those who took terror seriously and those who thought it was a passing fad.

Clarke's attempt to form a counterterror establishment was influenced by events abroad. The *jihadi* had scattered after leaving Afghanistan and then Pakistan in 1992. Osama bin Laden had moved to Sudan, where he continued his efforts to organize and support *jihad*. Other Afghani Arabs had volunteered in Islamic causes in the Balkans, the Caucasus and Central Asia. There were soon intense armed struggles in Egypt and Algeria. The Hezbollah Shi'ites remained active against the Israelis in south Lebanon. The *jihadi* underground, a pool of potential terrorists created by the war in Afghanistan, continued to spread out across Europe and the United States.

While there was great operational capacity, funds and patrons, a driving sense of purpose, there was no single *jihadi* command structure. Individuals like Sheikh Omar Rahman were involved even in prison. National movements like Hamas in Palestine or Hezbollah, funded by Iran, combined with front groups, charities and schools in Pakistan and mosques in London or Hamburg in the global underground. The fundamentalist Islamists produced newspapers, opened book stores, collected funds for new mosques, offered a base to the dedicated. There were transnational configurations like that of bin Laden's al-Qaeda and very small, narrow groups engaged in terror like Abu Sayyaf in the Philippines.

If many of the *jihadi* remained engaged in special places such as Egypt or Bosnia, the most attractive option for others was to strike at the Great Satan instead of local corrupt regimes. In 1995 the *jihadi* found an opportunity to attack both at the same time.

American troops were stationed in Saudi Arabia not only as a defense screen against the Iranian ayatollahs and Saddam Hussein, but also as an ally. Many Saudis did not want the infidels in the country. Early in 1995 there had been bombs in a small village far to the south of Riyadh to protest the regime's policies. After this, an effort had to be made to reduce the visibility of the U.S. force while still maintaining the mission. There was no sense of urgency about local terror attacks. Counterterror was a domestic matter handled by Richard Clarke in Washington.

In Riyadh, where the U.S. military advisors based at the National Guard headquarters trained Saudis, the Americans were a visible reminder of the regime's concession not only to Washington but also to Western ways and Western power. U.S. authorities assumed that the headquarters could be protected by security regulations enacted after the destruction of Pan Am Flight 103 over Lockerbie, Scotland. But these precautions took time and money.

Many embassies had been rebuilt. Other facilities had to wait their turn, the National Guard headquarters among them.

On Monday, November 13, 1995, a van containing two hundred pounds of explosives drove up to the headquarters opposite the ground floor snack bar at a time when the 378 Americans were eating lunch and the Saudis were at prayer. The van was parked as close as possible to the building. There was no challenge. The terrorists stepped out of the vehicle and fled, detonating the bomb by remote control. A huge explosion set off a secondary explosion in the gas tank of a nearby car, killing 6 people—5 Americans and 1 Indian—and injuring 37 other Americans, 6 of them critically.

Two groups took responsibility. One was unknown; the other, the Islamic Movement for Change, sent telegrams warning of action against Western interests in the kingdom. American ambassador R. E. Mabus said, "The only way people like this win is if you're intimidated or deterred, and we won't be intimidated or deterred." The zealots, however, didn't really care if the Americans were intimidated or deterred, but only that they were punished for being in Saudi Arabia. That aim had been achieved when the blast wave smashed into the building.

Washington insisted on participating in the effort to bring the bombers to justice; but the Saudis acted swiftly and unilaterally, arresting four local Islamic fundamentalists—three Afghani Arabs and a volunteer who had fought in Bosnia. The terrorists had smuggled the explosives in from Yemen, increasingly a center of *jihadi* support. They admitted ties to Osama bin Laden and to the Egyptian al-Gama'a. They were tried, convicted and beheaded with dispatch. Evidence was not shared and little information was made available to the FBI. What could Washington say? Justice had been done, or so it seemed.

The next year, on June 25, 1996, three American Air Force security guards were on duty on the roof of the Khobar Towers, a large, high-rise facility that housed American, British and French personnel assigned to the King Abdul Azia Air Base at Dhahran. Just before ten at night, they noticed a fuel truck parked outside the fence thirty-five yards from the complex. As they looked down, the driver ran to an escape car and drove off. The guards immediately assumed that the truck was a bomb, but they had only three minutes to rush down the stairs and urge everyone to evacuate before it smashed the north front of the building and left a crater 35 feet deep and 85 feet wide, killing 19 Americans and injuring 400 others including 250 Americans.

Secretary of State Warren Christopher changed his schedule in the Middle East to fly to the scene of the bombing, calling it a direct and deliberate attack on the citizens of the United States and our friends and allies. The next evening at dusk, standing in the shattered heap of rubble and broken glass, he added, "It's a very bleak day for all of us." The subsequent Pentagon report would indicate that a lack of urgency and priority by the commanding generals was responsible for the tragedy. The lesson that should have been learned after the bomb at the National Guard barracks the year before had not been applied. The concrete security fence had not been moved out to three hundred yards, the glass windows had not been laminated or shielded, and there had been no security filter to stop the gasoline truck.

The FBI again dispatched a team to help the Saudis, including John O'Neill, who had worked with Richard Clarke to get Ramzi Yousef, and now had his first real exposure to operating in an alien arena. The Saudis did not want to be seen allied to foreigners. The regime's primary goal was to minimize the attack and close the case. The Americans, however, were outraged and intended to see that the terrorists were found and all the ramifications of the plot were revealed. A reward of $25 million was offered for information leading to arrest and/or conviction of the guilty. The Saudis added another $3 million to the reward, but again were less than forthcoming with their intelligence. The FBI agents found the Saudis evasive and their procedures alien. Bureau director Louis Freeh flew to Saudi Arabia three times. He had hopes of Saudi cooperation, although John O'Neill did not.

Finally, in January 1997, Freeh, Attorney General Janet Reno and Secretary of State Madeleine K. Albright complained publicly about the lack of cooperation—to the dismay of the Saudis. When the suspected terrorists were arrested, tried and convicted, there was little FBI access. The terrorists had been *jihadi* but their contacts in the underground remained unknown. The Saudis did not want to dwell on Islamic opposition to the state.

Until the mid-1990s, most Americans had identified global terrorism with aircraft hijacking rather than attacks on American facilities. The hijackers had typically wanted to make a statement, not simply kill passengers, although from time to time there had been bloody attacks on the planes or in airport lounges. The most deadly terror operations had been bombs on jets, sometimes for political purposes as in the case of Pan Am Flight 103, downed over Lockerbie in 1988, and sometimes for criminal purposes as with the Avianca flight bombed over Colombia in 1988 by the cocaine dealer Pablo Escobar.

But after events in Saudi Arabia, American attitudes began to change. They began to understand that for the *jihadi,* terrorism was not propaganda, but as Ramzi Yousef had indicated, a way of killing as many infidels as possible in order to punish the West. The two bomb incidents in Saudi Arabia clearly had a link to the zealotry of the New York conspirators. A growing number of Americans began to accept the fact that there had been a paradigm shift in terrorism.

And increasingly there seemed to be zealots who would willingly sacrifice their own lives to punish Americans. On Christmas Eve 1994, the Algerian Groupe Armée Islamique hijacked an Air France Airbus A-300 flight in Algiers. After the terrorists had released some women and children but murdered three other passengers, the Algerian authorities permitted the aircraft to leave for France. So far the hijacking had been traditional. It soon became clear from the released passengers and other sources, however, that what the hijackers were planning was to crash the fully fueled plane into the Eiffel Tower or blow it up in midair over Paris. The hijackers were seized when they landed in France for refueling.

Crashing into the Eiffel Tower was like Ramzi Yousef's dream. In fact, during the Philippine operations, Yousef and Abdul

Hakim Murad had talked about crashing a plane into CIA head-quarters at Langley. Yousef later bragged about the concept to American agents and pointed out that, after all, small planes had in the past breached security in Red Square and at the White House.

In part because of the Saudi bombs and the abortive plot against the Eiffel Tower, the Clinton administration made further efforts to put safeguards in place to defend America from the new terrorists. Security was hardened and intelligence sought on anti-American plots. The Antiterrorism and Effective Death Penalty Act of 1996 increased terrorism penalties and enacted Justice's recommendation concerning illegal immigrants. The State Department was tasked to develop a list of foreign terrorist organizations; but State had other, more pressing items on the agenda and was slow to compile such a list. The Department of Defense did not want a terrorist mission and the FBI and CIA still did not share intelligence. With the exception of Richard Clarke, acting as unofficial terror czar, there was still no centralized control, no single pool of terror intelligence, no compatible computer databases. Some agencies were simply unprepared for the challenge—Freeh at the FBI had resisted computers. There was also no integration of local and regional authorities.

Each legislative response had to go through or around special interests. The new powers granted to the government to counter terrorism were too extensive for many concerned about civil liberties. In fact, although President Clinton signed the antiterrorism act, he later tried unsuccessfully to ease certain restrictions related to immigration because of the implications for civil liberties. There were also a variety of other obstacles in pursuing an active counterterror policy. Despite the spectaculars, bombings and hijackings, the terror had a limited narrative in the media. Television especially focused on the novel and spectacular, and then moved on to the next celebrity or the next disaster.

America had the power to intervene any place but not every place. No other power had ever been as dominant globally, but American hegemony rested on the capacity to extend power, the vast

technological and industrial sinews of an open and effective democratic society. Washington remained enthusiastic about the
prospects of globalization whatever the collateral costs, enthusiastic about the dot.com boom, confident that global order could
expand in an orderly and profitable fashion, and that China could
be brought into the system, the debris of the Soviet Union revived
and the needs of the Third World addressed.

Yet the new global order was filled with those who resented
the direction of history. Much of the developing world was gripped
by poverty and despotism. There were national, ethnic and religious differences beyond easy accommodation. There were small
wars and insurrections. In 1988, ten thousand United Nations
troops were deployed in peacekeeping chores. Ten years later,
eighty thousand were required.

No area generated more grievances or more violence than the
Middle East. The governments all had to balance the appeal of
Islamic fundamentalism with their regime's interests. Islam as the
answer to poverty and frustration had enormous appeal, even if
few would use violence in the Prophet's name. Certainly the governments were corrupt, authoritarian, often cruel and, worse,
ineffectual. Most of the time, in most cases, all they could offer was
repression and instability—and terrorists.

The most visible face of the new Islamic underground in the
1990s appeared in the armed struggles in Algeria and Egypt. The
two regimes had persisted in their resistance to the armed struggles initiated by the Islamists. The governments had no real
option. In Algeria, the generals in power had canceled elections
that the fundamentalists seemed certain to win in 1992. The result
was a violent insurrection that killed thousands. In Egypt at the
beginning of the decade, the surviving Islamists initiated an armed
struggle to destroy Mubarak's regime. The government, as always,
responded to provocation with violent repression. When the
Islamists in 1992 announced the existence of a liberated zone in
the Embaba quarter of Cairo, the reaction was swift, cruel and
effective. Beginning in December, the security forces smashed the
Islamists' pretensions—fourteen thousand soldiers arrested five
thousand suspects and remained in occupation for six weeks. There
would be no urban liberated zones nor, as it developed, a national

insurrection. There was, however, going to be the first real armed struggle along the Nile.

Most of the violence was in Upper Egypt. The attacks instigated by radicals were again on the small Coptic shops, jewelers or pharmacies. The police—country boys in ill-fitting uniforms —were ambushed. Still, the armed struggle proved sufficiently potent to put the government at risk—and so, too, President Mubarak. On June 25, 1995, while attending a meeting of the Organization of African States in Addis Ababa, Ethiopia, the president drove into an ambush. Egyptian zealots, operating out of a Sudanese haven, sprayed his bulletproof limousine with automatic weapons. He escaped to condemn Sudan and to persist in the repression of the Islamists, whose cause remained popular among the exile leadership and the *jihadi* abroad. In fact, on November 20, 1995, an attack on the Egyptian embassy in Islamabad resulted in fifteen dead and eighty injured. In Egypt the incident rate and kill rate went up.

In 1992, Sheikh Rahman in New York had sent videos to Egypt describing tourism as an enterprise of debauchery. The *jihadi* began to attack foreigners. There were bombs on a train and on a cruise boat on the Nile. In April 1996, the Islamists killed eighteen Greek tourists, including fourteen women, in a Cairo hotel. The country was appalled. The Islamic zealots shifted ground: The tourists had been mistaken for Israelis. A *jihadi* communiqué insisted, "The slaughter was just vengeance against the Jews, sons of monkeys and pigs...for the blood of martyrs who died in Lebanon." The horror still remained—as well as the implications of the ruin of the vital tourist industry. In July 1997, even the historic leadership of al-Gama'a in prison, including Sheikh Rahman in the United States, called for a truce.

Then, four months later, the zealots who persisted finally blundered fatally. Six gunmen made an attack on a large tourist party visiting the Pharaonic Hatsepshut Temple at Luxor above the Nile. They killed fifty-eight tourists—Swiss, British, Japanese —and four Egyptians. The police chased the killers into the barren hills near the Valley of the Queen and captured them. The Luxor massacre destroyed the $4 billion Egyptian tourist industry and put 700,000 jobs at risk; it also revealed the cost and horror of the armed struggle to all Egyptians.

The ringleader at Luxor, Medhat Abdel Rahman, 32, a member of al-Gama'a, had recruited several students including two from Assyut University. Amid the heaped bodies they had left a declaration, entitled "Havoc and Destruction," that focused on grievances and vengeance. No political program was offered; governance was not on the agenda, only revenge. The moral impact of the Luxor murders on the Islamists was profound.

Those in prison who had called for a ceasefire and had announced that tourists were not targets felt betrayed. There were splits within both Islamic Jihad and al-Gama'a. Ceasefires were announced. Aid and support dwindled away. The gunmen could only hide out in the sugar fields and a few safe houses, hoping for a better day. In Algeria the struggle cost even more lives, a long bloody massacre of the innocent often by anonymous killers and government terrorists. Over time the assets of the regime simply eroded the will of the Islamists and the killing slowed to a trickle.

The failure of the *jihadi* in Egypt and then in Algeria in the 1990s did not produce Middle Eastern stability or allow an accommodation in Palestine. There were Islamic victories as well, for the *jihadi* were active in central Asia and they supported the Taliban in Afghanistan. Hezbollah had forced an Israeli withdrawal from south Lebanon and the Islamists of Hamas and Islamic Jihad were beginning to dominate the Palestinian struggle. In other countries, failure simply meant that the militants were driven abroad. There, living in exile alongside Algerians or Saudis or Egyptians, they made new friends, sought new patrons, and hoped for new opportunities to attack the West. In the previous generation, similar exiles had found ways to operate. Sheikh Rahman, Professor Abdullah Azzam and Dr. Ayman al-Zawahiri had come to America and crisscrossed the country getting support. Their careers reflected the times. Azzam had been killed in Pakistan. Sheikh Rahman had ended up imprisoned at the federal medical center outside Rochester, Minnesota, being treated for diabetes and a heart condition, isolated from other inmates. And Dr. al-Zawahiri had decided to meld the Egyptian Islamic Jihad into al-Qaeda. Yet alive or dead, active or not, they offered examples. Azzam was a martyr; the sheikh was still in touch despite his isolation; and al-Qaeda had become crucial to the Islamic underground.

In the nineties, another generation of Arab exiles drifted toward the margin of the West, resentful and denied, eager for a mission. They were ready to be recruited into the covert world filled with Islamic ideologues, representatives of patron states, potential martyrs, individual prophets, agents for all sorts of enterprises. The faithful could be found in Madrid or Singapore. And instead of the one-man ideological adventures of Azzam or Sheikh Rahman, they were drawn into larger efforts. Some enlisted in groups like Hamas in Palestine, focused on one arena. Others formed organizations that operated globally, and to these Osama bin Laden's al-Qaeda could offer sanctuary, *fatwas*, funds, advice and volunteers.

The *jihadi* were global and elusive, and the American response remained conventional and parochial. Everyone in Washington could understand weapons, but few understood the Islamists or credited their intentions or could fathom their structure. One of the few who did was John O'Neill, who had been exposed to the problems in pursuing Ramzi Yousef almost as soon as he was placed in charge of the FBI counterterror operation. Then had come his involvement with the bombs in Saudi Arabia.

A career agent who had served for a quarter of a century, O'Neill was almost the polar opposite of Richard Clarke—and not even a very typical FBI agent. He was not an anonymous desk man and not amenable to standard operating procedures, although deeply loyal to the bureau. From his youth, when he drove a taxi cab for his father in Atlantic City, he had wanted to be an agent. He put himself through college and became a fulltime agent in Baltimore in 1976, at the end of the Edgar J. Hoover era. He did not, however, keep the Hoover ideal of rectitude: narrow ties, store-bought suits, anonymity. Instead he wore double-breasted black suits and pointy shoes, ate in good restaurants, had polished nails, exaggerated his harsh Jersey accent, drank expensive scotch, had an eye for the ladies and wore a 9-millimeter automatic in an ankle holster. With his flashy suits, slicked-back hair and expensive cigar, O'Neill was hard to miss. Yet he was very bright, a quick study. He could and did work around the clock. He could be devastating in his criticism but he engendered enormous loyalty. He was as painstaking in investigation as he often was flamboyant in his private life.

O'Neill was as colorful on the surface as Clarke was conventional; but both were ambitious, shrewd and analytical, and both had a late vocation in counterterrorism. Both suspected that Osama bin Laden's al-Qaeda had become a crucial factor in the *jihadi* underground.

Al-Qaeda offered cohesion amid the factions and splinters, the lone volunteers and the exiles in patron states. The organization was in some ways orthodox. It had leaders such as bin Laden, al-Zawahiri and, as military commander, the Egyptian Muhammad Atef; and it had members and contacts throughout the global underground. The group included a few of the famous, such as Mohammed Islambouli, the brother of Sadat's assassin, the remains of the Egyptian Islamic Jihad and Gama'a Islamiyya, the exiled scholars, and some of the Afghani Arabs along with new, anonymous recruits from Yemen and Saudi Arabia. At times al-Qaeda sponsored and directed particular operations, but the group was not a traditional underground movement in that many militants became involved only for one operation or only for a time. Much of the membership were simply zealots-in-waiting. They did not always form cells or engage in subversion, but waited to be activated, like those in New York. There was no cohesive campaign, only the exploitation of operational opportunities.

This complex and elusive underground only gradually became known to those it threatened. The French were victims of the overflow of the Algerian armed struggle and took a keen interest in the *jihadi*. American intelligence and law enforcement, on the other hand, even after the bombs in Saudi Arabia, knew very little about the Islamic underground or bin Laden, who would not declare war on the Great Satan formally until 1998. Al-Qaeda had not been involved in most of the attacks on Americans, but traces began to show up. In the spring of 1996, an al-Qaeda member, Jama Ahmed al-Fadl—who had been involved in the plots against America in Somalia—walked into the American embassy in Asmara, Eritrea, and for six months revealed what he knew of the *jihadi* underground. The CIA turned him over to the FBI, who put him in the witness-protection program. After each bomb in Saudi Arabia, however, the FBI and CIA found not a plot but loose ends. They had assumed that some sort of conspiracy might be involved, but could discover no hard evidence. There certainly had been no consensus that bin Laden's group was a major player or that the *jihadi* were pursuing a centralized strategy, so there had been no sense of foreboding. Exercises, simulations, warning notifications, action agendas in Washington did not produce a sense of urgency even after Fadl began to talk. John O'Neill, however, took al-Qaeda seriously and set up a special monitoring unit.

O'Neill had already gone global, creating a net of law enforcement contacts while flying to conferences, conferring with European police and intelligence sources. Unlike most in the FBI, he saw the threat as international and so made every effort to integrate the agency's policies with those of the CIA. For his part, as counterterror coordinator, Richard Clarke could most readily sell programs that were congenial to bureaucratic practice rather than necessarily effective defenses against actual threats. Clarke thought it was better to do something than nothing, to negotiate programs that could be implemented. And there were specific responses to provocation. For example, on July 7, 1998, President Clinton imposed a travel ban against the Taliban regime, whose leaders had expressed sympathy for *jihad*. The Kabul government's financial assets in the United States were also frozen. There seemed little else that could be done except pursue increased safeguards in the United States.

Then on August 7, 1998, the whole terror spectacular was repeated, this time with more than one target. Almost simultaneously, truck bomb explosions went off in front of the buildings housing the American embassies in Kenya and in Tanzania. In Nairobi the blast tore into the glass building and killed 224 people, including 12 Americans. In Dar es Salaam, 11 were killed. Over 5,000 people, mostly Africans, were injured in the two attacks. Hundreds of Nairobi office workers, sprayed with blasted glass, were blinded.

Once again, investigation showed what everyone had known: the plot involved the Islamists—emigrants, the Arab diaspora, a few men learning on the job. As usual the terrorists' tradecraft was flawed. They attracted attention, left evidence and didn't plan their escape well. None committed suicide as planned. The bombs, however, exploded as planned. The Islamic Army for the Liberation of the Holy Places claimed credit. Those involved in the bombings were tracked down and taken into custody; several began to talk, so Washington soon knew, as O'Neill had immediately assumed, that al-Qaeda was responsible.

By then, no longer welcome in Sudan (in fact, before then the Sudanese government had at one point approached the Americans with an offer to betray him), Osama bin Laden had moved on to Afghanistan.

After the twin bombings, al-Qaeda was taken very seriously. Yet the incidents in Kenya and Tanzania, like the World Trade Center conspiracies, were treated mainly as a law enforcement problem and not an act of war. The State Department offered a $5 million reward for information leading to bin Laden's arrest. Five of the suspects were flown to the United States. Three more were held in London. Eight suspects who were still at large, including bin Laden, were indicted as co-conspirators. Four of the terrorists were tried in New York. The government offered 92 witnesses and 1,300 exhibits, a compelling case that resulted in a guilty verdict.

According to the Taliban in Afghanistan, on December 24, 1998, Osama bin Laden commented, "I was not involved in the bomb blasts but I don't regret what happened there." The jury in New York did not believe he had not been involved. In August 1998, retaliatory missile strikes hit suspected al-Qaeda chemical warfare facilities in Sudan and guerrilla camps in Afghanistan. But like the attack on Iraq after the assassination attempt on former President Bush in 1993, the strikes were meant to reassure Americans rather than do serious damage to al-Qaeda.

In Washington the authorities received 650 threat reports in the seven months after the August 7 attacks. There were 264 other embassies and consulates to consider as targets. In response, State Department officials dispatched Emergency Security Assessment Teams, Security Augmentation Teams and Mobile Training Teams. More than one thousand new guards were authorized and countless barriers and blast walls, bomb detection units, "back-scatter" X-ray systems, closed-circuit recording cameras and metal detectors were constructed. More money was allotted to protect American officials abroad. Increasingly it was accepted that not only the State Department but all Americans were targets, especially abroad.

Immediate steps were taken to create a higher state of international alert for any future attacks. Arrangements with African and Middle Eastern intelligence and police services were put into place. The Saudis reluctantly recognized that even their Wahhabi regime, guardian of the holy places, was vulnerable to *jihadi.* And those outside the Middle East faced a similar threat. The European diaspora was a virtual nursery for gunmen and bombers. There were Afghani Arabs in the Balkans, in many of the successor states in the Soviet Union, and scattered throughout the world.

Washington was trying to seek aid in interdicting future operations. More American intelligence assets were allotted to antiterror and more talent was slowly recruited. John O'Neill had become a one-man action unit and Richard Clarke a source of counterterror initiatives, but while they had previously operated more or less alone, now other officials and agencies became more involved. There was still no central strategy for countering terrorism, but in 1998 President Clinton signed Presidential Decision Directive 62, making Clarke the national coordinator for counterterror. No longer content with eroding terrorists' vulnerabilities and erecting safeguards against them, Clarke had decided to harass suspected terrorists; and he got results.

On December 14, 1999, a millennium bomb plot was discovered when an Algerian named Ahmed Ait Ressam was stopped as he crossed from Canada into the United States at Port Angeles, Washington. A search revealed a carload of bomb-making materials for a Y2K operation against Los Angeles Airport. Ressam had left a long paper trail: he had entered Canada in 1994 on a false passport, applied for refugee standing and failed to appear, been arrested and released and then sought again after a new arrest warrant was issued in 1998. By then he had acquired a false Canadian passport in a false name.

After his arrest, Ressam began to assist the authorities. He helped convict another Algerian, Mokhtar Hourai, in July 2001. Most importantly he offered the authorities an extensive insight into the nature of the global holy war against America and the West and further information on the unfolding millennium *jihad* operation.

Jihad attacks had been planned for January 3, 2000, against buildings and tourist sites in Jordan and against the USS *Sulka* during a stop in Aden. Richard Clarke personally directed security measures to frustrate the plot. The suspects were arrested in America and Jordan, but nobody was sure if there were hidden terrorists in America planning to act on New Year's Eve. As the clock ticked down, Clarke waited in the secret communications vault at 1800 G Street NW in Washington. He was dressed for New Year's in his tuxedo, but waited until midnight came to California before sipping champagne. There was no millennium terrorist spectacular. As Clarke said a year later: "What if January last year had started with one thousand Americans dead at six or seven locations around the world? We came very close to having that happen."

Nonetheless, each terrorist spectacular always came as a surprise because Americans, even with all the evidence that men like Clarke and O'Neill were accumulating, found terror alien. It was hard to accept a secret threat, a blackworld of fanatics, or the impact a few can make by recourse to violence. There was still denial that terror could come to America. So Clarke pushed for what would be accepted as much as for what was actually needed.

The emerging war against terror was, indeed, asymmetrical. Elusive, loosely organized without a central command, pursuing an unconventional campaign of righteous murder, the *jihadi* were opposed by extensive, costly and complex American defenses that often did not address the challenge posed by irregulars. Despite the concerns of those like Clarke and O'Neill and the rising number of incidents, there was still a lack of urgency. Yet it was clear to those involved in the counterterror campaign that the *jihadi* sought any vulnerability, anywhere in the world, that would allow an action-group to succeed, and that they didn't need forward planning, formal programs or even many tangible assets.

On October 12, 2000, for instance, no one on the crew of the USS *Cole* guided-missile destroyer sitting at anchor on a friendly refueling visit to Aden had imagined that an act of terror was possible. The small boats were coming out for the mooring lines. Crewed by exotic locals, they hardly seemed a threat. Then one boat pulled up very close to the *Cole* at amidships and suddenly exploded in a flash of white, smashing a 20-by-40-foot hole in the side of the destroyer. Even though there had already been one plot against the USS *Sulka,* scheduled to visit Yemen the previous year, the small boat filled with C4 explosives had not been diverted. Seventeen American sailors were killed and thirty-nine others injured. Another surprise attack had killed Americans, somehow still unprepared, still innocents abroad.

As in the past in Lebanon and Somalia, a Pentagon investigation released on June 19, 2001, revealed that no one was really to blame for the small lapse of security and the lack of imagination that had led to the death and destruction. In effect, the system was to blame and so everyone was to blame for failing to grasp the dangers associated with the terrorist mind. Once again, disaster led to a renewed commitment that next time America would be prepared.

In the meantime John O'Neill and a three-hundred-man FBI task force, including fifty United States Marines with automatic weapons, descended on Aden. They filled the hotels, sleeping on the floors. By day they collected forensic evidence and questioned Yemeni through interpreters. In his eighth-floor bunker, protected by sandbags and Marines, O'Neill knew he had problems. Neither he nor the agents knew anything of Yemen. They spoke no Arabic. Will, determination and a driving sense of purpose were not sufficient. The FBI proceeded to investigate the crime as if it had been a mass murder in America. Ultimately, the FBI task force irritated the American ambassador in Sana'a, Barbara Bodine, who fretted that Yemeni-American relations would be frayed by the intrusive presence of so many Americans, often armed and dominating the local authorities. The Yemeni government in Sana'a made a real effort to cooperate. But no one was arrested. The task force went home, and Ambassador Bodine returned to more conventional diplomatic priorities.

The chief lesson the FBI learned—paralleling the Saudi Arabian experience—was that operating in the Middle East was complex and frustrating. In Aden, O'Neill and the FBI had by necessity relied on the American Navy and on Yemeni authorities for crime scene data, on the CIA for intelligence and on the State Department for in-country support. The most difficult obstacles arose from the clash of cultures and the limited FBI capacity for a Middle Eastern operation. Standard operating procedures did not work. Terror attacks did not fit easily into law enforcement practice.

But what the attacks in Africa and on the USS *Cole* proved beyond doubt was that there was a real *jihad* organization, al-Qaeda, with actual leaders like bin Laden and al-Zawahiri and a headquarters in the wilds of Afghanistan. Even if nobody could be arrested, the attack on the USS *Cole* involved Yemeni associated with al-Qaeda. Thus, the threat was finally tangible, with a name and a pattern of attacks. The counterterrorist agencies were increasingly focused on the next time—for they were certain there would be a next time.

When an umbrella organization for *jihadi* was announced in 1998, the name—International Front for Jihad against Jews and Crusaders—had seemed as weird as the declaration that it was the individual duty of Moslems to kill Americans, including civilians. But civilians had been killed. The *jihadi* capacity for damage had been proved, not only in the Middle East but also in New York City with its symbolic targets: celebrities, embassies, media headquarters, bridges and tunnels and famous buildings. Having grasped the implications of the new threat America faced— *jihad* was not a series of murders but an unconventional war—John O'Neill, as chief of counterterror, had moved to the FBI office in New York after the *Cole* investigation, fearful that the city would again be a target for the *jihadi*.

For over a decade the city had benefited from federal funds, from Mayor Giuliani's determination to be prepared, and from the political urgency generated by vulnerability. The potential scenarios that generated most federal aid were high-tech and high-impact: a nuclear device, Sarin in the subways, poison in the reservoir in Central Park. New York could do little specifically until the threat was manifest in the city. What New York could control was the way it responded to another incident—an incident that could well be far more deadly than a car bomb in a parking garage.

Mayor Giuliani ordered a 50,000-square-foot command-and-control post (Emergency Operations Center, EOC), for the Office of Emergency Management (OEM). The mayor's bunker was built on the twenty-third floor of the World Trade Center Building Number 7, across from the two towers, near One Police Plaza and not far from City Hall. Costing between $13 and $15 million, the EOC was bomb-resistant, bulletproof, and hardened to withstand hurricane-force winds. The bunker was stocked with thirty days of food and beds for the mayor's response team and eleven thousand gallons of drinking water that could be used for heating, ventilation and air conditioners. There were three backup generators and a ventilation system to waft away airborne biological or chemical materials.

The OEM operated on a 24-hour schedule, ready to coordinate the sixty-eight agencies representing the city, state and federal authorities as well as the forty thousand officers of the fire and police departments. There were state-of-the-art computers, video-conferencing secure phone systems and satellite contacts. The OEM monitored all emergency radio frequencies—UHF, VHF, 800 MHz trunked, conventional, and marine-band capacity—and had access to everything from the National Warning and Alert System to the National Weather Service. Through a hookup with the Coast Guard, the mayor's team could monitor all major waterways through microwave-assisted video. There were contacts prepared to all the utilities: water, fire, gas, cable television, telephone.

Some believed that too much money was spent on a bunker and too few other security measures were taken. All the exercises and simulations had indicated that the problems of overlapping jurisdiction remained. Many, especially in the police, for example, did not think the World Trade Center was much better prepared than it had been in 1993 or that many of the mayor's initiatives were wise. Public health people thought that law enforcement domination in any response to mass destruction was unwise and the National Guard teams were useless. Exactly what the state and the federal government would do in case of catastrophic disaster was uncertain. But despite the cavils, all agreed that matters had improved. The city had taken a variety of other remedial measures including the stockpiling of drugs, arranged for a Disaster Mortuary Response Team and incorporated New Jersey in any overall plans. Over $1 million was used by the city to purchase twelve mobile emergency vehicles filled with containment vessels that could isolate biological or chemical threats.

The city would be able to draw on the National Guard program for Weapons of Mass Destruction Civil Support Teams

—RAID. These teams, including those available to New York City, would be ready for action in 2000. But while the program was politically astute, involving 120 cities in counterterror, the cost and effectiveness were problematical. Each RAID was likely to be late on the scene. Each cost $3,500,000—the same as outfitting 2,333 hospitals with decontamination facilities. Yet each increased the antiterror constituency and gave evidence to American citizens that the government was constructing safeguards.

Supported by Washington funds and expertise, the city staged drills and gamed out scenarios. These indicated the existing flaws of the city's response. The problem of the flood of volunteers to any site was addressed and the city's first responders were sent to special training. New protocols were set up and the New York Police Department's famous Emergency Service Unit was assigned the lead role in decontamination in the event of a chemical, biological or nuclear attack.

Any national or local response to catastrophe would have to cope with the contingent and unforeseen. Some attacks would defy the skills and resources of the first responders. In New York City, as elsewhere, casualties caused by biological and chemical attacks would be quite different from those produced by bombs or air crashes. For a time no one might know that plague was loose or that citizens were being poisoned. Such conditions could be difficult to diagnose or require complex immediate treatment, and so be a matter of public health rather than police reaction.

Whatever might happen or however effective the planned response might be, money had been spent and programs initiated. And in contrast to the situation in 1993, when the bomb had gone off in the World Trade Center, a great deal had been accomplished.

In Washington, Richard Clarke's counterterrorism strategy group had also set in motion an integrated response to potential attacks. Federal spending had been doubled in forty relevant departments and agencies. Terror had moved up on the agenda of the CIA and the FBI, and the attacks in Saudi Arabia had focused minds at the Pentagon. The 2000 budget for antiterror had reached $10.2 billion, almost double the $5.7 billion spent in 1997. Congress had accepted extensive domestic funding: $6.8 billion on government security programs—including protection of buildings,

$1.8 billion for responding to weapons of mass destruction and $1.5 billion on defense of computer systems. The threat of further spectaculars by the Islamic zealots was a rising concern, but still not at the top of the list.

John O'Neill had made a splash in New York. He loved the city, the glamour and the glitz. He soon knew everyone, waved his way into Elaine's, knew Yankee players and crime reporters by name, was recognized in the clubs. He knew the headwaiters and the city politicians and the police on the beat. He still traveled abroad to meet law enforcement people from Paris and Italy and agents from the new Russia. Everyone seemed to know O'Neill. He flourished amid the famous, yet he also worked enormously hard, consumed by the threat of terror. But his style was a problem for the bureau. He had an indiscreet private life, was too visible in his sleek tailored suits moving through the club circuit. This was not an image the FBI found acceptable.

Even though he believed the prime enemy was al-Qaeda and feared the arrival of more of the zealots in America, O'Neill finally decided to leave government service rather than be shunted aside. He was not about to change his lifestyle. He was depressed that what sold best in the terrorism trade in Washington and even New York was not measures against the *jihadi* but safeguards against plague and plutonium. Washington feared the use of such weapons by rogue states, and so even after the *Cole* attack did not really pay sufficient attention to the doomsday scenario represented by *jihad*.

In any case, after the election in November 2000, the response to terror would be in the hands of a Republican administration. When George W. Bush arrived in Washington, counterterror was firmly established as a national priority, an agenda item. His administration made no fundamental change, not increasing spending but not reducing it either. Richard Clarke was moved sideways into cyberdefense. The White House had other concerns and didn't see terror as a pressing priority; nothing had happened since the USS *Cole*, and in any case there was less interest in Middle Eastern events in general.

With Clarke gone, there was no longer an effective antiter-ror czar who had the proper bureaucratic contacts. There was still no really coherent counterterror strategy. In May 2001 the presi-dent appointed Vice-President Dick Cheney to head a special group to study the issue and authorized a new office within FEMA, the emergency management authority that was a hodgepodge of agen-cies with little prestige or influence. Still, terror was not forgotten. In June 2001 the new attorney general, John Ashcroft, noted that terrorism was an administration priority. In the meantime, many experts suggested that absolute security was not only impossible but also undesirable—why should Americans withdraw into a bunker? Tomorrow's terror should not be allowed to dictate today's events and skew priorities.

Senator Moynihan called for reopening Pennsylvania Avenue in front of the White House, closed off after the 1995 Oklahoma City bombing, and removing the "visual blight" of con-crete barriers. Harry Truman used to take afternoon walks in front of the White House, but now a fortress had been created—and to what end? There had to be a balanced response, common sense deployed, other priorities considered. For many there had been no terrorist narrative that gave urgency to an escalating threat, no sense that America was truly vulnerable.

Little noted by either the old administration or the new one was the growing anxiety of the counterterrorism specialists. No one except Shoko Asahara of Aum and Timothy McVeigh had ever used weapons of mass destruction in the service of terror. The domestic anthrax threats against abortion clinics were all false alarms. A suitcase nuclear device had never been discovered. On the other hand, the Islamic zealots had spent a decade attacking American targets in Arabia, in Africa—and in New York City. They had narrowly been prevented from doing so again in Amer-ica when the millennium bomb plot failed.

What Richard Clarke had wanted was not simply to imple-ment a good defense for all contingencies but also to ruin al-Qaeda: "Our goal should be to so erode his network of organi-zations that they no longer pose a serious threat." John O'Neill in New York believed that an attack was imminent.

The conspirators always looked for some vulnerability: the

Marines carried unloaded weapons at their concrete headquarters near the Beirut airport; there was no security in the World Trade Center parking garage; anyone could hijack an airliner with a pen knife; a van could be parked below the American embassy in Nairobi. New York was filled with vulnerabilities. In fact, since America was an open society, much of the country offered opportunities to the *jihadi*. O'Neill was convinced that time was running out.

Some of the zealots in America needed only to make contact with a patron who could offer money and support, but take no further part. The Arab diaspora was filled with potential patrons, and with people eager to act. The *jihadi* volunteers didn't have to know each other, or have ties with the funding or even with the leadership. This time the *jihadi* had an idea that seemed worth the risks. Yousef had contemplated an attack by air, and any plane could be hijacked and diverted to a target. All that was really needed was dedicated volunteers to make such an attack possible. With time and a little money, volunteers could be recruited and could learn how to seize a modern jet airliner and fly it well enough to reach the target. With a few such "pilots" as well as volunteers to control the passengers, a huge missile could be launched at an appropriate target. With access to internet schedules and reservations, even a very complex operation could be projected. A truly spectacular attack that would kill a great many Americans and humiliate the Great Satan seemed a real prospect; and so preparations began.

The zealots in and out of al-Qaeda had repeatedly hit American targets, but for the most part there was no sense in Washington that the United States had been engaged in a holy war. Only O'Neill and other specialists were concerned not simply about "terrorism" but about a specific *jihadi* attack in America. In fact, Sheikh Rahman, isolated in his high-security prison cell, knew more about the intentions of the *jihadi* than American officials did. He knew the power of the Islamic dream, the necessity to kill, and the shape of the future.

Almost every spectacular terrorist operation arises from a single idea. There was now such an idea: have volunteer martyrs seize a jetliner using easily smuggled knives and box cutters, then guide it into the target. In fact, with enough volunteers they could hijack several planes. There was no defense in place and, most important, no one who was likely to imagine one was needed. Emboldened by brazen optimism, the *jihadi* believed that success was possible because of the novelty of the operation—and the flaws in the American security system.

As with many other *jihadi* attacks, this was compartmental-ized, involving only a few leaders with the usual elusive contacts for funding. The key was not an underground cell structure, a cen-tralized command center, money and time or even the availability of martyrs, but rather the idea. This operational idea had been cir-culating in the underground for some years. The Algerian Groupe Armée Islamique had even undertaken such an attack on Paris before the plot was aborted.

As long as a conspiracy was secure from informers and those involved were pursuing seemingly legitimate interests, the prospect of discovery was remote. In this case, little hierarchy of control was needed—a few agents circulating, an operational com-mandeer, the Egyptian Mohammed Atta, and ties with the funding sources. Some of the Arab conspirators were not even chosen until the last moment.

There had been rumors picked up by various federal agencies, rumors dispatched by friendly governments abroad; but there was no hard data. All sorts of indicators were floating within the sys-tem, but there was nobody who had access to all the data and could make sense of it all, and so there was no sense of urgency. The arrogance and confidence of al-Qaeda, the growing militancy of the *fatwas* and statements all boded ill for tranquility; but even those most concerned about it could not easily point to a specific threat.

Nobody was more concerned than John O'Neill. He was no longer the FBI's key player in the terrorist stakes, but he had stayed in New York and in the counterterrorism game. Early in 2001 he had taken a new job as head of security at the Port Authority and with it the World Trade Center. It was not only a lucrative position but also an influential one. He was delighted with the challenge and the change. And the first item on his agenda was the threat of the *jihadi*. In the summer of 2001, O'Neill was almost certain that something was about to happen. He hadn't yet had time to assess the requirements and powers of his new position, but he felt an intense urgency.

On the morning of September 11, 2001, O'Neill was en route to his new office on the thirty-fourth floor of the World Trade Center complex, confident that here he would make a difference.

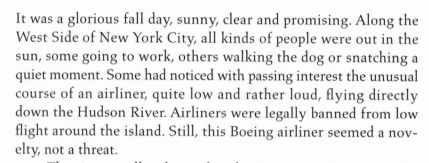

It was a glorious fall day, sunny, clear and promising. Along the West Side of New York City, all kinds of people were out in the sun, some going to work, others walking the dog or snatching a quiet moment. Some had noticed with passing interest the unusual course of an airliner, quite low and rather loud, flying directly down the Hudson River. Airliners were legally banned from low flight around the island. Still, this Boeing airliner seemed a novelty, not a threat.

The air controllers knew that the Boeing was American Airlines Flight 11, out of Boston bound for Los Angeles, which had been diverted down the Hudson by unknown skyjackers. On their screens, they could only watch Flight 11 approach the tip of the island at below 10,000 feet and just under 500 miles per hour. No demands had been made, no request for a landing site, and no name was given by the hijackers.

Down below, the pedestrians in lower Manhattan could see the plane tip slightly, waver and then swing toward the World Trade Center complex. The pilot would have to use manual control and rely on luck to turn Flight 11. In any case, he was risking disaster because of the high speed and low altitude.

Jules Naudet, 28, was standing in front of the lobby of the World Trade Center's north tower. Along with his brother Gedeon, 31, he was making a documentary film on the life of a probationary fireman named Tony Benatatos at Engine 7, Ladder 1, in a nearby station. That morning, Jules had brought his camera to the fire station, and then moved out with the battalion chief to check a gas leak. He was learning to film on the job. At 8:45 he was standing below the north tower, ready to begin the day's filming, when he heard a huge roar overhead.

People began to look upward. The plane was too loud, too

close. Automatically, Naudet tipped his camera up. The running videotape caught Flight 11 just as it smashed between the 94th and 98th floors of the north tower at exactly 8:46:26. Instantly there was a huge orange and red fireball, fed by 10,000 gallons of jet fuel.

There was a roaring noise, an incredible explosion, a great welt of flame, the concussion, and soon the clank and bang of falling bits: the plane's landing carriage, broken glass, ruined jet engines, luggage, building panels. Naudet's framing was crisp, focused, steady—the horror made into record. His images were the first captured, but were not seen publicly until six months later, when CBS aired the documentary on March 11, 2002. Almost from the moment of impact, others from the local media rushed toward the tragedy. The images they sent out through the networks almost immediately were to shape one of the most dramatic days of American history. *Jihad* had come again to America.

Word of the event spread; in 18 minutes there were 3,000 telephone calls to 911, many of them made on mobile phones from the burning tower. In the lobby of the north tower through the glass walls, Naudet could hear the dreadful crunch and splat of impact from those who leaped from the top stories rather than burn to death, the clatter and clank of falling debris, and see the writhing burnt victims caught in the flaming aviation fuel. The first responders, the firemen and the police, began to arrive. They and Naudet waited on instructions at ground zero. Burning aviation fuel had spurted over the plaza and poured down the elevator shafts. A few firemen started up to fight the fires—a hopeless task since it would take an hour for the heavily loaded men to reach the huge blaze and then there would be no water. At least the firemen could oversee an evacuation.

The others waited in the lobby, uncertain what was expected, what headquarters wanted, and what was happening elsewhere. People looking out from nearby high-rises saw a sky filled with bits of paper floating out over the city, and smoke. A few could see the flaming cauldron in the side of the tower. Farther away, the disaster was visible as a great plume of smoke drifting over the harbor.

The independent stations and networks soon moved downtown with their cameras running. CNN interrupted regular coverage and begin to run cameras live. Soon the disaster could be seen in hotel rooms in Budapest and Karachi, on the television sets in shop windows in Lima and San Francisco. Afternoon programs were canceled in Dublin and prime time in Singapore. The national stations in Norway and Japan picked up the New York feed. In the city, press photographers made their way toward the disaster, and journalists, stringers, hopeful amateurs with video cams, and foreign correspondents. The plume of smoke could be seen for miles as the fire continued to rage up on the side of the building. The fresh film was snatched up by television news producers and run alongside the constant live coverage. This time, unlike the 1993 bombing, the *jihadi* had produced something far more dramatic than a smudge of foul smoke rising from the entry of an underground garage.

Inside the north tower, the crash had shaken loose installation, ruined the sprinkler system and cut electricity. Water poured useless down the stairwells, many already impassible with debris. The flames, fed by the aviation fuel and unhampered by the fire-retardant panels that had been jarred loose, threatened the building's structural integrity, which had withstood the crash. The braces that held the external girders in place began to soften. Above the impact site on the 91st floor, 1,344 people were trapped. The tower's architect had not designed it to withstand the impact of a fully fueled Boeing 767-200, which had not even been designed when the World Trade Center was constructed.

And then, as the millions watched, twenty minutes later at 9:02:54, a second Boeing 767-200, United Airlines Flight 175, appeared going well over 500 miles an hour, faster than the previous flight. For a moment the Boeing trembled and tilted, then crashed into the south tower between the 76th and 84th floors. A second huge orange fireball blossomed from the tower. Again, great gouts of flaming aviation fuel splattered out of the ruins. Again, debris tumbled over and over and crashed into the street: landing gear, luggage, a jet engine. Again, there was the huge flaming hole in the tower's skin and the jumpers plummeting down the side of the building away from the flames, to die in the plaza.

In the streets below, stunned people looked up in disbelief.

One was John O'Neill, the security chief of the World Trade Center. He had anticipated an attack, but not on this scale. The second explosion far above made clear that his anxiety had been justified. One crash just might have been an accident, but two meant terrorism. Massive terror had come to New York not in the form of plague or nerve gas, but as two Boeing 767-200s transformed into missiles.

This time the image of the 767 flying into the south tower was seen live by tens of millions, seen in replay from various angles, over and over, for days. A terrorist spectacular was playing in New York, and seemed to evolve into an ongoing tragedy as a third hijacked airliner, American Airlines Flight 77, flew into the side of the Pentagon at 9:39 A.M., generating a third huge fireball and killing 189 people in the building. A fourth hijacked airliner, American Flight 93, crashed into a field near Shanksville, Pennsylvania, southeast of Pittsburgh, leaving a crater crusted with blackened debris and bringing the death toll for the four lost planes to 266. At least the passengers on Flight 93, learning of their certain fate from cell phone calls, had attempted to seize the plane and had prevented a fourth disaster as great as the others.

And then the towers imploded. The central internal supports in the south tower, weakened by the heat, began to fail from the top floors down: 56 minutes after impact, at 9:59:04, the south tower collapsed like an accordion. The television tower disappeared into a pillar of smoke. As the vast building cascaded into a huge heap, hidden by an enormous cloud of smoke and dust, those still in the north tower rushed to get out, some aware of what had happened in the other tower, others not, but all hurried along by the firemen and police.

Then, 102 minutes after impact, the outside vertical girders of the north tower could no longer bear the weight on them as their horizontal supports, softened by the intense heat, failed. The north tower collapsed at 10:28:31. The vast global audience could again watch the huge building, 110 stories, disappear into rubble.

In the ruins, hidden by the enormous, roiling smoke cloud, were the remains of those who had not escaped. No one knew how many were lost, injured, missing. No one could see into lower Manhattan. The grit and dust fell onto the streets, on the people, on crushed fire equipment and abandoned cars. It was hard to breathe. After escaping from the lobby with a few firemen, Jules Naudet kept filming, his lens soon covered in dust, wiped clean and clouded again. His tape revealed only a few glints of light in the dark and the sound of coughing. Further away, other television cameras caught the survivors rushing out of the expanding cloud that chased them up the streets. The great racing flood of smoke and dust caught up with the runners, blinded them, covered them with a thick gray powder. Survivors moved out and away. Some walked across the Brooklyn Bridge or uptown, shocked, caked with dust. Some boarded hastily gathered ferries and boats to reach New Jersey.

There were thousands killed in the towers, but no bodies. For a few hours casualties came into the nearest Manhattan hospitals, and then nothing. Nearly everyone lost had been pulverized, turned into dust. They left behind no physical evidence of themselves except DNA traces. Thousands of people had disappeared in two huge implosions, vaporized, blowing on the wind: as many killed in an hour as had been lost in the bloodiest day of the American Civil War at the battle of Antietam, and more than at Pearl Harbor.

Among the missing was John O'Neill. Upon arriving at the base of the towers soon after the first hijacked airliner struck the north tower, he contacted his friends and family by mobile phone from the base of the north tower, where a command center was being established, and assured them that he was all right. He telephoned out again after the second airliner hit the second tower, and then moved on toward the tunnel to the south tower. This was the last any survivor saw of him. He was reported among the missing, lost somewhere in the rubble, dead at ground zero.

EPILOGUE

After September 11, the United States declared a war on terrorism. It deployed massive military power against Afghanistan, engaged in missions against al-Qaeda cells elsewhere in the world, sought to increase the defenses of America by new technology and better training, and mounted a new crusade against weapons of mass destruction in the hands of Iraq and other "rogue states."

Various measures were taken to harass the terrorists and intimidate other zealots who might be inclined to emulate them. The U.S. strategy for dealing with the crisis was clear: the nation would rely on military power, diplomatic alliances, and technology deployed by special forces abroad, and on filters at airports, electronic intercepts and a beefed-up homeland security at home. But while all these responses were helpful and necessary, they did not really acknowledge the implications of a global *jihad*. The threat facing America was unprecedented, and could not be countered with organization, power and technology.

Much was made of the tentacles of al-Qaeda, but the *jihadi* did not rely on conventional power; they had few tangible assets, no military timetable or order of battle, no need to initiate new programs or procedures. If the Taliban disappeared overnight, if the cadres of al-Qaeda were all imprisoned, if Osama bin Laden was killed, the Islamists' lethal dream would persist. The *jihadi* didn't care if America returned to normal, rebuilt the Trade Center, made antiterrorist alliances abroad, railed against fundamentalist Islam, suppressed the new *intifada*, or took out Saddam Hussein. Their struggle was their mission. Military triumph was secondary;

even the stated desire to expel the Jews and the Crusaders from the Holy Land was a distant priority. They were not disheartened by operational failures, for more martyrs generated more soldiers.

The *jihadi* goal is absolute and cannot be accommodated by the elimination of grievance, through negotiation or by repression. The cause and core of *jihadi* terror is the conviction that only violence can assure the triumph of Islam and that such a triumph is possible. Either the whole world changes or the *jihad* continues. No one can kill or imprison the growing masses of the faithful who offer the few terrorists necessary for action against the Great Satan. Hundreds of millions of Muslims understand the *jihadi* and the dream that is spread by the wandering imams, the hardened Egyptian exiles and the other zealots, even if they might have reservations about terror as the proper means of achieving it.

The enormous power of the Islamic dream, first shaped for the contemporary era by the faithful along the Nile, is that it offers so much: an explanation of what hinders the Muslim world from its rightful success; who is responsible for this crime against Islam; and why they must be punished. The dream is a bloody one, yet for the dreamer it offers hope and a mission, which is why it attracts both the idealists and the outraged, the educated and the desperate. It will continue to attract them even if there are long periods between actions against the infidels of the West.

Somewhere in a dingy rented room in Dhaka or Detroit, a few men, some marginal and some with certificates and degrees, are likely, sooner or later, to find a way to inflict great damage on America. They won't need much in the way of resources. As long as the *jihadi* are tolerated by their own, hidden from view, dedicated to the dream and convinced that *jihad* is the only way into the future, America is at grave risk.

In the months after September 11, the world went back to normal. The leaders of al-Qaeda disappeared. In Japan, the Aum cult still exists and seems to be growing. In Egypt, Mubarak has largely emptied the prisons of those zealots who have accepted that Allah is not the answer—at least not now, not for them. The armed struggle in Algeria is winding down. Many of those who left the Nile valley for the global *jihad* have entered a closed underground and vanished, perhaps to find temporary comfort in private life before being mobilized once again for the dream. Yet boys still memorize the Koran in Pakistan's seven thousand *madrassa* schools. Radical sermons are still given in popular mosques in Cairo and Khartoum. Islamic migrants come and go, crossing international borders with the *jihadi* virus undeclared at customs.

The prisoners remain at Guantanamo in their orange jump-suits. Many detainees have been released. While a few new suspects have been captured, the sense of urgency is less. The turmoil of Palestine competes with global terror and homeland security. But there are reminders of how far we have come. Just outside Washington, D.C., in Langley, Virginia, there is a small concrete monument across the highway from the CIA that honors the two men shot by Mir Amal Kansi long ago, when the *jihadi* were a matter for a few experts like Richard Clarke and a few law enforcement officials like John O'Neill. There are daily discussions of Next Time—the dirty bomb or the smallpox or something else unimaginable.

And Sheikh Omar Abdel Rahman still makes the news on occasion. In April 2002, federal prosecutors charged that two years earlier, in May, his lawyer helped him send a message out of prison calling for an end to the ceasefire in Egypt. Even from within the closed cell of a high-security American penitentiary, the sheikh could still urge murder on the Nile. For him, blind in a closed prison cell, nothing has changed except for his temporary isolation from his congregation. For him, now more than ever, *jihad* is the way, his years in New York were not wasted, and the Great Satan remains the target of the dream of vengeance and redemption. The sheikh could take pride in knowing that what he helped begin in obscure mosques and upstairs rooms along the Nile has for millions become a vision of the future.

GLOSSARY

Ali, Mohammed: ruled Egypt, nominally in the Ottoman Empire, from 1820 to 1839, initiating modernization and the basis for nationalism.

Azzam, Abdullah: one of the first and most effective *jihadi* organizers, who traveled throughout the Islamic world and its diaspora, ending in Pakistan, where on November 14, 1989, he was assassinated at the gate to the Saba-e-Leit mosque by unknown assailants.

al-Banna, Hasan: founder of the Moslem Brothers in 1928 in Ismailiyya, Egypt; murdered by agents of the state on February 12, 1949.

bin Laden, Osama: from a Yemeni family, son of a Saudi millionaire, who became a fundamentalist and used his inheritance to support the *mujaheddin* in Afghanistan. Became a *jihadi* after the Gulf War and founded al-Qaeda, which merged with the Egyptian Islamic Jihad. Funded, advised or directed armed operations in a global *jihad* against the West.

Farouk, King: the last and increasingly corrupt Egyptian monarch who sought ineffectually to extend the power of the palace from 1937 until 1952, when he was exiled by the Free Officers under Nasser.

Fatwa: a religious declaration by an individual or group as a sanction or to assert the proper course of behavior.

Fedemin: the small village in upper Egypt where Sheikh Omar

Abdel Rahman's sermons first came to the attention of both the fundamentalists and the authorities.

Hamas: Islamic Resistance Movement in Palestine, waging a *jihad* against the Israelis.

Hezbollah: Islamic Shi'ite movement in southern Lebanon, supported by Iran and engaged in a campaign of terror and armed struggle against the Israeli occupation.

al-Ikhwan al-Muslimon: the Society of Muslim Brethren, or Moslem Brothers, from time to time legally recognized in Egypt and the model for similarly named organizations throughout the Middle East.

ISI: Inter-Services Intelligence Agency, the Pakistani secret service responsible for aiding fundamentalists and *jihadi* in Afghanistan, Kashmir and India.

il-Islambouli, Khaled Ahmed: Sadat's assassin, tried and executed. His *jihadi* brother Mohammed was leader of an Islamic student association; in exile after 1982.

Islamic Jihad: formed in Egypt and active in the armed struggle against the regime until repression drove most of the leadership into exile.

Jahiliyya: for the fundamentalists, the corrupt societies ruling the Middle East.

Jihadi: those fundamentals who insist that an armed crusade against either the corrupt Islamic regimes or the infidels, especially the West and the United States in particular, is the only way to achieve a just Islamic society.

Kahane, Meir: radical American-Israeli Zionist, assassinated in the ballroom of a New York hotel in 1990 by the Egyptian el-Sayyid Nosair.

LEHI: Lohmey Heruth Israel—Fighters for the Freedom of Israel, also known as the Stern Group or Stern Gang, the radical Zionists who chose personal terror as a strategy in their struggle against the British.

Lord Moyne: Walter Edward Guinness, senior British official in the Middle East who was assassinated by two members of the radical Zionist LEHI—the Stern Gang—in 1944.

Mubarak, Hosni: air force officer, vice-president of Egypt and president after Sadat's murder, 1982 to present; a repeated target of *jihadi* assassination plots.

Nasser, Gamal Abdel: leader of the Free Officers' coup on July 23, 1952, and of the new military regime as premier in 1954 and president from 1956 until his death in 1970. Dominated Egyptian politics as well as Arab nationalist sentiment. For many fundamentalists, however, he was always an evil pharaoh—a secular and so a discredited leader.

Nosair, el-Sayyid: Egyptian immigrant who assassinated Meir Kahane in New York on November 5, 1990. Arrested and tried, he was convicted only on assault and weapons charges.

Qutb, Sayyid: Arabist theologian and analyst who died a martyr when executed on August 29, 1966, by the Nasser government and whose *Signposts* became a key text for the *jihadi.*

Rahman, Sheikh Omar Abdel: Advocate of *jihad,* leader of the Egyptian Gama'a Islamiyya, international organizer for fundamentalist Islam. Involved in the New York City conspiracies. Arrested, tried, convicted and sentenced for the World Trade Center bombing of 1993, he is presently in an American high-security prison.

Sadat, Anwar: officer, nationalist conspirator, early friend of il-Ikhwan and the Free Officers, then vice-president and president of Egypt until his assassination in 1982.

Siddig Ali, Siddig Ibrahim: Sudanese exile in New York who took the lead in the bombing conspiracy that included Sheikh Omar Abdel Rahman. When all the conspirators were arrested in June 1993, Siddig gave evidence against them.

Stack, Sir Lee, Pasha: British commander of the Egyptian army, he was assassinated on November 19, 1924, apparently by nationalists.

al-Turabi, Hassan: leader of the Sudanese Nationalist Islamic

Front; radical fundamentalist presence in the Sudanese military government.

Wafd Party: arose out of the delegation headed by Saad Zagloul that was to have visited Great Britain in 1918 to urge Egypt's independence. Zagloul formed the party in 1919. In addition to espousing independence, the Wafdis called for extensive social and economic reforms.

Wahabbism: a fundamentalist sect that is the state religion of Saudi Arabia, whose establishment has funded a spectrum of fundamentalist organizations throughout the Islamic world.

Yousef, Ramzi Ahmed: a *jihadi,* apparently from a Baluchi family, who was instrumental in the first World Trade Center bomb conspiracy; he then escaped and in Manila planned, among other operations, to use mass airliner bombs and to attack the Pope. Escaped from the Philippines and was arrested in Pakistan and extradited to the United States, where he was tried, convicted and imprisoned.

Zagloul, Saad: Egyptian politician, prime minister, founder of the Wafd Party—the most effective modern Egyptian political party—and dominant nationalist from 1918 until his death in 1927.

al-Zawahiri, Dr. Ayman: Egyptian physician from a prominent family who organized Islamic Jihad; fled Egypt to Pakistan and then in Afghanistan merged his organization with that of Osama bin Laden.

SOURCES

Murders on the Nile is based on four decades of interviews and exposure to the implications of terror, on work in the field and a familiarity with the existing sources; but like most exercises in contemporary history, it can hardly be definitive. Nor have I attempted to supply a visible scholarly scaffolding. This list of sources indicates the kinds of materials that are available and useful, and suggests additional reading for those who are interested.

Any contemporary crisis generates a vast amount of paper: hundreds of newspaper and journal articles, printed interviews, government publications, commentary and analysis from research centers, swift books, tracts and pamphlets, in addition to electronic riches. There is television footage, video documentaries and all the resources of the internet. If you want to know the room rates at the Su Casa Guest House in Pakistan where Ramzi Yousef spent his last free night, the information is on the web. In short, there is an enormous body of information on the subject of terrorism. Even a clipping file on September 11, 2001, from a paper like the *New York Times* or the *London Independent* requires two hands to carry. The recent works aiming to summarize all this raw data, often by investigative journalists, often based on interviews, are sometimes useful, sometimes not, and tend to suffer from the flaw of detailing what is known rather than what is important.

For historians, social scientists and analysts there is often far too much raw data to use. Much that is available is for specialists only; the *United States Marine Corps Mid-Range Threat Estimate* may be compelling for the really keen, but not even for most specialists. What most readers want is data refined, clear and coherent, a plain narrative of events, not the specialist monographs or a plethora of primary sources.

Still, there is much information that is not available—official and unofficial sources that cannot be tapped. Governments wait generations to release documents, unless war (as in the case of Nazi Germany) or chaos (as in the case of the Soviet Union) reveals matters long held secret. Often the crucial evidence is only in the memory of individuals who may have no interest in being sources of information. In the case of September 11, 2001, many sources are closed, some—especially classified government material—for the foreseeable future and some for good. As for the people who are directly involved, they are likely to be fugitive, dead, restrained by government procedures or still participating in terrorist activity.

I want to stress again the special usefulness of research papers by four of my students: Joshuah Berman, "Ready or Not? U.S. Preparations for Biological and Chemical Terrorism"; Joseph Blady, "Biological and Chemical Events: Threat and Response in New York and New Jersey"; Andrew Galliker, "How Much Is Enough? Assessing the Adequacy of the Federal Response Plan for Consequence Management"; and Ronit Golan, "Terrorism."

Most of the data I have employed comes from the usual and expected sources—newspapers, government documents, years of interviews and so on; and these are generally not cited. Most of the direct quotations come from the *New York Times* or official press releases. In addition are these:

Chapter 2—"Our deed stemmed from ...": Gerold Frank, *The Deed* (New York: Ballantine, 1963), p. 261. "Finest suit of clothing...": Geula Cohen, *Women of Violence* (London: Hart-Davis, 1966), p. 62.

Chapter 4—"You should prepare whatever...": Peter L. Bergen, *Holy War* (New York: Free Press, 2001), pp. 70–71. "When you meet him you do not...": Bergen, *Holy War,* p. 203.

Chapter 5—"It may be that my presence in the belly...": interview by Ian Williams in *Washington Report of Middle Eastern Affairs,* February 1993. "Destroy them thoroughly...": Youssef Bodanksy, *Bin Laden* (Rocklin, Cal.: Forum, 1999), p. 296. "Hit hard and kill...": Jerusalem Center for Public Affairs.

Chapter 6—"Take two beakers...": William Powell, *The Anarchist Cookbook* (Secaucus, N.J.: Lyle Stuart, 1971). "When I looked around the sight...": I. D. W. Breckett, *Holy Terror: Armageddon in Tokyo* (New York and Tokyo: Weatherhill, 1996), p. 130. "I need a truck...": Richard A. Serrano, *One of Ours: Timothy McVeigh and the Oklahoma City Bombing* (New York: Norton, 1998), p. 130. "The slaughter was just vengeance...": Gilles Kepel, *Jihad: The Trail of Political Islam* (Cambridge, Mass.: Belknap, Harvard University Press, 2002), p. 295. "What if January...": *Washington Post*, December 24, 2000. "Our goal should be...": *Washington Post*, April 2, 2000.

Chapter 7—"You develop in the culture...": Jeffrey Toobin, "Aschcroft's Ascent," *New Yorker*, April 15, 2002, p. 536.

The long tale of Islamic *jihad* begins in Egypt. There is no single book that begins with the pharaohs and ends with the sheikh; but on modern Egyptian history there is a series of books, one or two of them indispensable and many interesting. Some areas have generated a substantial literature and some have not. As the narrative moves from Egypt into the international world of the *jihadi*, there are fewer authoritative works. For the last few years, one must rely on newspapers, the stories and rumors of participants, the undigested paper trail of a modern crisis, or a few books hastily published to meet an unexpected market demand. For slightly earlier times, there is much that is worthwhile. On matters related to the Islamic *jihadi*, including the Egyptian background, the available authoritative literature has been greatly expanded in the last decade. There has long been an academic concern with Islamic fundamentalism, the wars and troubles of Afghanistan and the impact of political Islam.

For a generation there has been intense interest in terrorism: over ten thousand published books and whole journals dedicated to the subject. There are good and useful popular works available. Yet mostly, one is very much like another: the same gunmen appear—the IRA or Black September; the same causes—ethnic separatism or militant nationalism; and the same threats—hijackers or people making a nuclear bomb out of stolen plutonium. The context changes and the particulars of the cases, but terror is still terror. Islamic fundamentalist terror has emerged only in recent years, so the library still has room for additions, many now undoubtedly in process.

Most of the work on terror is generated by opponents, potential victims, advocates of security—although apologists too are heard from. The policy interest in terrorism in general and weapons of mass destruction in particular sometimes gives context to the perceived Islamic threat. What is the threat? Where is the West vulnerable? What safeguards should be taken? These questions have generated an ongoing debate and another small library.

So there is much to be read on terrorism in general and a few books that specifically address the new threat from Islamic extremism. The terror events of September 2001 have inspired some to hurry their books into print, but the dynamics of al-Qaeda and the response to September 11 are still beyond easy reach—and may be so for some time.

The authoritative history of Egypt is P. J. Vatikiotiss, *The History of Modern Egypt from Muhammad Ali to Mubarak* (Baltimore: Johns Hopkins, 1991), stronger on intellectual and social matters than on day-to-day politics, but so far irreplaceable. There are works on the early al-Ikhwan: Ishak Musa Husaini, *The Moslem Brethren* (Beirut: Khayats College Book Cooperative, 1956); and the later, authoritative Richard P. Mitchell, *The Society of Muslim Brothers* (Oxford and New York: Oxford University Press, 1969); see also Christina Phelps Harris, *Nationalism and Revolution in Egypt: The Role of the Muslim Brotherhood* (The Hague: Muton & Co., 1964). No single narrative, however, brings al-Ikwhan up to date. On the newer *jihadi* groups there are, as yet, only journal articles.

There is a great deal on the political history of Egypt, especially by the British. For example, there are the relevant volumes of the Royal Institute of International Affairs. See as well John Marlowe, *Anglo-Egyptian Relations, 1800–1953* (London: Cressent Press, 1954); or Derek Hopwood, *Egypt: Politics and Society, 1945–1981* (London: George Allen & Unwin, 1982). Scholars and analysts concerned with modern Egypt have tended to focus on the Nasser-Sadat years; there are works on aspects of governance, but little political history until the arrival of the Free Officers. There are, in fact, a great many works addressing Nasser, Egyptian socialism, Egypt and Arab nationalism and the Palestinian problem. There is a substantial library of monographs and journal articles on most of modern Egyptian political, social and economic matters, on peasant politics, on the structure of Delta society, on the Sufis and the organization of the professional societies, on defunct political parties and the emergence of the Egyptian working class after 1882.

There is no comprehensive work on Egyptian assassins. There is one book by Gerold Frank, *The Deed* (New York: Simon & Schuster, 1963), on the Zionist assassination of Lord Moyne; and also the most recent printing of my more general *Terror out of Zion* (New Brunswick, N.J.: Transaction, 1991). There is not much on any of the other assassinations except Sadat's; see for example the Islamic context in Johannes J. G. Jansen, *The Neglected Duty: The Creed of Sadat's Assassins and Islamic Resurgence in the Middle East* (New York: MacMillan, 1986). For one view on the murder (and there are many) there is the exceptionally well-informed Mohamed Heikal's *Autumn of Fury: The Assassination of Sadat* (New York: Random House, 1983). The Egypt of Mubarak has attracted less attention; it is too recent, conditions are uncongenial and, as suggested in the title of Hamid Ansari's *Egypt: The Stalled Society* (New York: State University of New York, 1986), it is insufficiently dynamic. It isn't only the Egyptians who find the last pharaoh oppressive—and dull—but also foreign observers.

Egyptians, scholars and journalists, have often found contemporary events difficult to approach in an authoritarian society, and more recently in a society under siege by gunmen. The entire academic and analytical field of the Middle East is torn by ideological rather than methodological conflicts: Arabists and Arabs, advocates and apologists, the Zionists, the enormously fecund Israeli academics, those who favor the meek or Marx. Each product must be checked for the maker as well as the method. And in the Middle East, in Egypt, foreign scholars of whatever persuasion often have problems of access. Free inquiry is apt to be suspect, records closed, and participants not very forthcoming. And no one can readily associate with active gunmen or those in prison.

For the Middle East in general, where conditions on the ground are often less promising than in Egypt, this has not deterred the bold, who use what is available. There are, for example, a great many works on the rise of Islamic fundamentalism in general—books, articles, even whole annals, for instance, Charles E. Butterworth and I. William Zartman, eds., *Political Islam*, a special issue of the *Annals of the American Academy of Political and Social Science*, vol. 524 (November 1992). For the immediate present, one can do no better than read the quarterly *Middle East Journal* to keep up on events and even find articles on the elusive Egyptian gunmen.

The key analysis of the Egyptian origins of those gunmen is found in the work of the French scholar Gilles Kepel. His *Jihad: The Trail of Political Islam* (Cambridge, Mass.: Belknap, Harvard University Press, 2002) is the definite work on the subject, the very best book to read for the big picture. His *Muslim Extremism in Egypt: The Prophet and Pharaoh* (Berkeley and Los Angeles: University of California Press, 1992; first pub. Paris, 1984) remains the crucial analysis of the ideological foundation of the Egyptian *jihadi*. Two other books by journalists address modern, militant Islamic Egypt directly: Genevieve Abdo, *No God but God: Egypt and the Triumph of Islam* (New York and Oxford: Oxford University Press, 2000); and Mary Anne Weaver, *A Portrait of Egypt: Journey through the World of Militant Islam* (New York: Farrar, Strauss & Giroux, 1999). Weaver's extensive interview with Sheikh Rahman in the *New Yorker*, "The Novelist and the Sheikh," indicated the cultural obstacles to an understanding of the alien and the reluctance of the faithful to open a dialogue with the West. A third work with a wider scope is Judith Miller, *God Has Ninety-Nine Names: Reporting from a Militant Middle East* (New York: Simon & Schuster, 1996). For the general impact on America see Fawaz Gerges, *American and Political Islam: Clash of Cultures or Clash of Interests?* (Cambridge: Cambridge University Press, 1999).

There have always been those who detail the flaws and failures of Islamic, and particularly Arab, society, especially the political dimension. The most elegant—a must-read—is the recent study by Bernard Lewis, *What Went Wrong? Western Impact and Middle Eastern Response* (Oxford and New York: Oxford University Press, 2001).

When Afghanistan became a Cold War battleground that attracted Egyptians as well as others, another spate of works appeared in an arena formerly of concern only to a few scholars and those ruling in Kabul, the capital of a distant and unknown Central Asian state. For example: Diego Cordovez and Selit Harrison, *Out of Afghanistan: The Inside Story of the Soviet Withdrawal* (Oxford and New York: Oxford University Press, 1995); Robert Kaplan, *The Ends of the Earth: A Journey to the Frontiers of Anarchy* (New York: Vintage, 1997); William Maley, ed., *Fundamentalism Reborn? Afghanistan and the Taliban* (London: C. Hurst, 1998); Roy Olivier, *Afghanistan: From Holy War to Civil War* (Princeton: Princeton University Press, 1995), and also *The Failure of Political Islam* (Cambridge, Mass.: Harvard University Press, 1994); Ahmed Rashid, *Taliban, Militant Islam, Oil and Fundamentalism in Central Asia* (New Haven: Yale University Press, 2000); Barnett Rubin, *The Search for Peace in Afghanistan: From Buffer State to Failed State* (New Haven: Yale University Press, 1995).

Almost certainly the American war in Afghanistan against the Taliban—even if there is no closure—will produce a variety of works: history, analysis of strategy, the impact of weapons systems, the diplomacy required and the implications for Central Asia and Pakistan.

By the time the Afghan war involving the Soviet Union had become a historical case study for American policymakers, the implications of global terror were beginning to attract attention. There are thousands of books on terror, bibliographies and bibliographies of bibliographies—an extensive, international project. There is also a vast literature on weapons of mass destruction that might be used by contemporary terrorists.

There are books focused on policy options to defend against terror, on the techniques and organization of terrorists, on high-tech vulnerabilities, on the ideology of violence, on specific armed struggles. Some use the library, others statistics, some the experience of their former office. Many rely on official and unofficial archives and a few on interviews with participants or psychological probes of captives. Each conflict produces its own literature: thousands of books on the Irish Troubles and more thousands on the Palestinian armed struggle. The same has become true with the problem of weapons of mass destruction. In fact, there is an open literature reached on the internet, some of it supplied by the United States government, on the construction of such weapons; while atomic bombs are not for dummies, a trained mind can make an impressive beginning or find out where to buy a nasty virus or build an explosive device. The internet offers an array of material on terrorism, including bibliographies of the available literature, often accompanied by critics' choices.

Here are this critic's choices: For a general history of terror—without a definition if it—there is Walter Laqueur's *Terrorism* (Boston: Little Brown, 1977), which has come out in many editions; see also his *The Terrorist Reader* (Philadelphia: Temple University Press, 1978), also in many editions. The best recent work on terror is Bruce Hoffman's *Inside Terrorism* (New York: Columbia University Press, 1998); and for the threat from weapons of mass destruction just before the September attack, Jessica Stern, *The Ultimate Terrorists* (Cambridge, Mass.: Harvard University Press, 1999).

How terrorism appeared to one of those charged with making policy can be found in a book by Bill Clinton's first national security advisor, Anthony Lake, *Nightmares: Real Threats in a Dangerous World and How America Can Meet Them* (Boston: Little Brown, 2000). Terror has fascinated the orthodox; when Admiral Stansfield Turner retired as director of the CIA, he didn't want to write about intelligence, but about terrorism. Overall, little that is new has been offered recently, aside from the inclusion of more data in case studies and the application of various academic methodologies. Just as no one has presented a satisfactory definition of terrorism (see Omar Malik, *Enough of the Definition of Terrorism* (Washington, Brookings Institution, 2000), no one has suggested a universal antiterrorism policy acceptable to all. Most of the advice falls along the traditional spectrum of right to left, conservative hawks to liberal doves.

There are books on the history, construction and political implications of the World Trade Center—Angus Kress Gillespie, *Twin Towers* (New Brunswick, N.J.: Rutgers University Press, 1999), among others. There are several works that address the 1993 bombing, but there is no consensus on it as yet. Laurie Mylroie, in her *Study of Revenge: Saddam Hussein's Unfinished War against America* (Washington: American Enterprise Institute, 2000), incorporated the available records, including a detailed examination of the court records, finding in Iraq the culprit behind the attack. A Canadian journalist using slightly different sources, Simon Reeve, in *The New Jackals: Ramzi Yousef, Osama Bin Laden and the Future of Terrorism* (London: Andre Deutsch, and Boston: Northeastern University Press, 1999), does not see an Iraqi connection. There is also Jim Dwyer, David Kocieniewski, Deidre Murphy and Peg Tyre, *Two Seconds under the World: Terror Comes to America—The Conspiracy behind the World Trade Center Bombing* (New York: Crown, 1997).

For the two atypical terror attacks in Japan and in Oklahoma, there is contemporary coverage largely by investigative journalists.

For the Sarin gas attack in Tokyo, there is a massive literature in Japanese. In English there is: E. Kaplan and Andrew Marshall, *The Cult at the End of the World* (New York: Crown, 1996); and D. W. Brackett, *Holy Terror: Armageddon in Tokyo* (New York: Weatherhill, 1996). Survivor stories can be found in *Underground: The Tokyo Gas Attack and the Japanese Psyche* (New York: Vintage, 2001). The big picture is in Robert Jay Lifton, *Destroying the World to Save It: Aum Shinrikyo, Apocalyptic Violence, and the New Global Terrorism* (New York: Henry Holt, 1999).

For Oklahoma City there are several journalists' works on McVeigh: Brandon M. Stickney, *All-American Monster: The Unauthorized Biography of Timothy McVeigh* (Amherst, N.Y.: Prometheus, 1996); Lou Micheal and Dan Herbeck, *American Terrorist: Timothy McVeigh and the Oklahoma City Bombing* (New York: HarperCollins, 2001); Richard A. Serrano, *One of Ours: Timothy McVeigh and the Oklahoma City Bombing* (New York: Norton, 1998).

On terror and the West, especially America, there are not

only the books—shelves and shelves, entire publisher's catalogs (like that of Frank Cass, listing only works on terrorism and political violence), but also work in scholarly journals like *Studies in Conflict and Terrorism*, in journals of opinion and on websites. Terror is the subject of RAND reports, policy conferences and television documentaries. There are summaries by governments, parties, seminars and so on. The impact of the bombing at the World Trade Center in 1993 did not greatly heighten policy concerns, but was a penny on the scales for policymakers.

A selection of readings on the topic includes: Jeffrey D. Simon, *The Terrorist Trap: American Experience and Terrorism* (Bloomington, Ind.: Indiana University Press, 2001): Phillip B. Heymann, *Terrorism and America: A Commonsense Strategy for a Democratic Society* (Cambridge, Mass.: MIT Press, 2001); Paul R. Pillar, *Terrorism and United States Foreign Policy* (Washington: Brookings Institution, 2001). For intelligence in particular: Robert Baer, *See No Evil: The True Story of a Ground Soldier in the CIA's War on Terrorism* (New York: Crown, 2002); Loch K. Johnson, *Bombs, Bugs, Drugs and Thugs: Intelligence and America's Quest for Security* (New York: NYU Press, 2001); and Robert M. Gates, *From the Shadows: The Ultimate Insider's Story of Five Presidents and How They Won the Cold War* (New York: Simon & Schuster, 1996).

There is a whole spectrum of works on the defense response to irregular wars and unconventional challenges. One is David Halberstam, *War in a Time of Peace: Bush, Clinton and the Generals* (New York: Scribner, 2002). The same has not been the case for law enforcement, where the war against drugs and organized crime, especially the American mafia, has attracted most interest. With the FBI seeking the lead in the war against terrorism, this may change. In any case, nearly any aspect of policy response can be found someplace, offered by someone, and increasingly on the specific threat of Islamic terror—for instance, Karim H. Karim, *Islamic Peril, Media and Global Violence* (Cheektowaga, New York: Black Rose Books, 2001).

The threat from weapons of mass destruction has given rise to a separate literature, often concerned with vulnerabilities and safeguards. The work of Judith Miller, Stephen Engelberg and

William Broad, *Germs: Biological Weapons and America's Secret War* (New York: Simon & Schuster, 2001) has had an impact on policymakers and on conventional wisdom. The anthrax scare will generate further studies.

With the emergence of Osama bin Laden and his al-Qaeda, some have focused directly on him, using open sources, congressional testimony and Middle Eastern experience. Peter Bergen even managed an interview for television. Other pertinent books include: Mark Hubard, *Warriors of the Prophet and the Struggle for Islam* (Boulder, Co.: Westview, 1998); Roland Jacquard, *In the Name of Global Terrorism and the bin Laden Brotherhood* (Durham, N.C.: Duke University Press, 2002); Peter L. Bergen, *Holy War, Inc.: Inside the Secret World of Osama bin Laden* (New York: Free Press, 2001); Steven Emerson, *American Jihad: The Terrorists Living Among Us* (New York: Free Press, 2002). There is new information in *Ben Laden: La Vérité Interdit* by Charles Brisard and Guillaume Dasquié, but no English translation.

The early rush of publications after September 11 has produced mostly works for those who want photographs or a chronology disguised as a text. Some are better done than others, contain more data, are more accessible, and show less evidence of haste. One can find the front pages of the world's newspapers and the reaction of the staff of Reuters or *Der Spiegel*. In fact, various institutions have published the response of their staff: *New York* magazine, *September 11, 2001: A Record of Tragedy, Heroism and Hope* (New York: Harry N. Abrams, 2002); Magnum, *September 11* (New York: Power House Books, 2002); *Life* magazine, *One Nation* (Boston: Little Brown, 2002). A few individuals have collected and published their own impressions, including Dennis Smith, *Report from Ground Zero* (New York: Viking, 2002). Some have chronicled the art of the disaster, the role of the BBC in London, the implications for aviation, the structural impact of the Boeings on the two towers. There is a World Trade Center 2002 Memorial Wall Calendar for those interested in the visual record.

The season of analysis, recollection and admonition regarding September 11 has only begun: As'ad AbuKhalil, *Bin Laden, Islam, and America's New War on Terrorism* (New York: Seven Stories Press, 2001) strikes out quickly for the radicals. Others lay out the policy imperatives: Strobe Talbott and Nayan Chanda, eds., *The Age of Terror: America and the World after September 11* (New York: Basic Books, 2001); and James F. Hoge and Gideon Rose, ed., *How Did This Happen? Terrorism and the New War* (New York: Public Affairs, 2001). A great wave of works is anticipated with the autumn 2002 list, and this is likely to be simply a harbinger of a vast new literature. There is every reason to expect that the implications of September 11, 2001, will be a subject or a starting point of ongoing analysis and discussion.

For those with limited time to devote to the subject there is Bruce Hoffman, *Inside Terrorism* (New York: Columbia University Press, 1998), on terror; Jessica Stern, *The Ultimate Terrorists* (Cambridge, Mass.: Harvard University Press, 1999), on weapons of mass destruction; and Gilles Kepel, *Jihad: The Trail of Political Islam* (Cambridge, Mass.: Belknap, Harvard University Press, 2002).

For the future impact of global terror, the next time, there will be the evening television news, with details to come in the newspapers the next day, and soon thereafter new books on the shelf.

INDEX

Young Men's Moslem Association, 41, 42

Yousef, Ramzi Ahmed: bomb making, 125–26, 133; evades capture, 124–29; extradition/ conviction, 128–29, 147; hijack/crash plans, 153–54, 170; in Pakistan, 127–28; in Philippines, 125–27; plot against Pope, 126–27, 128–29; in U.S., 106–18; WTC 1993 bombing, 109–18, 127

Zagloul Pasha, Saad, 18–19, 21, 39

al-Zawahiri, Ayman, 61–62, 63, 82–83, 157; in Afghanistan, 83, 86; and bin Laden, 88; founds Islamic Jihad, 61, 82; imprisoned, 83; al-Qaeda leader, 159; and Rahman, 86–87

al-Zawahiri, Rabiaa, 83

al-Zindani, Abdel Meguid, 93

Zionists, 29–31, 55, 73, 76, 83, 84; Arab war against, 40–41; assassins, 31–38; Jewish Defense League, 102; Meir Kahane, 102–3